DATE DUE

D1451218

The Basics of Adoption

The Basics of Adoption

A Guide for Building Families in the U.S. and Canada

James L. Dickerson

and

Mardi Allen

PRAEGER

Westport, Connecticut
London

Library of Congress Cataloging-in-Publication Data

Dickerson, James.
   The basics of adoption : a guide for building families in the U.S. and Canada /
James L. Dickerson and Mardi Allen.
      p. cm.
   Includes bibliographical references and index.
   ISBN 0–275–98799–X (alk. paper)
   1. Adoption—United States. 2. Adoption—Canada. I. Allen, Mardi, 1951–   .
II. Title.
HV875.55.D53   2006
362.7340973—dc22   2006019255

British Library Cataloguing in Publication Data is available.

Library of Congress Catalog Card Number: 2006019255
ISBN: 0–275–98799–X

First published in 2006

Praeger Publishers, 88 Post Road West, Westport, CT 06881
An imprint of Greenwood Publishing Group, Inc.
www.praeger.com

Printed in the United States of America

The paper used in this book complies with the
Permanent Paper Standard issued by the National
Information Standards Organization (Z39.48–1984).

10 9 8 7 6 5 4 3 2 1

In memory of Mardi Allen's father, Edward Earl Allen, a man whose journey through life had more to do with others than himself

James L. Dickerson dedicates this book to R. S. Fenemore and the late Reg Barrett who gave him his first job as a social worker

Contents

Preface

This book began as an idea and quickly escalated to a passion.

The idea was that, of all the adoption books on the market, none were written by what we considered the best possible combination of authors: a social worker who has placed hundreds of children into foster and adoptive homes, and a clinical psychologist who has had more than two decades of experience dealing with parenting issues. Books written by adoptive parents, academics, and journalists are useful additions to the literature on adoption—indeed I have enjoyed a lively second career as a journalist—but they are limited, almost by definition, in the depth of information they can provide to prospective adoptive parents. When it comes to navigating the world of adoption, there is no substitute for guides who have real-world, professional experience.

What we have tried to do with this book, successfully we hope, is merge the sometimes competing professions of social work and psychology in such a way as to provide the sort of authoritative, behind-the-scenes information about adoption that is not available anywhere else. While we cover every aspect of adoption in this book, our focus is on adoption in the United States and Canada, and on the unique parenting challenges that face adoptive parents. Adoption is a lifesaver for the children affected by it, and a life builder for those who open their homes to these children. With nine years experience screening foster and adoptive parents for the Children's Aid Society of Leeds and Grenville County in Brockville, Ontario, and for Adoptions International in Memphis, Tennessee, I feel lucky to have participated in that process as a screener. My job required me to interview foster and adoptive parents, match children with parents, and supervise placements during six-month probationary periods. For me, this book is an opportunity to give back to a profession that has given much to me in myriad ways. Sometimes it is difficult to explain to other people the joy that one feels when helping someone realize the dream of parenthood. The thrill of physically handing an infant to his or her new parents is not something that is quickly forgotten. I would like to think that the experience I gained as a social worker helped me be a better father to my son, Jonathan; as a journalist, it provided me with insights that often were beyond the grasp of my colleagues.

My coauthor, Dr. Mardi Allen, is currently the Division Director of Professional Development for the Mississippi Department of Mental Health, where she is responsible for staff development and the training of nearly ten thousand mental health employees. Prior to that, she had experience counseling adopted children in Salt Lake City at the Neurology, Learning and Behavior Center. A licensed clinical psychologist, she has presented papers on attention deficit hyperactivity disorder, childhood depression, effects of divorce on children, positive parenting, child discipline, stress management, behavior intervention, identification and treatment of learning difficulties, teaching children social skills, and numerous other topics that affect the family. Mardi's professional expertise is in parenting, but she has a long-time personal interest in adoption and she views this book as an opportunity to merge the professional with the personal.

The writing of this book was severely tested toward the end of the process with the unexpected arrival of Hurricane Katrina, which threw us into darkness without food, water, gasoline, or electricity. Added to that was Mardi's brief absence from the project—as a state mental health officer she was called into service to assist the hurricane victims on the Mississippi coast—and my unexpected diagnosis of a life-threatening illness. Despite those disasters, we finished the book, and did it on schedule!

We hope that you, the reader, will feel the passion and energy we put into this book and find the information it presents useful in your quest to build a family through adoption.

James L. Dickerson

Acknowledgments

James L. Dickerson would like to thank Ida-Mae Tracey at the Adoption Council of Canada for her help in gathering information; Sandra Scarth, president of the Adoption Council of Canada, for granting permission to reprint her article on Aboriginal children and adoption; Robert Pickens, executive director of Family and Children's Services in Brockville and the United Counties of Leeds and Grenville, Canada, for his help in gathering information; David and Debra Rice, great friends of long standing who encouraged the book; the late Jean Gardner; the late Florene Brownell; Grant Fair; Barbara Kenny; Sidney Rosenblatt; Richard Sourkes; Pat Herlehy; Gilda Baird; Gail Perkins; my friend, Alex A. Alston; and our editor at Praeger, Elizabeth Potenza, who was a pleasure to work with.

Mardi Allen would like to thank Department of Mental Health Executive Director Randy Hendrix, who has always supported my professional pursuits; librarian Margueritte Ransom; Jan Smith and Janice Parker for their contributions; administrative assistant Christy Miller, whose friendship and support are tremendous; my family who always believes in me far beyond my abilities; Billye Bob Currie who during a practicum experience encouraged me to learn and grow as a therapist; Paul Cotten and John Lipscomb who pushed me to succeed early in my career; the Jaycee Evaluation Center team who have always encouraged me; Steve Szukula for his supervision during my internship at Primary Children's Medical Center; Sam Goldstein at the Neurology, Learning and Behavior Center who was a great mentor to me during my postdoctoral residency training; Austin, Matthew, Brandon, and Mark Ellis who thought it was cool for me to write this book; and my sweet but precocious cocker spaniels, Allie and Mattie.

1 Starting the Adoption Process

If you are among the thousands of people each year who decide to adopt a child, you are already at a crossroads. The path to adoption is filled with "forks in the road" that at times may seem confusing, infuriating, and overwhelming. The decisions that you make early on will determine whether your adoption efforts end in failure or success. Fortunately, you have more control over those decisions than you think. As with most things in life, information is power.

Adoption is a big deal in America, but no one knew exactly how much of a big deal until 2003, when the U.S. Census released its first ever adoption report. Of the 65 million children in America under eighteen years of age, 2.5 percent—or 1.6 million—are adopted. Most were born in America, but a surprising number—about one hundred and sixty-nine thousand—came from foreign countries, including forty-eight thousand from Korea, twenty-one thousand from China, twenty thousand from Russia, eighteen thousand from Mexico, and eight thousand from India.

That should not come as a surprise to anyone. America, like its neighbor to the north, Canada, is an immigrant nation. Both countries were built by "foreigners" who came to North America in search of a better life. International adoption is simply an extension of that ongoing process.

For years, the number of white, adoptable infants in America has declined—due largely to society's increasing acceptance of abortion and single moms—which has given rise to the myth that adoption is no longer possible. Clearly, that is not the case. Adoptions are processed daily by state agencies, private agencies, and private facilitators such as physicians and lawyers, finalizing each year an estimated forty-eight thousand domestic adoptions and eighteen thousand foreign adoptions.

In addition to the infants available for adoption, whether domestically or from foreign countries, there are an estimated one hundred and twenty-six thousand older children in foster homes currently awaiting adoptive families. The problem is that for every available child there are many prospective adoptive homes, which means that the process is very competitive. Whether applicants end up in the "approved" group or the "pending" group often hinges on the quality of the information available to them. Applicants are more likely to be approved for adoption than are applicants who do not understand the basics of adoption.

WHAT ARE YOUR CHOICES AS AN ADOPTIVE PARENT?

Once you've made up your mind to adopt a child, you have to decide how you are going to go about it. Should you apply at a public or a private agency? If you decide on a private agency, should you choose a for-profit or a not-for-profit one? Should you adopt from an agency that specializes in international adoptions? Should you inquire in your community about private facilitators that initiate adoptions? Do you want to pursue a traditional adoption, an open adoption, or a subsidized adoption? Is it important to you that your application is handled by an agency associated with a specific religion—such as Christianity, Judaism, or Islam?

As you can see, your first decision is to determine what kind of agency is best for you. Only when you do that can you intelligently work with the agency to determine what kind of child is right for you. The next decision you have to make is whether money is a consideration. Public agency adoptions are generally done free of charge, but some agencies charge small fees of less than $500 to cover court costs. Private adoptions, whether domestic or international, can cost anywhere from $10,000 to $100,000. Adoption placements arranged by physicians or lawyers typically involve only legal and medical expenses, but they can sometimes run several thousand dollars.

Pluses and Minuses of Public Agency Adoptions

If you don't have thousands of dollars at your disposal, you should consider applying at a public agency. The downside to that is that abortion and growing community acceptance of unmarried mothers have greatly reduced the number of infants available for adoption through public agencies. The children who are available at public agencies tend to be school age or late pre-school age, and sometimes have chronic health, physical, or emotional problems that require follow-up care.

The upside is that public agencies typically have more experienced adoption workers than you will find in a private agency, which means that they are often more successful with their placements. You may not think that is important now, but you certainly will if problems arise later in the adoption. Experience is an important consideration in resolving adoption-related family problems.

Of course, service and experience levels can vary greatly from state to state and province to province, which you should take into consideration when making your decision. If you are not comfortable with the services offered by the public agencies in your state or province, you should consider the alternatives.

The first person you will come into contact at a public agency is the intake worker. It may be someone who specializes in adoption, but it is more likely to be a person who deals with a variety of issues, anything from adoption to child abuse. At such a stage in the application process, the agency is more interested in providing you with information than in gathering information from you. The intake worker will take your name, address, and telephone number and provide you with an assortment of pamphlets and other materials about adoption. You also will be given an application form that will request information from you, such as the following:

- Contact information (name, address, telephone numbers, and so on)
- Citizenship
- Marital information
- Names of people who can be used as references, including a physician
- Employment information (where do you work and what is your annual income?)
- Names and ages of parents, brothers, and sisters
- Health questionnaire
- Housing questionnaire (do you rent or owe your home?)

Once you return the completed application, you will be given an appointment with the adoption screener (most likely that person will have a degree in social work or psychology). Before you meet with the screener, it is essential that you understand that his or her reason for being there is not so much to find you a child as to protect the interests of the children who are and will be in the agency's custody.

Your first meeting with an adoption screener will be devoted to the worker providing you with enough information to help you screen yourself. You will be provided with information about agency policies in some basic areas such as citizenship, age, marital status, arrests and convictions, and so forth. The adoption screener also will make his or her first judgments about your suitability as adoptive parents.

The adoption worker may become your best friend after a placement occurs, but during the evaluation process it will appear that he or she is not interested in such a relationship. Playing God with another human being's life is an awesome responsibility, one that adoption screeners take very seriously—and because of that it may seem as though they have adversarial relationships with their clients as they determine who may be considered "safe" parents for the children in their care.

At all times, you must keep in mind that the adoption screener's job is to find parents for children, not to find children for you. As a prospective adoptive parent you are an important part of the equation, but you are not the most important part. The adoption screener is mandated by law to put the needs of the child first. Your job is to convince the adoption worker that you are a good candidate for an adoption.

Pluses and Minuses of Private Agencies

There are two types of private adoption agencies—nonprofit and for-profit. The nonprofit agencies charge fees for adoption so that they can pay salaries and expenses. Typically, they will be affiliated with religious or philanthropic organizations that set up adoption agencies for altruistic reasons.

For-profit agencies are just that—agencies that charge fees with a view of making a profit. There is nothing wrong with that, of course. Everyone else involved with adoption—physicians, lawyers, nurses, social workers, judges, psychologists, and so on—profits financially from adoptions when their services are rendered, so there is no reason why private adoption agencies should not do the same.

You may be attracted to a private agency because you think it will be more tolerant and overlook some of your shortcomings in order to find you a child—an agency that will put your interests ahead of those of the child. If so, you should keep in mind that if an agency is willing to misrepresent your qualifications as parents, it may be willing to misrepresent the child's background in order to make you more accepting of the child. If you choose a private agency, do so for the right reasons.

The advantages of choosing a private agency include the following:

- There is less red tape. Private agencies must be licensed by state government, but they are not directly accountable to state legislatures and governors. Less public accountability equates to less paperwork.
- There are better odds of adopting an infant. Private agencies are more likely than public agencies to have infants available

for adoption. Mothers who give their children up for adoption sometimes feel more comfortable dealing with private agencies. The children offered for adoption by private agencies are available because the mother made a studied decision to give the child up. The children offered by public agencies sometimes are available because a judge has declared their mothers or fathers to be unfit parents. The birth parents may have fought the court order, which means they are not willing participants in the adoption process.

The disadvantages of choosing a private agency include the following:

- There is less supervision. Public agencies may have a wide variety of professionals on staff, including nurses, behavioral experts, relationship experts, and so on. If a problem arises, a public agency can provide a variety of services, even if it means calling in the services of other government agencies. Private agencies often cannot afford to offer a variety of services to their clients during the adoption process. Typically, the adoption worker at a private agency will oversee the placement and report to a supervisor, and deal with any problems that arise.

- There is less information available. Since private agencies have no investigative authority, they do not have the resources to gather a great deal of information about the child or the child's birth parents. The information they gather from the birth parents is voluntary and controlled by the birth parents. They may have comprehensive information about the child's medical history since birth, but little information about the parents' medical history.

Pluses and Minuses of Open Adoptions

In the beginning, adoptions were undertaken by the family patriarch. If a daughter or granddaughter had a child out of wedlock, the patriarch took it upon himself to find a suitable home for the child, especially if it was a female. Usually, he approached family members or neighbors and asked them to take the child. If it was a male, he might decide to raise the child himself in order to have another worker on the farm.

With the arrival of the Industrial Revolution, which dispersed families over a wider geographical area, out-of-wedlock births took place with greater frequency, usually in situations in which the family patriarch lived apart from the birth mother in another neighborhood or community. With the declining influence of the family, it became obvious that society had to set up a system to find homes for children who otherwise might be abandoned by their extended families.

The first laws regarding adoption were enacted by Massachusetts in 1851. For the first time in history, courts were asked to oversee adoptions. Prior to that, adoptions were treated much like land transfers. Adoptive parents were required to file a deed similar to those used for real estate transactions.

Legal adoption was a reaction to changing roles of women in society. The transition from patriarch-controlled placements to legal adoption was not without growing pains. Public sentiment was fraught with judgment and blame, causing problems both for those who wanted to adopt and also for those who were adopted. It was in the best interest of everyone to keep all records sealed and to pretend that the adoptive parents were indeed the birth parents. The truth was usually not an option.

In time, society became more tolerant of adoption. Once that happened, society considered it "the right thing to do" for unwed mothers to give their babies up for adoption. Until the 1990s, it was considered scandalous for unmarried women to raise "bastard" children. Adoption was the only recourse.

For many years, adoption professionals considered parental contact with an adopted child to be one of the greatest risks to a successful adoption, and they steadfastly refused to budge on that principle. It was thought to be in the best interest of the child to be adopted by a family with a mother and father who could not be threatened by interference from the birth parents.

For couples who could not have birth children, adoption became a popular option. Often these adoptive parents were considered special and were praised for their willingness to take a child whose biological family could not care for them. Birth parents often were considered misfits who could not conform to the standards set by society.

Under those circumstances, confidentiality was considered essential if the child was to have a normal life. Parents were not encouraged to ever tell their children that they were adopted—and many followed that advice religiously. Sometimes children discovered the truth despite the parents' best efforts to keep the circumstances of their birth secret. As adoption agencies learned more about adopted children, they decided that a better way of managing the emotional turmoil associated with adoption was for children to be told, at an early age, that they are adopted.

Of course, once children know that they are adopted, their first question invariably is "who are my parents?" Adopted children have a strong need for information about their birth parents. The motivation ranges from the fanciful to the practical. An example of a fanciful motivation would be the belief that the child's birth parents are famous movie stars, basketball players, authors, or supermodels. A more practical motivation would be one that addresses concerns about medical histories and physical characteristics. Children may wonder if they are going to grow up to be tall or short, athletic or sedentary, or bright or average in intelligence. And they may wonder if they have brothers and sisters.

With time, as the confidentiality of adoption was eroded by the basic instincts of children to locate their birth parents, new solutions were sought. The first step was for agencies to approve contact with birth parents on the condition that everyone's identity would be protected. Early in the "contact movement," birth parents were able to request and receive updates on their children's school progress, health, and activities. Letters, photographs, and other important information were shared with the birth parents.

The next step was to share information about the birth parents with the child. Opening up this communication among birth parents, adoptive parents, and the adoptee often began through an intermediary employed by the adoption agency that had access to the records of both families involved and made the decisions about what information would be shared. The adoptive parents would communicate with the intermediary, and only information that seemed appropriate would be passed along to the birth parent. It was a form of censorship.

Today the trend is to maintain an open communication between all involved through a type of adoption termed the "open adoption." Under this system, birth parents are involved in the selection of the adoptive parents and maintain contact with the child and the adoptive parents after the adoption takes place. It is a form of co-parenting, although ardent supporters of open adoption sometimes insist that is not the case. They make the argument that once the paperwork is done the biological mother's options are limited. Of course, human nature being what it is, biological mothers don't always respect the "paperwork" involved with their child's adoption. In essence, open adoption is a time-share style of parenting in which both sets of parents raise the child into adulthood. Before you decide whether this type of adoption is right for you, you should consider both the advantages and the disadvantages.

The advantages of open adoptions include the following:

- A sense of partnership with the birth parents is fostered. You don't have to live in fear that your child someday will discover the identity of the birth parents and reject you as a parent.
- The sharing of important medical information takes place. Medical histories are sometimes important to the diagnosis of life-threatening diseases. Traditional adoptions are able to provide that option, but only to the extent that the information was gathered prior to placement.

- Biological family ties are maintained. Children grow up knowing their biological parents, aunts and uncles, and grandparents.

The disadvantages of open adoptions include the following:

- There may be stress and emotional uncertainty for birth and adoptive parents. Sometimes birth and adoptive parents discover that they have nothing in common other than the child and find that they are unsuccessful in sharing the child as they had hoped.
- It may create stress and emotional uncertainty for children. Two sets of parents is a concept that sometimes is more attractive to adults than children. Dueling parents, especially on issues such as discipline, after-school activities, and religious instruction, can be devastating to a child who wants and needs firm, consistent guidelines.
- Legal uncertainty may arise. A botched open adoption can result in years of legal wrangling. Generally speaking, what one court can do with a decree, another court can undo with a second decree.

It is important for public and private agencies to provide unwed mothers with a choice of whether their children will be placed in a traditional or in an open adoption home. Confidentiality is an important consideration to many unwed mothers, and if they are not offered that choice during their pregnancy, many will opt for abortion instead of adoption. That is especially important in cases involving rape, incest, or mothers younger than eighteen years of age.

As an adoptive parent, it is important for you to understand all the possibilities associated with open adoption. What may sound like a great idea on paper is sometimes less than great in reality. If the birth mother is similar to you in age, ethnic background, and intelligence, the adoption will have a greater chance for success than if she is not. Possible areas of conflict include *age* (if the mother is a teenager, her views about you parenting her child may change by the time she reaches the age of majority); *the reason for the pregnancy* (if incest or rape, the mother may still have unresolved problems that could affect your relationship with her); *level of intelligence* (if the mother is of low intelligence, you may find communication with her difficult); and *ethnic and/or religious considerations* (the mother may be a member of a culture or a religion that has strong opinions about the role women should play in society and you may find yourself in conflict with those opinions).

The potential for legal difficulties is endless in open adoptions. Teenage mothers may change their minds when they become adults and petition the court for the return of the child. A father, thought not to be an issue when an adoption is finalized, may appear years later and demand the child, claiming that he had never been informed of the pregnancy. Understandings between a birth mother and an adoptive couple may seem firm at the time of placement, but can change with the passing of time.

In 1999, a Caucasian couple in Memphis agreed to take care of a married Asian couple's baby girl while they got their life in order. At the time, the father was charged with sexual assault by a student at the college where he taught, which led to his dismissal. With no income and no prospects, the Asian couple, who had met the Caucasian couple through a local church, agreed to name them the child's guardian. They were in the United States on an educational visa and didn't realize that they had relinquished their parental rights when they transferred guardianship.

The battle over the child continued for more than six years, with stories appearing in the *New York Times* and *USA Today*, depicting the battle as a racial and cultural clash. It was a nightmare, filled with public confrontations and picket lines outside the couples' homes. As the battle continued, the Asian couple put their life back together—the father was acquitted of sexual assault—and they made it clear that they wanted their daughter back so that they could return to China. The first judge ruled against the Asian couple and sent the case to the Tennessee Court of Appeals, which as of early 2006 had not yet handed down a decision. The guardianship transfer seemed a simple matter in the beginning, but it quickly spiraled out of control and resulted in emotional distress and financial hardship for everyone involved.

The point in relating this story is to help you understand that human emotions that involve children are complex and subject to change. The open adoption that you think was crafted in heaven may end up dragging you through hell. Open adoptions are wonderful for the child in situations in which the birth and adoptive parents are willing and able to trust each other . But if birth and natural parents do not have a high level of mutual trust and common interest, the resulting emotional carnage of a failed adoption can do great harm to the child.

When it comes to open adoption, it gets down to the question of whether you are a risk-taker or whether you are conservative in your decisions. If you are conservative by nature and have a history of playing safe bets, you may not want to roll the dice on open adoption.

Pluses and Minuses of Facilitators

There are few pluses to adoptions by facilitators such as physicians and lawyers. Frankly, these types of adoptions have always been of concern to professional adoption workers. The most obvious reason is because physicians and lawyers have no training in evaluating individuals as adoptive parents. Their areas of expertise, respectively, are in medicine and law. They are no more qualified to place children with you than adoption workers are to perform surgery on you or to represent you in legal matters. They have important roles to play in the adoption process, but they act beyond their capabilities when they make decisions about placements that bypass psychosocial assessments undertaken by professionals.

That is not to say that placements made by physicians or lawyers never work out, because obviously some of them will, based on the law of averages. But your odds would be just as good with a child placed by a mechanic or a bus driver. Physicians and lawyers can be important team players in adoption as long as their efforts are confined to their specific areas of expertise.

We know a physician who took a baby from one of his patients and gave it to another patient who was infertile and unable to have children. All he knew about the birth mother and the adoptive mother was what he saw when they came into his office to be treated for the flu or to receive exams. He knew about the baby's health because he examined the child. It seemed like a good match to him, so he asked his lawyer golf-buddy to do the paperwork.

The adoption breezed through court and the physician thought no more about it until he picked up the newspaper one morning and saw a photograph of the adoptive father. He was dead and his wife was charged with murder.

As it turned out, the adoptive father was also the child's biological father. When the adoptive mother learned of his infidelity, she drove a screwdriver into his heart while he slept. The mother went to prison and the child was made a ward of the state. The physician chalked up the tragedy to bad luck and continued to place infants for adoption.

There are success stories, of course. One of the most well known is probably the physician-advised adoption of Audrey Faith Perry, who was placed with a married couple, Ted and Edna Perry of Jackson, Mississippi, who already had two boys of their own. Shortly after Audrey started school, the Perry family moved to a small town named Star, where Audrey grew up in a rural community, attending grammar and high school. She was told at a young age that she was adopted, so young in fact that she later said she could not recall a time when she did not know that she was adopted.

Throughout childhood and her teenage years, Audrey had fantasies about her birth parents. Were they famous and rich? Were they royalty? Were they recording artists? Were they someday going to find her and take her off to a mansion?

Eventually, Audrey concluded that she would have to find herself before she could find her birth parents. She loaded up all her possessions and moved to Nashville, where she married a man named Daniel Hill and recorded an album using the name Faith Hill. She was driven to become a superstar, perhaps because she felt it would make her more attractive to her birth mother. The fantasy was that her birth mother would see her on television and contact her and erase all the years of uncertainty about her true identity.

Meanwhile, Faith enlisted the help of one of her brothers in locating her birth mother. They were able to find enough information to ask a judge to name an intermediary who approached the mother, asking whether she wanted to have a relationship with her daughter. As it turned out, she did want a relationship. Mother and daughter met in a park and introduced themselves to each other.

Faith was able to establish a loving relationship with her birth mother. Her physician-placed adoption had a happy ending, but it was due more to the adoptive family and Faith's determination than to the physician's skill as an adoption expert.

Are Subsidized Adoptions Right for You?

Public agencies have always subsidized foster home placements because it was felt that potential foster parents should not be penalized because they do not have the income to take additional children into their homes. In recent years, as the number of infants available for adoption has decreased, agencies have concluded that financial incentives are appropriate for adoptive homes in which certain classes of children are placed—those who are mentally and physically challenged, those who have diseases such as AIDS requiring long-term care, or those that are likely to have emotional problems that will require long-term treatment.

Subsidy payments are not a salary for taking care of an adopted child. Their purpose is to help pay some of the medical costs associated with raising a child with "special needs"—that is, those with chronic physical, learning, or emotional problems that require special attention on an ongoing basis. Without subsidy payments, some children would remain in foster homes or institutions until adulthood.

If an adoption agency suggests that you would be a good candidate for evaluation for subsidized adoption, they are not being critical of you as wage earners. What they really want to do is to consider you as potential adoptive parents for a special needs child. The real issue is not whether you should receive financial assistance from the agency, but whether you should parent a child with physical, mental, or emotional problems.

Agencies Run by Religion-based Organizations

Some individuals prefer to adopt through private agencies operated by religious organizations with which they feel a spiritual connection. They do so for many reasons. Some people are distrustful of government. Some feel that a religious organization, by definition, will be more compassionate toward them as potential parents. Others feel that if an agency embraces the same religion, it will be in agreement with them about child rearing practices and religious instruction, and more likely to see things their way.

Religion-based agencies have a long and admirable history of placing children into adoptive homes. There have been situations when they have stepped into a void and carried the entire burden of adoption. Today, there are agencies that represent just about every religious affiliation imaginable.

Advantages to Adopting through a Religion-based Agency

Religion-based agencies typically have the same level of professional competence that you would find at public and for-profit agencies. However, they are more likely to place a child born to a mother of a particular religion with adoptive parents of the same religion.

Sometimes that is just as important to birth mothers as it is to adoptive parents. Some birth mothers insist on guarantees of same-religion placement before assigning custody of their child to the agency. Sometimes they are even invited to participate in the evaluation process and help choose the right adoptive parent.

If you are a person of strong faith, you may feel that your adoption will be blessed if it proceeds through a religion-based agency. You may feel that it has your church's approval and is therefore more likely to be successful. Those are not advantages that could be argued with objectivity, because in matters of faith objectivity is an early casualty.

Disadvantages of Adopting through a Religion-based Agency

Religion-based agencies were created as a reaction to perceived biases and injustices. Protestants initially got involved in adoption because they believed that Protestants were being discriminated against by the courts. Roman Catholics got involved because they believed that Protestants were biased against Roman Catholic children and adoption applicants. Jews soon followed, based on the belief that Protestants and Roman Catholics were biased against members of their faith.

The biggest disadvantage to adopting through a religion-based agency is the possibility of bias if you are not of the same religion. In 2005, Bethany Christian Services, a national organization with offices in Jackson, Mississippi, attracted media attention when it rejected a Roman Catholic couple as potential adoptive parents because their religion conflicted with the agency's "Statement of Faith."

The agency director admitted freely that the couple had been rejected because they are Catholics. The director said in a newspaper interview with the *Clarion-Ledger*: "It has been our understanding that Catholicism does not agree with our Statement of Faith. Our practice to not accept applications from Catholics was an effort to be good stewards of an adoptive applicant's time, money, and emotional energy."

After coming under criticism for rejecting the couple, the agency's board overruled the director and voted to include Catholic families in its adoption programs. In a statement released to the media, Bethany Christian Services explained, "We realize that we took too narrow a view in assessing adoptive applicants."

It is admirable that the agency reversed its position, but that does not change the fact that religion-based agencies have displayed bias in the past and will probably continue to so in the future, though probably without the public honesty displayed by Bethany Christian Services.

Common sense argues that if you are of one religion and apply to an agency that embraces a different religion, you probably will not receive the same thoughtful consideration you would receive if you were of the same religion. The agency may have a policy against religious discrimination, but that does not necessarily guarantee that adoption workers will follow it.

THE INTERSTATE COMPACT: THE ELEPHANT IN THE ROOM

Whether you adopt through an agency, a for-profit private agency, a not-for-profit private agency, or an attorney or physician arrangement, you will have to deal with the Interstate Compact if your adoption requires you to cross state lines to obtain a child. The Interstate Compact, also known as the Interstate Compact on the Placement of Children, is an administrative organization that was formed to oversee reciprocal laws on adoption enacted in the fifty states, the District of Columbia, and the Virgin Islands.

Since each state's laws on adoption are different, yet similar—and there are no federal laws regulating adoption—the Interstate Compact was given the task of developing a uniform procedure for dealing with those differences. As a result, the Interstate Compact enters the picture whenever a child born in one state is adopted by individuals in another state. It is the same philosophy that was used to develop interstate commerce and trade agreements.

As an adoptive parent, what you need to know is that, in addition to the adoption requirements in your home state, you must meet the requirements established by the Interstate Compact if your adoption involves a child from another state. Typically, the following will be needed:

- The completion, in duplicate, of the Compact Request (Form 100A)
- Three copies of a family history on both birth parents; a family history is not the same as a home study, although it includes much the same information. The family history must include information such as age, religion, appearance, employment history, educational background, race, information on physical and mental health problems, and special interests or creative talents.
- A notarized statement from the birth parent or legal guardian that it is the intent of the birth parent or guardian to place the child with the prospective parents named in the Compact Request
- A notarized statement signed by the birth parents or guardian that they have been provided personal information about the adoptive applicants, including names, addresses, ages, religions, races, employment, and health histories, as well as similar information about any individual living in the home with the applicants
- A statement indicating how the financial and medical needs of the children are being met in a preplacement home or facility
- Written authorization from the birth parents or guardian for the adoptive parents to obtain medical treatment for the child while the adoption in pending before the court
- A statement identifying the names of the lawyers involved in the case

As you can see, the Interstate Compact is a bureaucracy, not a social services agency, so the only services it provides to you are administrative. It seems to be the most effective when public agencies are involved in the adoption. It seems to be the least effective in adoptions involving private agencies or private placements involving facilitators such as physicians, lawyers, or business executives. The reason for that is because state laws differ more widely for those types of adoptions than they do for agency adoptions, and that has made it necessary for the Interstate Compact to formulate more complicated procedures for dealing with those situations.

As a result of the complexity of the paperwork involved, the Interstate Compact often is accused of blocking adoptions that cross state lines. There have been many calls for reform of the Interstate Compact, but that seems unlikely as long as it is subject to fifty different sets of state laws. It makes sense to federalize the Compact and provide it with a uniform set of procedures supervised by a federal agency, but conservative states are opposed to that because of the perception that it transfers too much power from the states to the federal government.

Until the compact is changed, you must deal with it as it is. Individuals have attempted creative legal maneuvers to circumvent the Compact's authority—such as having the pregnant mother move to the applicants' state to have the baby—but they have thus far not met with much success. This is because state governments view challenges to the Compact's authority as challenges to state authority. Failure to comply with the Compact's regulations is a serious violation of the law and could result in the child being returned to the state of origination.

WHAT TYPE OF FAMILY ARE YOU?

Are you single or do you have a traditional male-female family? Are you gay or straight? Are there already children in the home? Whatever your family situation, there is an adoption agency somewhere that will work with you.

If you are single, homosexual, in your fifties, or already have one or more birth children, your first priority should be to locate agencies that have a stated policy of serving clients like yourself. If you approach an agency blindly, without research, you are more likely to be rejected. Why undergo the trauma of rejection when you can increase your odds of approval by simply doing your research in advance?

WHAT KIND OF CHILD IS RIGHT FOR YOU?

When they first start thinking about adoption, most people envision an adopted child as bearing a strong physical resemblance to themselves. There is nothing wrong with that. It is human nature. However, the reality is that that is not likely to happen. Adoption is not a way to duplicate yourself. Before meeting with an adoption worker you need to ask yourself the following questions:

- Can you accept a child of a different race?
- Can you accept a child with serious health problems? If so, where do you draw the line? Heart disease? Cancer? AIDS?
- Can you accept a child who has or is likely to have learning problems at school?
- Can you accept a child who has anger problems?
- Can you accept a child who has been sexually abused?
- Can you accept a child who has sexually abused other children?
- Are you flexible when it comes to the child's age? Can you accept an older child, or have you made up your mind to adopt an infant only?
- Can you accept a child whose parent or parents are in prison?
- Would you be comfortable raising a child who has been forcibly removed from a family because of abuse?
- Can you accept a child from a different culture?

WHAT IS YOUR MOTIVATION FOR ADOPTING A CHILD?

There is a sad but common belief among women who cannot have birth children that they are somehow undeserving of parenthood. It is a hurdle that many women have to overcome before proceeding with adoption. Sometimes such women can be overheard saying, "If God wanted me to have a child, I guess I would have a child."

If women have a self-image handicap entering into adoption, it will only become more of a problem as the adoption proceeds. Adoption is not a cure for a broken self-image or a broken heart or a broken marriage. Adoption cannot "fix" problems or make life worth living. When you adopt a child you make a pledge to give of yourself. Adoption is about giving, not receiving.

The first thing you need to do before talking to an adoption agency is to honestly examine your reasons for wanting a child. If you are adopting as a couple it is essential that you and your partner be open with each other about your reasons for adding a child to your relationship. There may be times in your relationship that you keep your opinions to yourself in the interest of harmony, but adoption cannot be one of those times. For adoption to work, both partners have to be open and in total agreement.

Before ever talking to an adoption worker, you should ask yourself the following questions (write down your answers, put them away for a week or so, and then reread them to see if they hold up):

- Have you exhausted every possibility of having a birth child? Is one partner infertile? Does one partner have an aversion to sexual intercourse?

- Why is having a child important to you? Is it because all your friends have children? Is it because you feel incomplete without a child? Is it because your partner feels you should have children? Is it because your relationship is in trouble and you think a child will strengthen it? Is it because you have extra love to give to a child?

- Is anyone in your family opposed to adoption?

- Do you believe that applying for adoption makes it more likely that you will become pregnant?

2 What They Want to Know about You

Applying to adopt a child, whether at a public or private agency, will be unlike anything you have ever done in your life. It is a little like applying for a bank loan or for a job at a top-secret military installation, only many times more intense. The reason for that is because you are opening up the most intimate aspects of your life for scrutiny by strangers who will pass judgment on whether you are honest and worthy of being an adoptive parent. Adoption can be an intimating process for the unprepared.

"Why are they asking so many questions?" one frustrated applicant was overheard asking. "Anyone with half a brain can get a girl pregnant, or get pregnant, so why am I being singled out and treated like a criminal? I'm trying to give a home to a child!"

If the adoption screener is asking you a lot of personal questions that sometimes make you wince with painful self-examination, it is because he or she has a responsibility to effectively play God with a child's life. Other than a judge, society has given no one else the power to determine how a child will be raised. Mistakes in judgment can destroy lives. There is also the fact that in neither the United States nor Canada is there a constitutional right to adopt, or be adopted. Adoption is a privilege, like driving a motor vehicle, and as such it is regulated by the state, which has the power to set the standards for adoption.

You will encounter two types of social workers in the adoption process: those who screen adults as adoptive parents, sometimes called home-finders or screeners, and those who work with the family after placement during the probationary period, sometimes called caseworkers or adoption workers. In smaller agencies, both jobs will be performed by the same individual, but in larger private and public agencies the two jobs may be separate and performed by different people.

The adoption worker you first encounter will be the person who screens applicants. To avoid confusion, we will refer to that person as the screener and the person who supervises the adoption placement as the adoption worker. If the screener does not seem as friendly or embracing as you expected, or as encouraging and accepting as the adoption worker later proves to be, you should keep in mind that screeners are gatekeepers and their job is to prevent applicants who might abuse or mistreat a child from entering the system. They are less interested in becoming your friend than they are in protecting the children in their charge.

Screeners may or may not have had prior experience working with children. That's because they are hired to work with adults, not children. Their job is to write a psychosocial profile on you called a "home study," the purpose of which is to address your strengths and weaknesses as a prospective adoptive parent.

The basic elements of a home study are the following:

- Family background
- Medical background
- Employment background
- References
- Relationship background
- Prior experience with children
- Your lifestyle
- Your psychological strengths and weaknesses
- Attitudes about adoption
- Prior history of emotional, sexual, or physical abuse in your family

The home study process will involve several interviews, beginning with your introductory joint interview. If you are married, the interview will be with you and your spouse. If you are single, but living with a significant other, the interview will be with you and your partner. The purpose of that first interview is to allow the screener to inform you of all the agency's policies involving adoption. While that is taking place, you will be screened for inappropriate body language and comments, and you will be asked about your preferences in a child. If you are only interested in adopting a child of the same race, that is fine and there is no penalty for that. However, if you make disparaging comments about people of another race or religion, you may be shown to the door.

After the initial interview, the screener will contact your references by telephone or mail, and send a questionnaire to your physician and ask if he or she recommends you as adoptive parents based on your health history. If you have undergone therapy with a psychologist or psychiatrist, either as an individual or a couple, your therapist will be contacted after you have signed the necessary release forms.

In the weeks that follow, you and your spouse will be interviewed separately. The goal is to see how you respond to the same questions and to evaluate your separate strengths and weaknesses as potential adoptive parents. You will be asked some very personal questions about areas of your life that you may not have discussed with your partner. Generally speaking, the only information that will be disclosed to your spouse by the screener will be attitudes about adoption and child rearing. Personal information involving your sexual and social history will be kept confidential and not shared with your spouse.

Once the individual interviews are completed, you and your spouse will be interviewed together, this time to probe answers to questions that you gave during your individual interviews. The screener will use what he or she has learned to ask you more detailed questions about your relationship with each other and with your families.

Once the interviews are completed, the screener will write up a home study and present it to a supervisor and an adoption placement board. The screener will recommend that you be approved or rejected, and the supervisor or board will either agree or disagree. If there is agreement that you should be approved, you will be notified by telephone, letter, or both. If you are rejected, you will be notified by letter and invited to discuss the matter with the screener or supervisor if you have any questions.

Most public agencies do not provide the applicants with copies of the home study, nor do they provide them to the judges who approve the final adoption order. The reason for that is simple: although you have the right to know why you were rejected or approved, you do not have the right to read what your spouse, family members, or physician provided to the agency on grounds of confidentiality.

That guarantee of confidentiality also extends to the judge, who is not trained to evaluate the psychological nuances inherent in a home study. The judge may direct questions of his or her own to the agency or to the adoption applicants, based on the report provided by the agency, but cannot base those questions on information provided in confidence to the agency. In both the United States and Canada, rights of privacy come into play, which is why adoption laws have recognized the separate confidentiality needs of the agency and the court.

Some private agencies do provide applicants with copies of the home study. If this applies in your case, you should approach it with caution. If the screener included the confidential information received from your spouse, family members, or physician, it could have a very negative effect on your relationship with those people. If the screener did not include that information in the home study, then what you have is a watered-down version of a home study that almost certainly does not contain the real reasons why you were approved or rejected. Our experience has been that agencies that do not provide applicants with copies of their home studies generally are more professional in their evaluations and more successful in their placements.

If you are approved for adoption, you will feel an immediate sense of joy. Then as the days go by, you will realize that you are on a waiting list with many other applicants and may not hear from the agency again for months or even years. How quickly you hear from the agency will be directly proportional to the flexibility you showed when you were asked what kind of child you could accept.

If you specified a white infant boy with a good health history, then you will likely wait for years. However, if you stated that you could accept a child of either gender or any race, or one with possible "special needs" related to physical, emotional, or mental challenges, then you will hear from the agency fairly quickly.

A LOOK INSIDE THE HOME STUDY PROCESS

When you go for your interviews, dress appropriately. By that we mean don't show up in jeans, sandals, and a T-shirt, or dressed like you are on your way to a formal event. Don't overdo it in either direction. Women should avoid low-cut blouses or mini skirts, and men should dress conservatively. Pretend you are playing adoptive parents in a movie and dress the way you think the wardrobe department would instruct you to dress. Avoid extremes of any type.

When talking to the screener, look him or her in the eye and be careful not to interrupt when the screener is speaking. You would think that this goes without saying, but do not flirt with the screener. If you are there with your spouse, make certain that he or she is included in the conversation. If you do not have a spouse, that will raise a red flag for the adoption worker, who will then pay greater attention to your friendships and family relationships to determine whether you are too socially isolated to raise a child.

Don't make jokes at your spouse's expense or criticize embarrassing things he or she has done. Don't correct your spouse. And, most importantly, don't argue with your spouse, especially about issues related to adoption or to your relationship.

When Skye showed up with her husband Bob for their initial interview with a male screener, she was wearing a revealing tube top, large dangling earrings, and tight-fitting slacks. She seemed nervous and she crossed and uncrossed her legs almost constantly. Throughout the interview, she flirted with the screener, commenting on how "nice" he looked. She asked if he was married. Several times she leaned over to adjust her shoes, altering the contour of her tube top in a revealing manner.

For most of the interview, she held Bob's hand, but when the interviewer asked them to describe the kind of child they wanted to adopt, Skye released Bob's hand and said, "Bob's only interested in an infant, but I'd be willing to take a child up until school age. He can be so narrow minded sometimes."

The interviewer looked at Bob. "So, you wouldn't be interested in a child older than an infant?"

"Well....," Bob began.

"Of course he would," interrupted Skye.

Bob lowered his head and stopped talking.

Skye continued, "Bob and I will talk about this more at home. But you can go ahead and put us down for a child up to school age."

"Is that all right with you, Bob?"

"I guess."

After pausing to make a few notes, the interviewer moved on to a different subject. He addressed his next question to Bob. "Would you be interested in a child who has special needs?"

"What does that mean?"

"A child who has a chronic health condition, such as heart problems, or a child who may not test in the normal range on an intelligence test. Or a child who has a brother or sister."

"I don't know why not."

Skye sighed and rolled her eyes. "Bob can be so naïve sometimes. I swear, I don't know what I ever saw in him."

Needless to say, Skye and Bob self-destructed before their application was ever seriously considered for approval.

The "L" Word—Don't Use It

Screeners have no way to determine how much love you have to give to a child. There are no tests and no interview techniques that can measure love. As a result, the "L" word often falls on deaf ears. The day of your interview, the person doing your evaluation may already have heard someone say they "love" pizza, or they would "love" to take a vacation in the Bahamas. The "L" word has little meaning in today's culture.

Don't say you have a lot of love to give. Instead, say simply that you have a lot to offer to a child. Then explain what you feel you have to offer. Since no two people will ever agree on a definition of love, be specific when you are selling yourself to the screener. Do you have a nice home with plenty of room for children? If so, mention that, but mention it last, since the screener will be much more interested in what you and your spouse have to offer emotionally and intellectually.

Will either you or your spouse be a stay-at-home parent? If both you and your spouse work outside the home, tell the screener in specific terms your plans for physically caring for the child. Are you hiring a nanny? Do you have a first cousin who is going to help you care for the child? Think this through carefully before setting up an appointment with the screener. There is nothing wrong with both parents working, but if your schedules are such that your child-care plan is to let someone else raise the child, what motivation does the screener have to remove the child from a foster home, only to have you place the child in what amounts to another foster home?

If you have experience working with children, either as a professional or as a volunteer, you should let the screener know. If you have a close relationship with the children of family members or friends, let the screener know.

You may be the CEO of a corporation that has hundreds of employees, but for the duration of your interviews with the screener you are not in charge, so don't try to be authoritative since it will make you look resistant to the screener. For the most part, allow the screener to ask the questions. At the first interview, limit your questions to those that focus on agency policy. Are they required to place children into homes of the same religion? Do they give preferences to stay-at-home mothers? Is citizenship required to be an adoptive parent?

If you hear an answer you don't like, don't argue with the screener since agency policy is beyond his or her control. Don't try to impress the screener with your knowledge about adoption. Don't correct the screener, even if he or she is wrong. Don't put yourself in a position where you attempt to impress the screener at his or her expense. Be respectful.

Sell yourself at every opportunity. Before going in for the interview make a list of the things that you think will make you attractive as an adoptive parent. Do you have the support of your friends? Do you have a flexible work schedule? Do you have experience working with children? Have you had classroom experience as a teacher? Have you prepared your home for the arrival of a child? Is your extended family excited about the possibility of adding a new family member?

Also, keep in mind that while the screener is interested in what you have to offer a child, he or she is also interested in whether you have the potential to harm a child—and that will be a major focus of efforts to evaluate you as a parent.

Money Talks, but Not Necessarily the Way You Think

The agency will need to verify your income so that it can determine if you can provide for a child's basic needs. Once your income reaches that basic level, the screener loses interest in exploring your income and will move on to another subject. The screener doesn't care whether you are a millionaire or not. He or she doesn't care if you are the top zipper sales person in North America. The screener just wants to know if you can provide for the child.

If you think that you earn more than your interviewer, the less you say about your financial resources the better off you will be. If your plan is to establish a trust fund for your child and use it to educate him or her in Europe, then tell your close friends and not your interviewer. Most agency screeners earn less than $40,000 a year. If you earn more than that and talk about it in such a way that you seem to be bragging, you may cause resentment that could affect your application in subtle ways.

If two individuals are under consideration for the same child—and one individual is wealthy and the other is not—it is highly unlikely that the wealthy individual will be given a preference simply because he or she has more money. Since adoption workers don't enter the profession for financial reasons, you can be certain that financial factors will not influence their decision about you as a potential parent, at least not in the way you might think. When it comes to financial matters, answer only what is asked.

Did You Just Ask Me about My Sex Life?

An important part of the home study will be a discussion of your sexual relationship with your significant other. In order to determine if you have healthy sexual attitudes and practices, the interviewer will want to know how often you have sex, whether it is a fulfilling experience, whether you have ever undergone counseling for sexual dysfunction, how many sexual partners you have had, and so on.

Married couples that are experiencing relationship problems sometimes apply for adoption in the hopes that a child will bring them closer together and save their marriage. Or they may feel that caring for a child is a substitute for a fulfilling sex life.

The screener will ask you questions about your sex life because he or she knows there is a strong correlation between the quality of sex in a relationship and the longevity of the relationship. The screener will also attempt to ascertain whether you want to adopt a child because of sexual problems in your relationship. The questions will be blunt, so prepare in advance and answer honestly and without hesitation.

You Are the Sum Total of Your Diseases

The agency will ask your physician to fill out a questionnaire about your health problems and certify that you are in good health. The purpose of this is to ascertain whether you have any diseases that could be transmitted to a child or that would affect your ability to raise a child to adulthood. You may be asked to waive confidentiality so that the agency can discuss health issues with your physician.

The diseases that would be of interest to an adoption agency include anything that is potentially life threatening—heart disease, cancer, kidney disease, liver disease, AIDS, and so on. Also potentially threatening to your approval by a screener are diseases that could affect your ability to physically care for a child.

Have you ever been hospitalized or treated as an outpatient for emotional problems? Have you ever taken medication for nervousness or anxiety or depression? Have you ever been treated for an addiction? Has your driver's license ever been suspended for DUI? Have you ever been arrested for alcohol or drug-related offenses? These are issues that could affect your adoption application.

Health insurance is also an important issue. If you have health insurance, is everyone in the family included? Does the insurance company exclude adopted children for any reason? Find out if you are not certain. If you don't have health insurance, do you plan to get insurance by the time you adopt a child? Insurance may be a condition of placement, so find out all you can about your coverage—or lack of coverage—before you fill out your application and have that first interview. Of course, health insurance is not a problem in Canada, which has a national health care program; but it is a big problem in the United States, where many people find health insurance unaffordable or unavailable due to prior health problems.

References: Yes, They Are Important

The agency will ask you for a list of people, both friends and family, who they can contact regarding your suitability as adoptive parents. The agency contact will begin with a letter, but it may be followed up with telephone calls and face-to-face meetings with the people you listed. It is important that you discuss your adoption application in advance with the people you choose as references.

First, you want to make certain that you have their permission. Adoptions sometimes are sabotaged by references that resent the use of their names without their permission. Second, you want to probe your references for unhealthy attitudes about adoption. If you have never discussed adoption with them, you will not know whether they are opposed to adoption in general, or opposed to certain types of adoption, such as those that involve children of different races or cultures.

Most agencies will guarantee confidentiality to your references so that they will feel free to respond honestly. In a way, your first test as an adoptive applicant is the judgment you show in selecting your references. If one of your references responds to the agency with scathing comments about your potential as an adoptive parent, the screener will have to determine whether the comments are based in fact or merely an expression of the reference's personal hostility toward you. You lose in either case. If the screener concludes that the comments are not based in fact, he or she will still wonder about your judgment in choosing such a person as a reference.

Sometimes applicants choose references based on their standing in the community and not on the depth of their relationship with them. That is often a mistake since individuals with high profiles who don't have a close relationship with you may be hesitant to go out on a limb to recommend you.

The best way to approach the reference is to select only close friends and relatives that you think have a high opinion of you. If you ask a friend for permission to use his or her name, and he or she responds, "Do you want me to tell the truth?" or "Let me think about it," move on to the next name on the list. Be alert to his or her reaction: Is this person happy or perplexed by your request? Be alert to body language and listen carefully to what he or she has to say about adoption. You also will want to screen a potential reference about his or her opinion on hot-button issues such as interracial adoption, children with special needs, or children of a different religion.

Family Relationships Tell the Story

There are no tests that an agency can give you to determine if you have "love" to give to a child, but they can assess the love that you have given to your parents, siblings, and extended family members. Good adoptive parents invariably have good relationships with their siblings and parents.

Sometimes individuals apply for adoption in the hope that adoption will repair bad relationships within their families. They think that an adopted child will give them a new start. Anyone contemplating adoption should make an effort to repair damaged relationships with siblings and parents before applying for adoption.

One of the worst things you can tell an adoption worker is that you have a bad relationship with your parents or siblings and hope that adopting a child will give you someone with whom you can have a "good" relationship. That would be a definite red flag to the screener.

If the bad relationship you have with a family member is not your fault, the best thing you can do is to be up front with the screener about the relationship. Perhaps you have a sibling who is jealous of your success and thinks that you are the favored one with your parents, which has hurt your relationship with him or her. Or perhaps you loaned your stepfather money that was never repaid, and he is resentful of what he sees as his weakness and, as a result, he finds fault with everything that you do. In any case, explain the situation to the screener before he or she hears about it from another source.

Bad family relationships do not exist in a vacuum. They exist for a reason. Regardless of who is at fault, they should be repaired. If your relationships with your parents and siblings are so bad that they cannot be repaired, you might want to reconsider applying to adopt a child.

Significant-Other Relationships

Good adoptive parents know how to argue within the rules, without resorting to flight, physical abuse, or threats involving the withdrawal of love. That is important because couples tend to argue with their children in the same way that they argue with each other. Since adopted children tend to experience more behavioral problems than children that live with birth parents, knowing how to handle conflict is an essential skill for an adoptive parent to possess.

Adoption workers will want to know how you resolve conflict with your significant other. They will ask for detailed descriptions of recent conflicts, and they will observe you with your significant other during joint interviews, sometimes creating stressful situations based on leading questions to see how you react as a couple.

Think about this before you go in for your interview: Do you see yourself in any of the following?

Couple Number 1. Ted and Alice are proud of the fact that they have been married for ten years and have never had an argument. If one does something the other doesn't like, he or she simply ignores the offending behavior. "My parents argued all the time," explained Alice. "I swore to myself that when I got married that would not happen." Ted felt the same way: "When I hear couples argue, I want to leave the room—and sometimes I do. Nothing is worth arguing about."

Couple Number 2. Robert and June are just the opposite. Whenever they argue, their friends scurry away with promises to return when "things calm down." June is proud that she has never let Robert off the hook when he's done something to offend her. "Just the other day, he left the milk out on the table all night," she explained. "I had to throw it away the next morning." Robert laughed. "Yeah, she gave me hell for that. Of course, I deserved it."

Couple Number 3. George and Barbara were always pleasant around their friends. It was when they were alone that sparks flew. George was an introvert who disliked confrontation. Barbara was just the opposite. She instigated confrontation over even the smallest issues. She pushed and pushed, often getting into George's face to scream at him. George took it and took it until he reached a breaking point—and then he exploded, a reaction that always sent Barbara leaving the room in tears. Once the situation returned to normal, Barbara always rehashed the argument over and over until George apologized for losing his temper with her.

You've probably figured out by now that it is couple number two that has the best chance of being approved as adoptive parents. It is normal for couples to argue from time to time. What is not normal are situations in which one or both of the individuals in a relationship bury their feelings to the point of ignoring problems, or vent their disagreements so vehemently that physical and verbal abuse become part of the pattern.

It takes two to have a relationship. If one of the partners withdraws in the face of conflict—and the other partner uses that withdrawal as a tool for dominance—it solves nothing and merely creates resentment that will build over time. On the other hand, if both partners vent their emotions at every opportunity, arguing becomes the foundation of the relationship and that is ultimately a dead-end street.

As in most things, moderation is the key. If you have a disagreement with your spouse, or if he or she has a disagreement with you, the healthy response is to talk through the problem in an attempt to reach a resolution.

Don't withdraw. Don't lose your temper and say things you later will regret. Don't throw things. Don't hit the wall. Don't bring up old arguments.

How you resolve conflict with your partner is the best guide a screener has to determine how you will resolve conflict with a child. If you withdraw from your partner, you will withdraw from the child. If you are abusive toward your partner, you will be abusive toward the child.

If you have problems resolving conflict with your spouse or with co-workers, you should seek therapy before applying for adoption. Sometimes relationships reach a point where they cannot be salvaged, but it is never too late to learn how to resolve conflict.

What If You Were Sexually Abused as a Child?

Nicole was sexually abused by her foster father's brother from the age of ten until she started high school. Neither her foster parents nor her social worker ever knew about the abuse because she kept it a secret for fear of being removed from the home.

She suffered from a variety of emotional disorders that could be attributed to the abuse—depression, inability to sustain romantic relationships, employment difficulties, and so on—and she was in her mid-twenties before she met a man to whom she was able to relate at a deep emotional level. After they were married they tried right away to have a family, but without success. A series of medical tests revealed that she was infertile and would never have children of her own.

By the time Nicole and her husband decided to adopt she was twenty-eight years of age. "Let's go to the agency that supervised me in my foster home," she said, barely able to contain her joy. "They were always so nice!"

As luck would have it, when they arrived at the agency for their first joint interview, they encountered Nicole's old caseworker in the hallway. They embraced and the caseworker told her how happy she was that she was married. The interview with the screener went well, and they left optimistic about their chances of getting a child.

The following week, when Nicole returned for her individual interview with the screener, she confided that she had been abused while living in the foster home. "I haven't been able to tell a soul—not even my husband, but I want you to know since I think you will understand. I've prayed about it and I think a child will help me forget the pain I feel over the abuse."

"Why haven't you told your husband?" asked the screener.

"I am afraid he won't love me anymore."

"How would you describe your relationship with your husband?"

"Good."

"In what way?"

"He doesn't get angry when I get emotional. He says he understands."

"But he doesn't understand, does he?" asked the screener.

Nicole looked down at her hands, which lay knotted in her lap. "No," she said. "But he thinks he does—and that counts for something."

After more discussion, the screener explained to Nicole that he would be unable to give additional consideration to her application because of the abuse she experienced.

"I don't understand!" she sobbed. "I'm one of your children and I've come here for help. You owe me that much. If you had put me in a better home I would not have been abused."

The screener sighed. It pained him deeply to tell her that she was not acceptable as an adoptive parent. He tried to explain. "I just think you need to resolve your feelings about your abuse before you think about having a child in the home."

Nicole understood at one level, but at another level she felt betrayed. "All I'm asking for is a little help," she said, tears rolling down her cheeks.

"I know," said the screener. "And I can put you in touch with someone who can help you. Please trust me that adoption is not the solution that it appears to be."

Nicole's devastating experience points out the obvious: Individuals who have not experienced childhood sexual abuse are considered better candidates for adoption than those who have been abused. It may seem unfair that adoption agencies would reject a would-be parent because that person has been a victim of sexual abuse, but it happens routinely. That's because, statistically, adults who have been sexually abused as children are more likely to repeat that abuse on their own children when they become parents.

Rules like that are unfair to would-be parents, who otherwise have a great deal to offer, but the rules are in place to protect the children and not to protect the sensibilities of would-be parents. The first responsibility of the adoption agency is to find the most stable home possible, even if that runs counter to the needs of the applicants.

Motivation Is Always the Bottom Line

As an adoption applicant, the first step you should take before applying for adoption is to identify your reasons for wanting a child. If you cannot explain your motivation to yourself, you will never be able to explain it to a screener—and of all the responsibilities the screener has, the most important is to understand your motivation.

One thing to keep in mind is that it is very difficult to fool an experienced screener about your motivation for wanting to adopt. If the screener has had more than three or four years of experience, he or she has probably already seen it all. Since the agency is not looking for perfect parents, honesty carries a lot of weight with the people you are trying to impress. If you depict yourself as perfect, you are more likely to be rejected than if you freely admit your flaws.

Acceptable Reasons for Wanting to Adopt a Child

To experience a more complete family life. It is probably safe to say that most couples enter into a relationship with expectations of starting a family. If it turns out that one of them is unable to conceive a child, it is natural for them to consider adoption, provided both individuals are capable of loving another person's child.

To contribute to the development of another human being. This is a rare motivation, admittedly, but one that is deserving of consideration. It is no secret that most children are born of a passion that is totally unrelated to a desire to contribute to the development of another human being. However, sometimes couples deliberately set out to have a child, doing everything possible to increase their odds of pregnancy, for the purpose of bringing a child into the world. If they cannot have children of their own, they may see adoption as an acceptable substitute. Couples that cannot have children of their own are free to contemplate how they wish to spend their advancing years. Some focus on building a business or establishing a profession. Others devote their lives to the arts. Sometimes couples come to the conclusion that contributing to the development of another human being is something that is very important to them. Individuals who approach adoption from that perspective often make excellent parents.

To accept parental responsibility. Wanting to adopt to contribute to the development of another human being and wanting to adopt to accept parental responsibility represent two different motivations. Those who adopt for this reason have more of a *need* to contribute to the development of society as a whole. They feel that society needs them to accept parental responsibility to help raise children who have been abandoned by society. This is not the best reason in the world to adopt a child, but all other tests having been passed, it is an acceptable reason.

Because you are capable of giving and receiving love. We discussed this earlier, so you may be surprised to encounter it again. We suggested that you not use the "L" word since screeners hear it so often that it sometimes grates on their nerves a bit. What does attract the attention of a screener is when your references use the "L" world. Your capacity to love and be loved is critical to the success of an adoption but it is not the sort of thing for which you can take credit. If you have the capacity to love and be loved, be certain to choose references that will make this clear to the screener. The "L" word needs to come from them, not from you.

Unacceptable Reasons for Wanting to Adopt a Child

To make your marriage stronger. This is the sort of thing that seems reasonable during times of stress. You and your partner have drifted apart. The great passions you once shared—music, art, sports—no longer serve as a bond. Or one of you has grown more than the other. You think that if you both are able to focus on a new passion, namely a child, it will restore your relationship and you will live happily ever after.

To compensate for abuses you experienced as a child. You were sexually, physically, or emotionally abused as a child and you want to right that wrong by demonstrating the "right" way to raise a child. You see it as a second chance for yourself. You feel it will provide you with an opportunity to prove yourself worthy of love.

To give love you never received. Your parents were cold and unforgiving and presented you with a bleak, colorless childhood. You want to prove how deficient they were as parents by raising a child in the proper way.

To promote a religious agenda. Your priest, minister, rabbi, or mullah has told you that God expects you to raise a family. You aren't sure if you can love another person's child, but you are afraid you will displease God if you do not pursue every avenue possible to obtain a child.

To please a partner who wants a child more than you do. You don't feel a strong need to have a child in your life, but it is very important to your spouse and you very much care that he or she is fulfilled in life. You rationalize that you will learn to love the child. Having a child is a sacrifice you are willing to make.

To give meaning to your life. Everything in life has disappointed you, including yourself. You thought you would be more successful at this point in your life. You thought that you would have more close friends than you do. You feel like a failure, your good qualities overlooked or rejected by society. You feel that raising a child will counterbalance your failures in life.

To confirm your beliefs about the debate over nature vs. nurture. You are of the opinion that environment trumps genetic makeup, or you are of the opinion that the opposite is true—that is, you are the person you are genetically programmed to become. You are white and you want to adopt a black child to prove that the child can be raised to have "white values." Or just the opposite: you are a person of color and you want to raise a white child to prove that skin color does not determine the kind of person you become.

Because all your siblings have children and you feel left out. You have been competitive with your siblings your entire life. The only area in which they have been able to outperform you is by having children. You have none and your brother and two sisters have a total of seven children. You feel left out at family gatherings when stories about children are exchanged. You sometimes have to leave the holiday dinner table because of headaches.

Because you are sexually attracted to children. Most pedophiles spend a lifetime denying the truth, even to themselves. It is a myth that they are all single, weird-looking, effeminate men. They are often married and have children. In appearance, they look no different than your neighbor. If you have applied for adoption, you are the only person who knows for certain if you are attracted to children. However, you should know that this is an area that receives a lot of attention from screeners. They may or may not ask you outright if you have ever been sexually attracted to children, but you can be certain that they have less direct ways of obtaining that information from you.

We once were asked to do a home study on a grandfather who wanted to adopt his deceased son's preteen daughters. The girls had become wards of the state after their mother had abandoned them. The grandfather had a lot to gain by putting himself across in a positive manner to us, but from the beginning he was belligerent, angry that the state would intrude into his so-called private business.

Hostility is always a red flag during the home study process. Sometimes it indicates consciousness of guilt. Other times it indicates a level of intolerance that is incompatible with child rearing. It may also be used as a defense to discourage questions in sensitive areas.

In the grandfather's case, hostility was an indicator for all three of the above. We were able to determine, though interviews with him and his neighbors, that he fit the profile of an unrepentant pedophile. By that, we mean someone who had a history of inappropriate behavior toward preteen girls who lived in his community.

When his application to adopt the girls was rejected, he angrily filed a lawsuit to press the issue, thus opening the courthouse door on his earlier transgressions. The girls who were molested by him had since become adults and came forward with testimony that not only backed our assessment of his potential as an adoptive parent but also resulted in criminal charges against him. For his efforts, he got ten years in prison.

Since pedophiles tend to be obsessive, they are prone to overcompensating when confronted with criticism. They disagree with society's definition of inappropriate behavior, and they often feel a high level of righteous indignation over being singled out for engaging in behavior that they consider acceptable. It is the main reason why rehabilitation is not successful in changing their behavior. They go to their graves convinced that they have done nothing wrong.

Financial Assistance: Money Is Available

The federal government offers an adoption tax credit of $10,000 that can be applied to qualifying expenses involved in a child's adoption. Various organizations offer varying amounts of financial assistance in the form of loans and grants. Typically, this assistance is to be used for private domestic or international adoptions, or for public adoptions involving children with special needs.

For example, the National Adoption Foundation has a $9 million fund from which it provides unsecured loans to adoptive families, as well as grants that range from $500 to $2,500. The program is open to all legal adoptions, whether public, private, special needs–related, or international. There is no income requirement. The only requirement is that a home study be completed or underway at the time of application.

The Hebrew Free Loan Association, a California-based organization, offers interest-free loans of up to $10,000 to qualifying Jewish families who have applied for adoption. The main requirement is that the money be repaid.

Many employers will help with employee adoption expenses by providing cash benefits. If your employer doesn't advertise this service, ask anyway. You may be surprised at the response. The U.S. military will reimburse active-duty personnel up to $2,000 on adoption expenses for one child or $5,000 for siblings.

All states offer financial assistance for "special needs" children as a result of the Adoption Assistance and Child Welfare Act of 1980, which was enacted to remove the financial disincentives to the adoption of children with special needs. Children may receive a federally funded subsidy under Title IV-E or a state-funded subsidy as determined by each state's guidelines. The amount of money received is based on each state's foster home rate and varies from $325 to $400 per month in Mississippi to $846 to $1,283 per month in New York. The amounts vary because each state has different cost-of-living indexes, and medical and housing expenses vary widely from state to state.

To qualify as having special needs under the federal legislation, a child must possess one or more of the following characteristics: 1) a physical disability; 2) a mental disability defined as an IQ of 70 or less; 3) a developmental disability; 4) emotional problems; 5) membership in a sibling group of two or more that are placed together; 6) be aged 6 or older; 7) belong to a hard-to-place racial or ethnic group; 8) have a chronic medical condition; or 9) have a history of sexual, emotional, or physical abuse.

Grounds for Rejection

Once your screener completes your home study (it will be fifteen to thirty pages), he or she submits it to a supervisor, along with a recommendation. The screener is more than merely a recorder of information; he or she is a psychosocial profiler who must evaluate the information gathered. The screener must examine you as an individual and, if you have a significant other, as part of a couple. He or she must balance your strengths with your weaknesses and come to a conclusion about your suitability as an adoptive parent. In small agencies, the decision to approve or reject will rest with the screener and supervisor. In larger agencies, there may be a board composed of social workers, psychologists, and health professionals who vote as a group whether to approve your application.

Many times the supervisors may read something in the home study that raises questions that they want answered. In those situations, they will address questions to the screener, who may or may not have the information on hand to provide answers. If the screener doesn't have the information, he or she will call and set up another interview with you. If that happens, do not be overly concerned. Most of the time additional questions do not indicate that your application is in trouble. Extra questions may simply mean that the screener forgot to ask you something that the supervisor considers important.

If your application is rejected, you will probably be notified by mail (if approved, you will probably get a telephone call). A rejection delivered by the postal service is not the agency's way of being cold and distant. Rather, it is to satisfy legal requirements that your rejection be in writing so that there will not be confusion about the status of your application. It is also done to give you space in which to come to terms with the rejection.

The letter will state the reasons for your rejection in general terms. You can be rejected for lack of financial resources, sexual abuse in your past, characteristics of pedophilia, alcoholism, drug addiction, inadequate socialization, a history of spousal abuse, alienation from family members, membership in a radical organization that advocates violence, a history of unresolved marital difficulties, for having made hostile statements or having hostile attitudes toward the country of origin of a prospective adopted child, arrest due to drug use, conviction of assault or other crimes, and so on.

What If You Are Rejected?

If you are rejected as adoptive parents, you should request a face-to-face meeting with your screener and have the reasons explained to you. If you take exception to the grounds for rejection or feel that third parties may have maliciously provided incorrect information, ask for an opportunity to provide the agency with additional information.

If you are dissatisfied after talking to the screener, ask for an appointment with his or her supervisor. The task for the agency is to make certain that you understand the reasons for your rejection. If you do not understand, the supervisor may assign a caseworker to you to help you through what may be a difficult period. If you do understand the reasons—and want to challenge the information upon which the rejection was based—you may appeal the agency's decision to the agency's governing board.

If you are unsuccessful with your appeal within the agency, then you have the right to apply to another agency, the right to file a lawsuit, or both. Filing a lawsuit against an agency that has rejected you usually is counterproductive since, even if you win the lawsuit, the agency still maintains control of the selection process and can withhold a child from you indefinitely by passing over you on a case-by-case basis.

The problem with a lawsuit is that you have no constitutional right to have a child, so you cannot base a legal challenge on a rights violation. Your lawsuit would have to be based on some form of agency negligence or wrongdoing, and that type of charge is extremely difficult to prove. If the agency that rejected you is a public one, then it most likely did not provide you with a copy of your home study.

Obtaining your home study from a public agency is difficult, since it made guarantees of confidentiality to third parties during the home study process and courts are reluctant to override confidentiality agreements. If your rejection came from a private agency, then you probably were given a copy of your home study.

Many lawsuits are initiated by private agency applicants when they can find no real reason for rejection in the home study. There may be a reason for that. If a screener knows that you will read the home study, he or she may withhold all information that would be a violation of the confidentiality agreements made while gathering information about you. As a result, the reasons for your rejection will be stated and discussed off the record.

Before you file a lawsuit against an agency over a rejection, you should know that the most common sources for rejection are the spouse or an immediate member of the family. Examples of that would be the husband who confides that he is simply not interested in raising another man's child and knows that if he tells his wife his true feelings, it would end their relationship. Another example is the mother who confides that her daughter's marriage is in real trouble and she doesn't think that adoption is the solution. A final example is the uncle who suspects his nephew has molested other children. The screener will protect those sources at all costs for obvious reasons, and because you would be devastated by the truth and it would most likely destroy your relationship with loved ones.

You should view a rejection as a caution light that provides you with an opportunity to reassess your strengths and weaknesses as a potential adoption parent. If, after going through the appeal process you still feel that a mistake has been made, you have the right to apply at another agency. There is no adoption blacklist that is passed from agency to agency, so you may reapply at a different agency and get a fresh start. The exception to that would be if the screener at the new agency asks you point-blank if you have ever been rejected for adoption. If that happens, we strongly advise that you tell the truth. It is never wise to build a family on a foundation of lies.

3 They Gave You a Child: Now What?

When that telephone call or letter arrives informing you that you have been accepted as adoptive parents, it will be one of the happiest days of your life. We have seen men and women left breathless by the news.

Of course, acceptance is merely the first step in a long process. Your first response, if you have been contacted by telephone, will be to say, "Thank you so much!" Unless you have prepared for the event by writing questions on a notepad by the telephone, you will probably forget to ask the question that is most on your mind: "When do you think we will get a child?"

Once you have your wits about you again, you will call back and ask a whole series of questions, including the following:

- When do you think we will get a child?
- If you call and we aren't home, will you call back or will you move on to the next applicant on the list?
- How much notice will we get before we see the child?
- Once we view a child, how long do we have to decide?

The screener will tell you that there is no way of knowing when you will be called about a child, and he or she will assure you that you will not be penalized if you are not there to answer the telephone. As far as notice is concerned, the screener will tell you that it varies, depending on a variety of factors: the age of the child, whether the foster parents have a vacation planned, and so on. Once you view a child you will be expected to make a decision within a week, hopefully within a day or so. It is not a good sign if you have difficulty making up your mind.

WHAT HAPPENS AT THE AGENCY AFTER YOU ARE APPROVED?

Once you have been notified of your approval, the screener and supervisor will review the list of children that the agency has available. They will review the various files that have been compiled on the infants—medical reports, physical descriptions, family histories, reports of the infant's progress in the foster home—and they will select a child who is a good match based on family background, hair and eye color, race, personality, and development in the foster home.

Once a candidate has been identified, the screener will visit the child in the foster home to see the child and talk to the foster parents. The screener also will talk to the caseworker who supervises the foster home. Sometimes the caseworker for an infant will be a nurse and not a social worker. That is because the problems that foster parents face during the first year with an infant are almost always health related and some agencies prefer that nurses supervise the home.

If you have requested an older child or a child with special needs, the process will be much different. Instead of the screener and the supervisor reviewing the files, they will meet with the caseworkers that supervise the children in foster care. The screener will describe the adoption applicants and the caseworkers will describe their children. The caseworkers will usually have a good idea what kind of parents their children need based on the type of problems that have been encountered in foster care. Through that process, the most likely prospects for adoption are identified. The screener and the caseworker will usually visit the foster home of each child considered so that the screener can meet the child and the caseworker can deal with the child's fears or apprehensions about the meeting, and so they can discuss the child's development with the foster parents.

Once the screener, the supervisor, and the caseworker are in agreement, plans will be made for a viewing (if the child is an infant) or a visit (if the child is older). If none of the agency's children seem right for the applicants, they will be added to the waiting list. It is impossible to predict how long an applicant will remain on the waiting list. It could be weeks, months, or years.

What to Expect at the Viewing or Visit

When the screener calls to invite you to the agency for a viewing he or she will also make it clear to you that you should not feel pressured to accept the child who is presented to you if you have doubts or misgivings about that particular child. It will not be a "take it or leave it" situation. The last word in adoption belongs to you.

When you arrive at the agency you will be asked to remain in the waiting room until the child is ready. What you see when you enter the viewing room will depend on the age of the child. If it is an infant, you will see the screener and a caseworker holding the child. If it is an older child, you will see the screener, the child or children, and the caseworker. The foster parents will not be present. That is because the agency does not disclose the identity of adoptive parents to foster parents unless the children are school age or older.

Once everyone is at ease, you will be left alone with the child. The length of the visit will depend on the age of the child. The older the child, the longer the visit. For infants, fifteen or twenty minutes are usually enough. For older children, thirty or forty minutes would be more appropriate, depending on the comfort level of the child.

After the visit, you will discuss your reactions to the child with the screener and caseworker. If you have questions, they will try to answer them for you. You should be straightforward with the agency about any reservations you have. If you did not have a positive reaction to the child and do not feel that you can be accepting, it is important that you discuss it in a frank manner. If your response was positive, the screener will set up a time for the child to visit you in your home.

Of course, if you view a child and then say no you will want to make your reasons very clear. You will not arbitrarily be ruled out for another child, but your rejection of the child will be carefully examined and you may be asked to attend another interview. The reason for a postviewing interview is to make certain that you and your spouse are in agreement about adoption in general. Once the agency is satisfied that you are in agreement, it will want to analyze your reasons for the rejection of the child. It is important for you to be honest with the agency so that future viewings will not end in rejection. If you reject two or three children, the odds are not good that you will be invited back for a return visit because the agency will begin to question your motivation.

What You Can Do to Prepare for the Home Visit

We have never encountered adoptive parents who were not joyously anxious about the arrival of the child for the first visit, so it is not a bad sign if you are on pins and needles about the child's arrival. Visitation is not a complicated procedure, but there are certain things that you should do to ensure that it goes smoothly:

- If the child is an infant, make certain that you have all the diapers, lotions, oils, food, and so on that you will need for an all-day visit. Your spouse may or may not be at home for a portion of the visit and you do not want to find yourself in the position of having to drag the child to a store or having to leave it with a sitter while you run errands.

- If the child is older, make certain that you have an assortment of lunch possibilities on hand—or, better yet, ask the screener or caseworker to ask the foster parents what the child prefers to eat for lunch.

- For older children, plan activities that you can enjoy together—and we don't mean watching television. Talk to friends and relatives who have children the same age and ask for their advice on how to entertain the child. What you don't want to do is to ask a six-year-old to sit on the couch so that you can say, "Tell me all about yourself." Children communicate through play. They are not very good at question-and-answer conversations.

- Ask friends and relatives to wait until another time to schedule their visit. Subsequent visits—and the agency may require three or four, depending on the age of the child—are usually more relaxed. As the visits progress, it is all right to introduce the child to your friends and family. Just be careful not to overwhelm the child. Children are small people and the sight of large people rushing forward to hug or embrace them can be a frightening experience.

Home Visits: Joyful or Intimidating?

Whether your visits are joyful or intimidating will depend entirely on you. You are in control of the process from this point onward. The agency has already passed judgment on you. Now you will pass judgment on the child. Things can go wrong during visitation that could result in the agency taking that control away from you (we will discuss those situations later). But unless something extraordinary happens, you will be the person who decides the child's future.

The most important thing for you to remember is that the purpose of the visitation is not for you to impress the child. Just be yourself. The child will be nervous about the visitation, not knowing what to expect. The child senses that it is a test of some kind, but doesn't know what he or she is supposed to do to pass the test. The child will look to you for guidance.

For that reason, you should go out of your way not to make the child respond to questions he or she doesn't understand.

Here are some suggestions that you may find helpful:

- Give the child a walk-through tour of your home, but do not say, "This will be your room," since it would put pressure on the child. The child will be able to choose a room without your help.

- Ask the child what he or she wants for lunch. If he or she is too shy to give you an answer—"I don't know"—then give the child a choice: "Would you like to go get a pizza, or would you like for me to make you a sandwich?"

- If your spouse cannot be there for the visit, take the child to your spouse's workplace, if possible, for a brief visit.

- Invite friends and relatives over to met the child, but caution them about being too demonstrative with their affections.

At the end of each visit the screener will talk to you about what happened. You must be honest about your feelings concerning the child. If you have reservations, you should discuss them with the screener. If you decide you do not want to continue with the remaining visits, you should express those feelings clearly to the screener. Likewise, the screener will discuss the visits with the child. If he or she senses that the child does not feel comfortable in your home, the screener may terminate the visits.

Surviving the Probationary Period

If the visits go well, the child will be placed in your home for a period of supervised probation that will usually last from six to twelve months (different agencies have different probationary periods). The purpose of the probationary period is twofold: to protect the child, and to provide you and the child with casework support should any problems arise. It is important that you not view the probationary period as a threat. The agency wants it to work out as much as you do.

The person who supervises your adoption during the probationary period may be the screener or it may be the child's caseworker, depending on agency policy. Visits will be made to your home at regularly scheduled times, with unscheduled visits also a possibility. During the visits, the caseworker will observe the child, talk to the child in private if the child is old enough, and discuss with you any problems you might be having with the child. Do not be afraid to ask the caseworker's advice if you have questions about discipline, health concerns, or eating problems. You will be encouraged to take the child to your physician for a checkup, especially if the child is an infant.

Finalizing the Adoption

At the end of the probationary period, you will have a frank discussion about making the adoption permanent with the caseworker who supervised your placement. You can be certain that if the agency left the child in your home for the duration of the probation, they will not oppose finalizing the adoption. If, on the other hand, you feel you did not become attached to the child, you have the right to terminate the proceedings and ask that the child be removed from your home. That is rare, but it happens. In that case, the agency will devise an strategy for the child to be removed with as little emotional damage as possible.

If the adoption proceeds to finalization, the next step is to file a petition with the court in the jurisdiction of your residence to approve the adoption. If you are adopting through a public agency, the paperwork will be handled by the agency. If you are adopting through a private agency, the paperwork will be handled by the agency or by a lawyer whom you choose, depending on the agency's policy. If the adoption placement was initiated by a facilitator or by the child's birth parents or guardian, you will have to hire a lawyer to handle the adoption petition. Some lawyers have more experience in this area than others, so shop around for one who has a reputation for dealing with adoption issues.

State laws differ, but most states require a postplacement investigation and report before an adoption can be finalized by the court. Typically, public and private agencies provide the report, but in the case of adoptions initiated by facilitators or the child's birth parents or guardian, the courts may hire a social worker or psychologist to prepare the report.

Once all the paperwork has been done, and the necessary reports filed, the judge will conduct a hearing in his or her office or in a courtroom. If there are no problems and no opposition to the adoption, the judge will sign a decree or order that names you as the legal parent of the child. This part of the adoption process is usually anticlimactic, with your presence not required.

Things to Do Immediately After Finalization

You may want to have a celebration party or dinner that involves the child, depending on the age of the child and his or her comfort level discussing the adoption. Older children sometimes do not want their parents to make a big deal out of the fact that they have been adopted.

Once your jubilation subsides, you need to attend to the business end of the adoption. Here are a few of the things you will need to do:

- Apply for a Social Security number from the Social Security Administration. To do that you will need proof of the adoption and proof of residency for you and the child.

- Have an attorney draw up a will or trust that will ensure that the child will be provided for in the event of your death. State laws differ, so you must be certain that your will takes note of your child's adopted status.

- Include the child in your health insurance coverage. Sometimes adoptive parents forget to change their policies from individual to family coverage and only learn that their child is not covered during a health care emergency.

- If you don't have life insurance, you should take out a policy as soon as possible. If you already have a life insurance policy, make certain that the child is listed as a beneficiary and pay particular attention to the language of the policy since some use limiting terms such as "descendants" or "heirs of the body." Tell the insurance company that you have adopted and ask for written confirmation that the child is included in the policy.

- Some adoptive parents who adopt through expensive private agencies take out a life insurance policy on the child, fearing that they would not have the money to pursue another adoption if the child passed away.

- If you did not take the child to a dentist or physician during the probationary period, you need to do so as soon as possible so that you will have established health-care contacts in the event of illness. Let the physician or dentist know your child is adopted. Some physicians are uncomfortable treating children when a full health history is not available. Find out in advance if the physician you have chosen for your child has any negative attitudes about treating adopted children. We think it is a good idea for a child to receive a complete physical, including blood tests, especially if he or she has been adopted from abroad. Children can carry Hepatitis B, syphilis, tuberculosis, and other infectious diseases. In the case of Hepatitis B, a serious disease that can cause permanent liver damage later in life, the child can be infected and show no symptoms and still transmit it to unsuspecting family members.

4 International Adoptions

With eighteen thousand foreign adoptions processed every year in the United States, it is clear that international adoptions have become a major alternative for Americans unable to have children of their own and unwilling to go through domestic adoption agencies. Those who adopt through international agencies have two things in common: they are primarily interested in infants or toddlers of European or Asian ancestry; and they have enough disposable income to be able to afford the $10,000 to $30,000 that overseas adoptions can cost.

That is not to say that older children are not also adopted—they are being chosen in increasing numbers—or that other ethnic groups, such as Hispanic or African, are not represented. Each year nearly five hundred children are adopted from Ethiopia, two hundred and thirty from Haiti, and three hundred from Colombia, but those numbers fall far short of the eight thousand adoptions from China and the forty-six hundred adoptions from Russia.

International adoptions have all the ingredients of domestic adoptions—home study requirements, for example, and good health and employment verifications—but they are much more complicated and require the participation of the Citizenship and Immigration Service division of the Department of Homeland Security and the U.S. Department of State. On a complexity level, the difference between the paperwork associated with domestic and international adoptions is the difference between filling out a change-of-address form at the post office and filling out an income tax return.

For those willing and able to overcome those obstacles—and savvy enough to deal with the occasional instances of fraud or incompetence that arise in international agencies, both in the United States and abroad—international adoptions can be a rewarding way to build a family.

Cast of Characters

United States Bureau of Citizenship and Immigration Services

United States Department of State

U.S. International Adoption Agency of Your Choice

Foreign Adoption Agency (or a Private Facilitator)

Foreign Orphanages

Foreign State Departments

Licensed Social Worker or Psychologist (U.S.)

Local U.S. Senator or House of Representatives Member

SIX STEPS TO INTERNATIONAL ADOPTION

The first revelation you will discover about international adoption is that it involves a lot of "hurry up and wait" procedures. You rush to get something done and then you wait forever for signs of progress. Unlike domestic adoptions, where you usually go through the entire process dealing with one bureaucracy and two individuals at most, international adoptions require dealings with several bureaucracies and the cooperation of dozens of people, most of whom you will never meet.

The best way to approach international adoption is one step at a time.

Step One: Selecting an Adoption Agency

International adoption agencies in the United States are licensed, but that does not necessarily mean that they are regulated. Each state has different standards. Your first step in adoption should be to contact the international agencies in your state and request information about their adoption programs.

Some agencies specialize in the adoption of children from a specific country or region. Others work with representatives in various countries. If you are only interested in children from a particular country, you need to make certain that the agency you have selected has experience with adoption in that country. If there are no agencies in your state that offer the choices you want, you should contact agencies in surrounding states.

If you have several choices there is nothing wrong in meeting with representatives of all the agencies. At this point, you are interviewing them, and you have a right to expect full disclosure from them. When speaking with the agency's representative keep an open mind. The odds are that they know more about adoption than you do.

If you have your heart set on a child from China and the agency representatives suggest that you also consider children from the Philippines, Korea, Thailand, or Vietnam, listen to what they have to say and ask them to explain why they are recommending children from other Asian countries.

It is appropriate for you to ask how many adoptions they do yearly, which countries they deal with, and how much they charge for their services (if they seem vague or hesitant to answer this question, then you might want to consider going elsewhere). You also need to know whether they plan to do your home study in-house or refer you to a licensed professional, and information about the work experience of the people employed at the agency.

One word of caution: not all international adoption agencies are created equal and the fact that an agency has been licensed by the state is not a guarantee of ethical representation. All a license means is that the agency has met minimum standards insofar as organizational and educational requirements are concerned. Since private adoption agencies do have a history of wrongdoing—indeed, there have been instances of corruption and actual child selling—you should run a background check on the one you have chosen to represent you (they will be doing the same to you). You can do that by making inquiries at the Better Business Bureau and at the state attorney general's office.

An analysis of the agency's staff qualifications will give you a good indication of its potential to serve your needs. If it is heavy on love, but light on professional experience, you might want to consider an alternative since it takes more than love and tender mercies to make international adoption a reality.

Charles and Dolly Garrison were past forty and the parents of two teenage sons when they did the unthinkable: they decided to adopt a daughter. "I didn't want to go through life without a daughter and I couldn't have any more children," Dolly explained to a newspaper that interviewed her for a feature on adoption. Since they knew that American agencies, public and private, would not give a high priority to their application because of their ages and because they had two children of their own, they decided to pursue an international adoption.

As a result, Charles and Dolly adopted a two-year-old girl from Korea. The adoption went so well that they adopted a six-year-old Bolivian boy and then followed that up with the adoption of a four-month-old girl from Bolivia.

After their second adoption, they decided that one of them should stay home with the children. Charles volunteered to quit his job so that he could care for the children. That arrangement worked out well and he never regretted giving up his job. The same year that Charles and Dolly finalized their third adoption, they decided to expand their adoption efforts by starting up an international agency named Adoptions International, Inc. It was only the second international agency ever to be licensed in Tennessee.

One look at the background of the personnel at the agency and you knew it was serious about adoption. Dolly, with her degree in business administration, assumed the title of executive director and coordinated communications among the individuals and agencies involved and handled the agency's business matters. Dolly's sister Sharon Gary, the president and casework supervisor, was a psychologist, as was the clinical director and a consultant who provided guidance in the area of childhood development. Then there was the agency's liaison to Central and South America, a Bolivian native who once worked for the Bolivian government in its efforts to assist homeless children. An experienced public-agency screener with business contacts in Russia also was hired.

Adoptions International got off to a strong start by arranging placements from Bolivia, but less than a year after the agency was founded, Charles died quite unexpectedly. One day he was fine and the next he was dead, killed by a flesh-eating bacteria that seemed to appear from nowhere. One week later, Dolly underwent heart bypass surgery. These tragedies only made Dolly more determined to help others realize their dreams of adoption. After she recovered from her surgery, she continued with her work at the agency with the help of an Argentine friend who moved in with her to care for the children. Raising the three adopted children without the help of her husband was not something she had planned on. One thing that helped was a poignant message that Charles had left in the drawer of his nightstand on top of his Bible. On a piece of paper he had written, "Children are a gift from God." Everyone tried to keep the agency going, especially Dolly, but it eventually succumbed to the inertia of a tragic beginning, proving that sometimes it is impossible to recover from life's cruelest blows.

There are two lessons to be learned from the Adoptions International story. The first is that it can serve as a role model for how international agencies should be structured. The head of the agency should have a passion for adoption. Operating an adoption agency is not a job so much as it is a mission. You don't want the head of your agency to be a nine-to-fiver. You want someone who believes in what he or she is doing. Adoptions International's mixture of psychologists, social workers, and facilitators who effectively served as liaisons to countries targeted for adoption was a necessity for successful placements.

The second lesson is that it offers an example of how quickly an adoption placement can be transformed by events from ideal to tragic. Dolly had the savvy to build a support network that could help her with her children, but many adoptive parents do not have the knowledge or means to do so and their families are usually torn apart by tragedy. It is one reason why foreign countries are sometimes obsessive in demanding progress reports and assurances that the adoption is working out. The prospect of a child traveling halfway around the world to live with an American adoptive family, only to have the child end up in foster homes because the adoptive family did not plan for the child's future in the event of their deaths, is a tragedy that can be avoided with proper advance planning.

Step Two: The Home Study

Whether you go through an agency or a facilitator, or both, you will want to begin the home study process as soon as possible. Facilitators are people who act as go-betweens in international adoptions. They are not social workers or psychologists, but rather lawyers with expertise on the legal aspects of international adoption or private individuals who have extensive contacts with public officials and orphanages in the countries targeted for adoption.

International adoption is basically a private matter between the applicant and a foreign court, which oversees that country's adoption rules and regulations. However, whether you initially go through an agency or a facilitator for your adoption, you will still be required to go through the home study process.

Depending on when you get your first appointment with the screener, it could take two months or more to complete the home study. That is because you and your spouse will be scheduled for a series of interviews, some which will take place in an office and others of which will take place in your home. In addition to the interviews, references will be requested from friends, relatives, and a physician who is familiar with your medical history—all of which takes time.

Home studies for domestic adoptions and international adoptions differ in the following important ways:

- Adoption screeners at domestic agencies will want to know your attitudes toward different countries, ethnic groups, religions, and races in the event that a child of a different race, religion, or ethnic background becomes available for adoption. Adoption screeners for international adoptions know in advance that you have decided to pursue a child of a different race, religion, or ethnic background, and they will spend more time exploring your attitudes in those areas. They will want to know what experience you have with individuals from the targeted country and why you have chosen that race, religion, or ethnic group to provide you with a child. Don't be annoyed if they press you on this issue. There have been cases where individuals have chosen a particular race or ethnic group because they despise it and want to prove that their race and ethnic group are superior to the child's by raising the child to repudiate his or her own racial or ethnic background. The screener will want to make certain you are not one of those people.

- The home studies themselves are different since they are essentially public documents. You will receive a copy, along with court and immigration officials. Unlike domestic home studies, where everything discussed during the interviews is written up in the report, international home studies censor information about your sexual or personal history that would embarrass you if read by strangers. As in agencies themselves, there are wide gaps in professionalism among screeners. An incompetent screener will gloss over your relationship or personal problems and give you a report that will cause no waves. A competent screener will want to discuss your problems in detail and be certain that you are not a threat to a child before approving you for adoption. If the screener feels that you are not a suitable adoptive parent, he or she may tell you before the report is written and suggest that you undergo counseling with a therapist before proceeding, or he may advise you to withdraw. Or the screener may write up the situation as he or she sees it and send you the finished product without warning you in advance that it contains negative information about your potential as an adoptive parent. Either way, you will have paid for the home study in advance. Prices can vary from $500 to $3,000.

Step Three: Bureau of Citizenship and Immigration Service

Before you can bring a child from another country into the United States, you must receive a visa for the child from the Bureau of Citizenship and Immigration Service (BCIS). If you have located a child in a foreign country you cannot simply go to the U.S. Embassy and request a visa. The proceedings must be begun in the United States prior to the location of the child. The BCIS has two forms that apply:

- Form I-600 is used if you have located a child in a foreign country and want to obtain a visa.
- Form I-600A is used if you have not identified a particular child and want to go abroad to locate a child for adoption.

The purpose of the I-600 forms is to initiate the process by which the BCIS evaluates your suitability as adoptive parents (by means of your home study), to determine if there are any preadoption requirements in your state of residency for finalization of an adoption order (this applies in instances in which the child is adopted after entry into the United States; some countries require that the adoption take place in their jurisdiction before the child leaves the country), and to determine if the child you want to adopt meets the legal standards for being an orphan. In addition to a home study, the BCIS requires the following:

- Fingerprints of the adoptive parents and every adult who lives in the household; the fingerprints must be checked for any criminal records by state and federal authorities
- A police report that the applicants have no record of child abuse
- Employment verification
- A medical report on the applicant

If the BCIS is satisfied that all requirements have been met, it will notify the U.S. State Department through the embassy or consulate that processes visas for residents of the child's country. While that is taking place, the approved I-600 or I-600A will be sent to the National Visa Center in New Hampshire, where it will be coded with a tracking number and sent to the appropriate U.S. consular office abroad.

If you filed the I-600A form, you will be notified if it is approved and notification of your approval will be sent to the appropriate U.S. mission in the country where you have indicated a desire to adopt. Once you locate a specific child, you will have to file an I-600 petition either at the local BCIS office in the United States or with the U.S. consular office overseas. At least one parent who is a U.S. citizen must be physically present to file the I-600 petition overseas. The petition cannot be filed on your behalf by a third party, even if that person has your power of attorney.

Step Four: Foreign Adoption Agency or Facilitator

While you are dealing with the BCIS, your adoption agency or facilitator will be establishing contact with a counterpart in the foreign country. It doesn't matter whether your contact is an adoption agency or a facilitator; he or she will expect money from you. That shouldn't come as a surprise. This person is working for you just as your U.S. agency or facilitator is working for you and will locate children of the gender, age, and health status that you have specified. Most likely, the contact will find several children considered to be appropriate. If so, he or she will send photographs and identifying information to your U.S. agency or facilitator for presentation to you. That part is pretty straightforward.

The dicey aspect of international adoption begins once you have made your choice. The gatekeeper who stands between you and the child may be a public official or an orphanage director. This person will expect money from you in order to release the child. That sounds unseemly, but you should know that public officials and orphanage directors in many countries have such meager salaries that they must solicit "donations" from those they deal with in order to make a living wage. Before you get too outraged at that system, you should know that those "donations" are no different from the "donations" that flow to American elected officials from people who want favors. When foreigners request money, it is sometimes called a bribe, but when American officials do it, it is called a campaign contribution. Whatever you call it, just have your checkbook ready.

Once you have identified the child you want to adopt, the foreign agency or facilitator must gather the proper documentation to satisfy the BCIS and the appropriate foreign officials that the child meets the legal definition of an orphan. This is an area where you must be careful. Just because the child's country has labeled the child an orphan does not mean that the orphan status will be approved by the BCIS.

The United States defines a child whose parents are dead or a child who has no parents due to several other circumstances as an orphan. If the child is in an orphanage, there probably will not be a challenge of his or her orphan status. However, if the child was given to you or an adoption agency by his or her parents, the child will not be classified as an orphan.

While that is going on, your foreign agency or facilitator will arrange for the child to be examined by a physician designated by the BCIS. The examination will focus on a list of serious contagious diseases or disabilities that may be a basis for a visa rejection. The examination will not detect serious psychological problems or whether the child has ever suffered sexual, emotional, or physical abuse. If you have concerns about diseases and conditions not on the BCIS checklist, you can arrange for a physician whom you choose to examine the child before it leaves for the United States.

Step Five: The State Department and Citizenship

It seems like a backward way of doing things, but if you finalize your adoption in the child's country of residence, the first step in your child acquiring American citizenship is the State Department's approval of a visa for the child. Under U.S. law, the adopted child of a U.S. citizen automatically becomes a U.S. citizen upon entry into the country. If you do not adopt in the child's country of residence, your child will be granted permanent residency upon entry into the United States and will become a citizen when the adoption is finalized in the United States. Either way, the visa is key to your child obtaining citizenship and you must be careful to address all the concerns and questions posed by U.S. Embassy officials, even if they seem unnecessary to you at the time.

If you do not adopt in the child's country of origin, you will have to file for adoption in your home state. You will need a lawyer to do that. Before your child leaves his or her country of origin you will have to request a visa named the IR-4. Before it can be issued, the embassy must be certain that the child will be eligible for adoption in your home state (each state's laws are different, if only slightly). To be safe you should check with officials in your home state before ever leaving the country. You don't want to be thousands of miles away from home and realize that you cannot adopt in your home state.

Step Six: When You Return to the United States

If you finalized your adoption abroad, your child was granted full U.S. citizenship the moment you stepped foot on American soil with the child. There is no need for you to apply for either a passport or a Certificate of Citizenship for your child. The child has all the rights that you possess under U.S. law, and there is no probationary period for the adoption. Many people are surprised at the ease with which a child adopted abroad by a U.S. citizen can be granted citizenship.

If you finalized your adoption when you returned, you will have to apply for a Certificate of Citizenship from the BCIS for your child. In order to do that you will need the child's foreign passport or resident alien card; a certified copy of the final adoption decree; and valid identification that confirms that you are a U.S. citizen (birth certificate, Social Security number, or other like documents). Whether your child was adopted abroad or in the States, you will need to apply for the child's own Social Security number.

Some countries will not allow you to adopt the child before you remove him or her from the country. The reason for that is so that they can monitor a probationary period for a specified number of months (typically six months, but it can be as long as two years). During that time, the child welfare authorities in your state of residence will be required to follow up on the adoption and issue periodic reports on the child's progress in your home. In those cases, you cannot file an adoption petition until the probationary period is over.

Some states require that a child adopted abroad be readopted in a state court. We think readoption is a good idea, even in those states that do not require it. Readoption gives you additional legal protection for your child and it allows you to apply for a new birth certificate in your state of residence.

WHAT IF SOMETHING GOES WRONG?

The U.S. government can do many things to facilitate your adoption. It can provide you with information about adoption in countries around the world. It can protect you if you are discriminated against by foreign authorities. And it can make inquiries of foreign officials about the status of your adoption.

The U.S. government cannot become involved in the adoption process in another country. It cannot represent you in court, whether foreign or domestic. It cannot order that an adoption take place or that a visa be issued. And it cannot protect you against fraud.

It is the responsibility of your adoption agency or facilitator to protect you against fraud and you must use good judgment in selecting individuals you can trust. Adoption is a lucrative business, both in the United States and abroad, and although most agencies are honest and straightforward, some are not. The types of fraud you must be vigilant about include the following:

- Agencies that promise you a particular child and cannot deliver
- Agencies that offer you a healthy child with fraudulent medical documentation, so that only later do you learn that the child is seriously ill
- Agencies that require prepayment for a nonexistent or ineligible child
- A foreign contact that scams your agency and gives you a child that has been stolen from his or her parents

Sometimes unethical behavior occurs that may seem to be to your advantage. In reality it never is. Prior to 2001, Romania was a major source of children for adoption, but that was because children were being released to adoptive parents without any regard for child welfare safeguards and practices. Adoptive parents traveled to Romania and went directly to the orphanages to make a deal, or to meetings with the child's birth parents, and then left with the children.

When the U.S. government issued a report in 2001 stating that the adoption program was "susceptible to corrupt practices and ... many of the financial resources generated for child protection programs through the inter-country adoption process were being ... misappropriated," the Romanian government declared a moratorium on adoptions.

Shortcuts of the type used in Romania prior to 2001 opened the door for scam artists to sell children to the highest bidder, and they allowed children into the adoption pipeline who had unrevealed diseases or, in some cases, were not actually available for adoption. Shortcuts may seem attractive at first, since they cut through bureaucratic red tape, but if they result in a child whom you cannot legally bring into the United States, or a child who is dying of an undisclosed disease, what have you gained?

If you suspect that you have been scammed, or if you are approached with adoptions that are suspect, you should report the activity to the district attorney in your home state and to the BCIS, which will involve federal law enforcement agencies if needed.

If the BCIS has made an unfavorable ruling in your case or is taking too long to process your paperwork, you should contact your local member of Congress and ask for his or her help. In an ideal world, agencies such as the BCIS and the State Department are supposed to be immune to the influence of members of Congress, but in the real world, they routinely intervene with federal agencies at the request of their constituents.

TOP FIFTEEN COUNTRIES FOR INTERNATIONAL ADOPTION

The nature of international adoption is that individual countries change their rules and regulations on a regular basis. The information in this section is based on details gleaned from various sources, including the U.S. State Department and the Bureau of Citizenship and Immigration Services, and it is offered not as legal advice, but rather as reportage on the basics of adoption in each country. The information is subject to change. You should contact qualified legal counsel before initiating any contact regarding adoption with any of the following countries.

Russia

Russia has been a major source of adopted children for several years now, alternating between the number one and number two supplier of children to American adoption applicants, but that may be coming to an end because of recent scandals in the United States involving the adoption programs. In one instance, a Chicago woman was sentenced to twelve years in prison for beating her 6-year-old Russian adopted child to death. In another instance, an American woman was charged with the murder of a 2-year-old girl she had adopted in Russia. The autopsy showed that the child died after being hit in the stomach.

As a result of cases like those, some Russian leaders are pressuring their government to exert more control over international adoption programs.

Already authorities have suspended accreditation for three U.S. adoption agencies because they failed to supervise the adoptive parents after they returned to the United States. Some Russian officials are urging that all foreigners wanting to adopt Russian children be required to undergo psychological testing to determine their emotional stability.

Despite the concern in Russia, authorities are not likely to restrict the adoption program too severely because there are an estimated two million orphaned children in that country who need permanent homes. It is difficult to place them with Russian families because adoption carries a stigma in that country and because there are few families that can afford to adopt additional children.

As it now stands in Russia, children must be registered in the state database for three months before they are considered for international adoption. U.S. citizens who want to adopt in Russia must first apply at a regional Ministry of Education office, which then directs them to an orphanage that has available children. Adoptive parents are asked to travel to Russia to meet the children and once they have made their choice they are directed to apply for a court date. The parents may return to the United States until the court date, but the child they have selected must remain in Russia.

When the parents return to Russia for the court date, they will most likely obtain the adoption certificate and a new birth certificate that bears the child's new name after the court hearing. Before they can take the child to the United States, the parents must obtain an immigrant visa to the United States and register with the Ministry of Foreign Affairs.

There are no age requirements for adoption in Russia, and singles and divorcees are permitted to adopt. However, there are some restrictions for singles. They must show proof of above-average income and offer a childcare plan if they are currently employed, they must be at least sixteen years older than the child, and they are only allowed to adopt one child at a time. In addition, they are required to submit a psychiatric evaluation to the Russian government certifying them as good risks for adoption.

The U.S. government advises Americans adopting in Russia that visa requirements for foreign travelers in Russia are restrictive and complicated, and they are subject to change without notice. Since the Russian government does not recognize the standing of U.S. consular officers to intervene in visa cases, the U.S. Embassy is forbidden to act as a sponsor for an American applying for adoption. It also cannot request that visas or migration cards be corrected or replaced. Americans are reminded to protect their passports and visas from theft since it is not possible to leave Russia without a passport and a valid visa. It is also recommended that travelers kept their documents with them at all times since police officers have the authority to stop people and request their documents at any time without cause. If a traveler does not have proper documentation, he or she is subject to detention and heavy fines.

China

China is the largest supplier of children for adoption in the United States, with about thirty thousand children placed with American parents over the past five years. Because of discrimination against females in that country, the majority of children available for adoption are infant girls since they are considered less valuable than infant boys.

China is open to single men and women who apply for adoption, but its preference is for married couples between the ages of thirty and fifty-five. Single women who apply must be between thirty and fifty years of age and should not be more than forty-five years older than the child. Single men must be thirty to fifty years of age for the adoption of a boy and forty to fifty years old for the adoption of a girl. Applications from gay applicants are not accepted.

All adoptions are processed by the Chinese Center for Adoption Affairs, which matches individual children with adoptive parents whose applications have been submitted by a licensed U.S. adoption agency, which has credentials on file at the center. Once a child has been located, the center will send a letter of introduction about the child, along with the child's photograph and medical record.

If the child is accepted by the adoptive applicants, the center will provide the prospective parents with a formal notice and permission to proceed to China. Upon arrival, the applicants will undergo a series of interviews with Chinese authorities. Before the adoption is completed, the applicants will be permitted to see the child. They also may be permitted to have the child examined by a physician on the U.S. Embassy's list of approved physicians before finalizing the adoption.

Before completing the adoption contract, adoptive parents will be expected to make a donation of $3,000 to $4,000 to China's Children's Welfare Institute. Once the adoption is final, the adoptive parents are responsible for the child. If they return to the United States and decide that they cannot keep the child, they cannot return the child to China.

Americans traveling to China are reminded that they place themselves under the jurisdiction of local courts upon their arrival and can expect little in the way of assistance from the U.S. Embassy if they run into difficulties.

South Korea

South Korea is the fourth largest supplier of children for adoption in the United States, with approximately eight thousand children placed with American parents over the past five years. Under South Korean law, all overseas adoptions must take place through an adoption agency authorized by the Korean Ministry of Health and Social Affairs. A list of authorized adoption agencies can be obtained from the U.S. State Department.

The first step in adopting a Korean child is to apply to a U.S. adoption agency so that the home study process can begin. That should be followed up with contact with the BCIS to initiate the preprocessing of the child for an immigrant visa.

Once the placement has taken place, the child will leave Korea in the care of a U.S. adoption agency that is affiliated with one of four South Korean licensed agencies. It is not necessary for the adoptive parents to travel to Korea. The adoption agency will oversee the case in Korea and arrange for the transportation of the child to the United States.

Once the child is in the United States, the adoption agency will supervise the placement and make a series of visits at six-month intervals, sending reports to the responsible agency in Korea. At the end of the first year, the American family is expected to apply for adoption in a court in their home state. After the adoption is finalized, the adoption agency will remain in constant contact with the family until the child becomes a naturalized U.S. citizen, a process that usually takes two years.

Under Korean law, American adoptive parents must be eligible to adopt in their home state, and they must provide proof that they have been married for at least three years and are between the ages of twenty-five and forty-four. The age difference between the man and the woman cannot exceed fifteen years. Exceptions to the age requirement will be considered for applicants who have previously adopted a Korean orphan or who are willing to adopt an orphan with serious medical problems. Single applicants are not encouraged to apply.

Guatemala

Guatemala is the third largest supplier of children for adoption to the United States, with about eighteen thousand children placed with American parents over the past five years. Guatemalan adoptions are processed under a "notarial" system operated by Guatemalan attorneys who perform the role of an adoption agency. Under this system, an attorney will refer an orphan to prospective adoptive parents via their U.S. adoption agency. The agency then provides the attorney with power of attorney if they accept the referral. The attorney will act on their behalf to complete the adoption and represent the adoptive parents, the birth parents, and the child in Guatemalan government proceedings.

In some respects the adoption requirements in Guatemala are liberal compared to other countries. Applicants can be married or single and up to fifty years of age. They impose no limit on the number of children already in the adoptive family's home. Adoptive parents can specify the gender of the child they want to adopt. Despite many liberal viewpoints on adoption, Guatemala will not place children with gay applicants.

It is important to remember that an adoptive parent's agency and attorney are the only contacts for the progress of the adoption. The U.S. Embassy, which issues about thirty-five hundred immigrant visas a year to Guatemalan children adopted by U.S. citizens, does not receive information on the status of individual adoptions, nor does it have the authority to intervene in court in Guatemala adoptions. When questions arise, adoption applicants are advised to direct them to the agency or attorney who represents them.

Ukraine

Ukraine does not allow adoption agencies to operate in that country or locate a child for adoption, but facilitators are allowed to assist with translation and interpretation services. The only Ukrainian authority empowered to handle adoptions is the Adoption Center, a division of the Ministry of Education. The Adoption Center is involved in the process from the moment adoption applicants apply for registration until an adoption hearing is held in court. For that reason, the Adoption Center insists on direct contact with prospective adoptive parents or their facilitators or interpreters. All conversations with the center must be held in either Russian or Ukrainian.

The U.S. State Department suggests that prospective adoptive parents use caution in hiring a facilitator or interpreter and discuss all fees and expenses in great detail. While the U.S. Embassy cannot vouch for the professionalism of a specific facilitator or interpreter, it does maintain a list of adoption translators known to work in Ukraine.

Both married and single applicants are acceptable in Ukraine. They must be eighteen years of age or older and the difference between the age of the adopting parent and adopted child must be at least fifteen years, although waivers have been granted in special circumstances. It generally takes two to six months to be matched with a Ukrainian orphan after the home study has been submitted to the Adoption Center. Applicants can expect a three- to four-week wait between the initial filing of the adoption in local court and the issuance of the final adoption order. Applicants cannot remove the child from Ukraine until the adoption has been finalized.

India

India is the eighth largest provider of adopted children to the United States.

India requires couples interested in adopting an infant to be between the ages of twenty-five and forty-five, with a combined age of no more than eighty-five. Couples interested in toddlers or school age children may be up to age fifty-five. Single women up to age forty-five may be approved on a case-by-case basis. Adoptive applicants with four or more children are not eligible.

Americans are not allowed to adopt Indian children in India, but they are eligible to apply for legal guardianship of a child who meets the Indian government definition of destitute and abandoned. Once that has been granted, they are free to take the child out of India and adopt the child in the United States, as long as they do so within two years.

American applicants are required to work through an American adoption agency chosen from a list of agencies approved by the Indian government. It is recommended that an Indian attorney be hired by the applicants to oversee the process in India.

Americans must finalize the adoption in their home state.

Colombia

Colombia is the ninth largest provider of adopted children to the United States, with 865 adoptions processed over the past five years. Since private adoptions are not permitted, children must be adopted through the Colombian Family Welfare Institute or through approved adoption agencies. Only married men and women are eligible to adopt in Colombia. They must be between twenty-five and thirty-eight years of age and married for at least three years (five years is preferred but not mandatory). They may have no biological children in the family and they must provide proof of infertility. Newborns are given to younger couples and older children to older couples.

All of the children available for adoption reside in a private orphanage that is staffed with physicians and child psychologists. Adoptive parents receive a full medical report that includes testing for HIV and Hepatitis B. Older children are given a socio-developmental evaluation that is made available to adoptive parents.

Adoptive parents must be present in Colombia when the adoption is presented to a family judge, a process that takes up to four weeks or more. Once both parents have appeared before the court, one of the parents is allowed to return to the United States, but the remaining parent must remain in Colombia until the visa can be processed. Typically, the entire process from application to completion takes from eighteen to thirty months.

The U.S. Embassy maintains a list of adoption agencies licensed by Colombian authorities to process international adoption, but it does not investigate the competency or integrity of the agencies and assumes no responsibility for their actions.

Philippines

The Philippines is the tenth largest supplier of children for adoption in America. Couples applying for adoption must be married three years or longer and must be between the ages of twenty-seven and forty-five. Single men and women applying for adoption must be no more than forty-six years older than the child they wish to adopt and they are prohibited from adopting children younger than four.

It is not a legal requirement, but authorities in the Philippines historically have shown a strong preference for adoptive parents who have a Christian church affiliation. The average length of time between application and placement is about six to twelve months. Authorities require applicants to travel to the Philippines twice, with the first visit expected to last one week and the second visit to last about ten days.

U.S. consular officers, in an effort to protect the rights of the adoption applicant, the birth parent, and the child, give each adoption application consideration on a case-by-case basis to ensure that the complex legal requirements of both countries have been met. The U.S. Embassy is prohibited from providing legal advice to adoptive applicants and it cannot assist adoptive parents charged with violating local laws.

There are exceptions, of course, but generally Americans are granted custody of the child in the Philippines and asked to return to the United States to finalize the adoption in the applicant's home state. There is a six-month probationary period in the United States, at the end of which applicants have six months to file an adoption petition with the court.

Kazakhstan

There is no age or marital status requirement for adoption in Kazakhstan. The only major requirement is that a prospective adoptive parent must be at least sixteen years older than the child. Adoption is open to single men and women.

Kazakhstan does have a requirement that adoptive parents must reside with the child for a minimum of two weeks at the child's place of residence in Kazakhstan prior to the adoption. There is also a fifteen-day waiting period after the court hearing before the adoption becomes final. That is to allow anyone who objects to the adoption time to file an appeal. Because of the visitation and waiting period requirements, adoptive parents can expect to spend anywhere from forty to sixty days in Kazakhstan.

Adoptive parents are free to work with any private adoption agency they choose, but it is strongly recommended that the agency notify the Ministry of Education prior to applying for adoption. According to the U.S. State Department, adoption costs in Kazakhstan run between $18,000 to $25,000 per child.

Although adoption agencies may provide adoptive parents with photographs and biographical information about a particular child, the Kazakhstan government does not match a child to the parents until they arrive in that country. Upon arrival, adoptive parents must select a child in person and apply to a local court to adopt the child.

Ethiopia

Adoption in Ethiopian is open to married couples if at least one spouse is at least twenty-five years old. Single persons can adopt if they are female and at least twenty-five years old. Some single American men have been approved on a case-by-case basis. There is no age limit for adoptive parents per se, but Ethiopian practice is to limit the age of the parent to no more than forty years greater than the child. There are no residency requirements for adoptive parents and travel to Ethiopia is not required.

All adoptions go through the Ethiopian Children and Youth Affairs Office, which requires a home study and supporting information. Adoption in Ethiopia is a time-consuming process that requires the involvement of several U.S. government agencies and at least five Ethiopian government agencies. All documents must be translated into Amharic in the United States and into English in Ethiopia. Most of the documents must be certified and authenticated. As a result, adoptions can take up to two years to complete.

According to the U.S. State Department, some prospective adoptive parents who have worked with adoption facilitators have reported problems, including the following:

- Learning after the adoption has been finalized that the child is infected with HIV or AIDS

- Learning that a prospective adoptive child does not exist

- Discovering that fraudulent documents have been submitted to the court on their behalf

- Learning that they child they are adopting does not qualify as an orphan under U.S. law

If there are concerns about a particular child, the U.S. Embassy in Addis Ababa will conduct a full field investigation to determine the orphan status of a child involved in an adoption if a known unscrupulous individual or organization is involved.

One of the most famous Americans to adopt a child from Ethiopia is Hollywood actress Angelina Jolie, who found herself at the center of an adoption scandal in 2005 after it was learned that the teenage mother of her child was not dead as thought. It is a violation of Ethiopian law to adopt nonorphan children. The birth mother told reporters that she was happy that her child had been adopted by Jolie, but under Ethiopian law Jolie had to reapply for her adoptive rights since the initial paperwork was incorrect.

Haiti

Despite the issuance of a 2004 U.S. State Department warning about travel to Haiti—and the evacuation of nonemergency personnel at the U.S. Embassy there—U.S. citizens requested 231 immigrant visas for orphans to travel to the United States for adoption in 2005, showing a slight increase from an average of two hundred children per year, a figure that Haiti has maintained over the past five years.

All adoptions in Haiti are handled by the Institut du Bien Etre Social et de Research (IBESR), which is also responsible for accrediting adoption agencies and orphanages in that country. If you plan on adopting in Haiti, it is essential for you to obtain documentation from IBESR and the proper Haitian courts. The U.S. Embassy cannot issue U.S. passports to Haitian children since they are not U.S. citizens, and the wait for a Haitian passport can be as long as three months.

Haiti will place children with both married couples and single parents, but the applicant must be older than thirty-five years of age. If the applicants are married, one prospective parent may be under age thirty-five, provided the couple has been married for ten years and has no children.

Adoptions typically take from two to six months, but they have been known to take as long as one year. Applicants are strongly advised to engage the services of a competent Haitian attorney. A list of attorneys can be obtained from the State Department or the U.S. Embassy.

Haitian law does not allow adoptive parents to take a child out of Haiti until the child has been adopted in a Haitian court. That involves three steps: First, applicants must obtain a release from the Tribunal de Paix (Justice of the Peace), stating that the surviving parents or the orphanage has legal custody of the child. Second, the release must be submitted to the IBESR, which is responsible for investigating the psychological and medical well-being of both the applicant and the child (if approved, the applicant will be issued a document known as the "Autorisation d'Adoption"). Third, the applicants or their attorney must present the IBESR authorization to the Tribunal Civil (Civil Court) and request an adoption decree. At that point, adoptive parents can apply for a U.S. visa to travel to the United States with the child.

Liberia

Despite a travel warning issued by the U.S. State Department, Americans adopted more than two hundred children from Liberia in 2005, a figure that was considerably greater than that of previous years, making it the twelfth largest exporter of adopted children to the United States. One reason may be because Liberia has no gender, marriage, or age requirements for adoption. The selection process is also relaxed: any minor child in that country may be adopted.

All adoptive parents are required to engage the services of a U.S. adoption agency before beginning the adoption process. Once a specific child has been located, the adoptive applicant must obtain a letter of approval from the Ministry of Health. The next step is to file a petition for adoption with the Probate Court, which will require information about the petitioners and the child, as well as the written consent of the biological parents if the child is not an orphan. If the child is sixteen years of age or older, the child must consent to the adoption.

Once the petition has been filed, the court will serve notice on all interested parties and initiate an investigation. After the report has been filed by the investigator, the court will schedule a hearing. All hearings are held in closed court. If the court is satisfied that the "moral and temporal interests" of the child will be provided by the applicants, it will issue an adoption order.

Of course, before a child adopted by an American citizen in Liberia can be taken to the United States, the child must be issued a visa by the U.S.

Embassy. In order for that to happen the embassy must be satisfied that one of two criteria has been met. The first is that if the child is under the age of sixteen, he or she must have been in the legal custody of the adoptive parent for at least two years, which means the adoptive parent would have to establish residency in Liberia for at least two years. The second is that the child must meet the embassy's definition of an orphan. Applicants unwilling to reside in Liberia for two years should check with the U.S. Embassy before finalizing a Liberian adoption so that they can be informed of the current definition of an orphan for immigration purposes. The fact that Liberia classifies a child as an orphan does not necessarily mean that the U.S. Embassy will accept that classification.

Taiwan

Taiwan is the thirteenth largest supplier of adopted children to the United States, supplying one hundred-plus children per year. Taiwan will accept applications from couples or single parents, but the applicant must be at least twenty years older than the child. If there are two adoptive parents, both must be at least twenty years older than the child.

Persons wishing to adopt in Taiwan are advised to work through a Taiwan-based adoption agency, a list of which is kept by the U.S. Embassy. The agencies in Taiwan may be contacted through a U.S.-based adoption agency or by a private facilitator.

Once a child has been located, adoption applicants are expected to submit an application to the Taiwan Supreme Court, which appoints an officer of the court to process the adoption, a step that can take up to eight weeks. After that has been done, the applicants will receive a notice to appear from the court. Before a hearing is held, a social worker from the Children's Bureau of the Ministry of Interior will interview the adoptive applicants or review the home study prepared by a licensed adoption agency. If the court makes a favorable ruling on the adoption, applicants will be instructed to register the adoption at the Taiwan Registrar's office.

Documents required to finalize an adoption in Taiwan include the following:

- Home study
- Taiwan household registration for the child
- Notarized contract between the biological parent and adoptive parent
- Power of attorney, in the event the adoptive parent does not appear before the court

- Certified statement from the adoptive parent that addresses the provision of U.S. law under which the child is being adopted

Mexico

Mexico allows U.S. citizens to adopt Mexican children, but the adoption must take place in Mexico in accordance with Mexican law. Approximately one hundred children per year are adopted in Mexico by American citizens.

Mexican authorities will place children with married couples, or with male or female single applicants, provided they are over twenty-five years of age, possess "good moral character," and can demonstrate that they have the financial resources to provide for the child. Children over fourteen years of age must consent to the adoption. There is a six-month trial period during which the child must live with the applicants. The child cannot leave Mexico during the trial period unless the judge waives that requirement, a frequent occurrence in international adoptions. If the judge does not waive the requirement, it would be necessary for the adoptive parents to reside in Mexico for six months.

Since adoption is regulated on a state-by-state basis in Mexico, it is important that U.S. adoption applicants work through a Mexican agency or select a U.S. agency that is knowledgeable in the laws of each state. Overall, adoption laws in Mexico are similar in each state, but there are important variations that make it necessary for agencies to form strong working relationships with individual states since authorities in some jurisdictions are stricter than in others.

There are two types of adoptions in Mexico: public agency adoptions that are processed by the Full Development of the Family (Desarrollo Integral de la Familia), also known as the DIF, and private adoptions that are handled separately by facilitators who work directly with the adoption applicants and the birth parent.

The DIF handles children who have been verified to be orphans because they have been abused or abandoned by their birth parents. Private adoptions are arranged with mothers prior to the birth of their children. Typically, the mothers are provided with medical care, living expenses, clothing, and food during the term of their pregnancies.

American applicants will need the following documents to adopt in Mexico:

- Certified copy of the applicants' birth certificate, or a U.S. passport
- Certified copy of the marriage certificate, if applicable

- A letter from the applicant's employer that states salary, years of service, and position
- A recent income-tax return
- Two reference letters
- A certificate from the state police in the applicants' home state stating that they have no police record
- One 3-by-3 inch color photograph of each prospective parent
- Two 3-by-5 inch photographs of the applicants in their home

Thailand

Over the past several years, Thailand has, on average, sent about seventy-five children a year to the United States for adoption. Procedures in that country are complex and lengthy, and applicants are advised to work with an international agency in the United States that has experience working with authorities in that country. It is rare that Thai authorities approve adoption for abandoned children under the age of one year, and U.S. officials report that they seldom see children under two years of age placed with overseas parents.

Thailand does not place children with single applicants. Successful applicants will be married, at least twenty-five years of age, and at least fifteen years older than the child to be adopted. Applicants who are not legally qualified to adopt in their home state are automatically ineligible to adopt in Thailand.

All adoptions are processed through the Child Adoption Center of the Department of Public Welfare (DPW), the only government organization in that country responsible for the adoption of Thai children. The Adoption Center has licensed three nongovernment adoption agencies to process applicants from the United States:

Holt Sahathai Foundation
850/33 Sukhumvit 71
Bangkok 10110
(66) 2-381-8834

Thai Red Cross Foundation
Chulalongkorn Hospital
Corner of Rama IV road and Rajdamri road
Bangkok 10300
(66) 2-252-8181

Pattaya Orphanage
Pattaya City, Chonburi 20151
(66) 38-422-745

All documents submitted to the DPW must be authenticated by the Thai Embassy in the United States and they must be in English or Thai. Applications should include a completed home study, a marriage certificate, a copy of the adoption agency's license, photographs of both applicants, birth certificates of both parents, proof of termination of any previous marriages or deaths of former spouses, and references from two responsible persons.

Once the applicants have been matched with a child, they will be free to take the child to the United States, provided the child's orphan status meets U.S. guidelines. Once three bimonthly reports have been submitted to the DPW, the adoption application can be referred to the Child Adoption Board for final approval. Once the applicants have been notified of the Board's approval, they have six months to register the adoption at the Thai Embassy in the United States.

Vietnam

Until 2004, Vietnam was one of the top ten suppliers of children for adoption to the United States, with more than thirty-three hundred children placed from 1999 through 2003. Perhaps because of the complexity of adoption in Vietnam—all adoptions must be approved by the People's Committee in the birth mother's province—the number of placements with American applicants has declined.

Problems sometimes arise over the definition of orphan. Vietnamese law does not define "orphaned" or "abandoned," which sometimes creates difficulties for U.S. Embassy officials who must determine the orphan status of a child. Many of the children in Vietnamese orphanages do not meet the standard of law to be eligible for adoption.

Despite its loose-knit socialist structure, which places more emphasis on local autonomy than on centralized institutions, adoption authorities in Vietnam are surprisingly flexible. Children can be placed for adoption by orphanages or by individual mothers. The Vietnamese do not discriminate against singles or gay parents.

One of the best accounts we've read of the emotional aspect of international adoption was written by Kevin McGarry, a single gay man who adopted two children in Vietnam. After completing the necessary paperwork for adoption, he traveled to Ho Chi Minh City to take custody of a male child whom he named Andrew. The "Giving and Receiving" ceremony took place in the presence of a government official who presented both McGarry and the birth mother with papers to sign. McGarry thought that the mother, Kim Hoa, was pretty. In his book, *Fatherhood for Gay Men*,[*] he wrote:

> Today was the first time I met her. Although she was all smiles, there was some uneasiness about her—you could see her heart breaking just under the surface. In the very beginning of the ceremony, I gave her Andrew to hold and she played with him for the entire ceremony.... While I was watching her hold him, I was thinking about the extreme emotional bond that must exist between a mother and her child and how difficult it must be for her to let him go. However, I must admit that the most painful emotions swirling around in my heart that day were not about Kim Hoa and her sacrifice, but about the risk that she would change her mind. This consumed me because I had fallen in love with her little boy and I could not bear it if she decided to keep him.... When we went outside, Kim Hoa was still holding Andy. We stood around a bit and I was about to cry when she came up and handed Andy to me. It was a very symbolic gesture, as I am sure she intended it to be. She did not look me in my eyes—if she had she might have seen the tears there.

Later, after his return to America, McGarry received a letter from Kim Hoa. Since it was written in Vietnamese, he had it translated by two Vietnamese Americans. Hoa wrote: "Because of poverty, I am resigned to sever my parental links, for what mother could bear giving up her child without breaking to pieces inside? Because his ill-fated life started out without the man who made him and because as a single mother I cannot afford to raise him, I have to give him up. Now, since you will adopt him, he will escape a life of want and wandering.... As long as he is happy, I will be indebted to you for the rest of my life."

It is extremely rare for adoptive applicants pursuing international adoption to ever have contact with the birth mother. In their excitement to receive a child, adoptive applicants sometimes forget that the birth mother ever existed, much less think that she is a person who once had dreams for her child. McGarry's account of his meeting with Andrew's mother is a reminder that adoption is often composed of equal parts heartbreak for the birth mother and joy for the adoptive parent, with the child sometimes relegated to straddling the emotionally fragile dividing line between the two.

---

[*] McGarry, Kevin. *Fatherhood for Gay Men*. New York: Haworth Press, 2003.

5 Adoption in Canada

Each year there are about two thousand domestic adoptions and about two thousand international adoptions in Canada, with most of the children for international adoptions arriving from China and Vietnam. About one hundred children a year go to Canada from the United States. By contrast, only a handful of Canadian children are adopted in the United States.

There are no laws per se restricting Canadian children from entering the United States. The imbalance is due to the fact that Canadians have better information about adopting in America than Americans have about adopting in Canada. The purpose of this chapter is to provide useful information to Canadians about domestic and international adoptions in Canada, as well as to provide information to Americans about adopting children in Canada.

Canada has one of the most professional and sophisticated child welfare systems in the world. It is a system that dates back to the 1800s, when individual provinces started enacting legislation to protect apprenticed children. It grew from that into a network of children's aid societies that offered protection services to children, counseling to unwed mothers, and adoption for children who became wards of the state (in Canada they are referred to as wards of the Crown).

There is no national oversight of Canada's social services network. Each province is responsible for passing legislation and establishing social service agencies to address the needs of its children. Laws vary from province to province, just as laws vary in the United States from state to state, but the provinces are more alike than unalike in their approach to providing services to children. Each system is based on the belief that it is the responsibility of the province to protect the rights, health, and welfare of children who are in need of a helping hand. Accordingly, each province has established a network of children's aid societies that are empowered to act quickly to protect children against physical, emotional, or sexual abuse.

One of the things that make Canada unique is its willingness to provide parental adoption leave of up to thirty-five weeks (some provinces offer up to fifty-two weeks). Most of that leave is unpaid, but an adoptive parent is entitled to two weeks of paid leave and another ten weeks of paid leave at 95 percent of his or her salary. The main requirement is that the parent be enrolled in Canada's Employment Insurance plan, which is similar to the Social Security plan used in the United States.

Social workers are given special rights to enter homes in which there is suspected child abuse, rights that traditional law enforcement officers do not have. They also have the right to remove children from their parents' home and place them in foster or group homes until a judge can hear the case. If the courts rule that parents have forfeited legal rights to their children because of abuse or abandonment, the children are made wards of the Crown and placed for adoption. Generally speaking, individuals who adopt children in Canada can be assured that the children have received the best care possible.

AMERICANS WHO ADOPT CANADIAN CHILDREN

American law permits citizens to adopt children in Canada, provided the adoption laws of both countries are observed. For the past decade, only one or two Canadian children per year have qualified for adoption in the United States. That number would be much higher if Americans were better educated on adoption opportunities in Canada.

The first challenge for Americans who want to adopt in Canada is to qualify in that country for adoption. Each province has different requirements. British Columbia, Alberta, Saskatchewan, Manitoba, Ontario, Newfoundland, New Brunswick, Nova Scotia, Yukon, and the Northwest Territories require that all adoption applicants be residents of the province in which they apply for adoption. Quebec and Prince Edward Island currently are silent on the issue of residency, but that could change in the future.

Canada's residency requirement can be met in one of two ways:

1) Americans couples interested in adopting a Canadian child can simply establish residency in Canada, an idea that is not as far-fetched as it may seem, and then apply for adoption through a local public or private agency. In most provinces, a six-month residency is sufficient to qualify you for adoption.

Canadian immigration authorities are receptive to Americans who enter the country to live, provided they have job skills that are in demand (Canadian employers cannot offer jobs to Americans unless there are no Canadians who could hold the position) or provided they have the means to support themselves without taking jobs away from Canadians.

There are several types of residency, but the major types of interest to Americans are permanent residency, which occurs when you enter Canada for the purpose of obtaining citizenship; temporary residency, which occurs when you enter Canada for a specified period (students fall into this category); and business residency, which requires you to support yourself without taking a Canadian job.

Business residency identifies three types of persons who are eligible for permanent resident status. The first type is the investor with a net worth of at least $800,000 and who agrees to invest $400,000 to be used by the provinces for job creation (you get the money back at the end of five years). The second type is the entrepreneur with a net worth of $300,000 who agrees to own and manage at least one-third of a business that contributes to the Canadian economy. The third type is the self-employed individual who can show the ability to become economically established in Canada by creating his or her own employment. This type of residency was created for authors, dancers, professional athletes, coaches, and those interested in purchasing farms in Canada.

2) Each province has a provision that allows the residency requirement to be waived, provided that special circumstances justify a waiver. An example of a special circumstance would be a child with special needs. For most Americans, this is the most realistic option to adopt a Canadian child. As in the United States, the term "special needs" applies to a wide variety of possibilities, from a child with siblings to one with severe mental, emotional, or physical challenges.

If you establish residency in Canada, you will not need a lawyer to adopt, since your adoption will be processed by a public agency. If you apply directly as a resident of the United States to request a waiver, then you will need to contact a private agency in Canada to process your application and retain a Canadian lawyer with immigration expertise. It is possible, but not likely, that a private agency will be able to find you a special needs child who is in the care of a public agency. What you will have going for you is the fact that at any given moment there are more than twenty thousand Canadian children in foster homes in need of adoptive parents. Public agencies are desperate to find permanent homes for those children and may be persuaded to request a waiver in your case.

Sometimes private agencies are aware of mothers who do not want to give their children to public agencies for various reasons. If a private agency finds you such a child (in most instances the child will be an infant), you still will have to go through a public agency to be approved as adoptive parents. If the public agency agrees with the private agency that you would be a good parent for the child, the public agency may be persuaded to request a waiver of the residency requirement, which would be to your advantage.

If you are able to locate a child in Canada and then successfully complete the home study and residency requirements, your next challenge will be with the U.S. Department of Immigration. Before starting that process—you will need an American lawyer who is familiar with immigration law to do that—you should contact U.S. consular officials in Canada to obtain a U.S. immigrant visa for the child. There are two types of visas available: those for previously adopted children under age sixteen who have already lived with the adoptive parents for at least two years, and those for children who qualify for orphan status.

The United States defines an orphan as a child under sixteen who meets one of two requirements: the child has no parents because of abandonment, or the death or disappearance of the birth parents; or the sole parent is incapable of providing proper care and has signed a legal document releasing the child for adoption.

Before issuing the visa, the consular official will review the case to make certain that the following appropriate procedures have been followed:

- If the adoptive parent is married, the spouse must also be a party to the adoption.
- If the adoptive parent is single, he or she must be at least twenty-five years of age.
- The adoptive parent or parents must be U.S. citizens.

Once you get the child into the United States with an immigrant visa, your next step is to follow the laws and regulations of the state in which you live to proceed with the finalization of the adoption by a court in your jurisdiction. State laws vary, but the odds are that you will need to work with social workers at the public agency that serves your community. You must also keep in mind that your child has entered the country as an alien and you must notify authorities of any change of address. After the adoption is finalized by the court, you will need to apply for U.S. citizenship for your child and that means revisiting the Bureau of Citizenship and Immigration Service (BCIS). Your adoption is not truly over until your child is granted U.S. citizenship.

CANADIANS WHO ADOPT AMERICAN CHILDREN

The situation for Canadians who want to adopt American children is much different. In any given year, the United States ranks sixth or seventh as a supplier of children to Canada, behind China, Haiti, Russia, Vietnam, India, and Korea. Almost all of the Americans placed with Canadian families are African American. Most are placed with families in Ontario, Quebec, or British Columbia.

Canadians cannot initiate adoption procedures in the United States until they have located a child who is available for adoption. To do that, they must contact private agencies in the United States that specialize in international adoptions. The Open Door, a private agency based in Georgia, has placed more than two hundred black children in British Columbia alone. Some of the placements are for open adoptions in which the birth mother maintains contact with the adoptive family and travels to Canada on a regular basis to visit her child. Canadian adoptive parents who have done media interviews report few problems with this type of adoption.

Canadian law allows you to adopt a child from another country if you are a Canadian or a permanent resident. Since adoption is the responsibility of each individual province, the Canadian government's only involvement in the process is through Citizenship and Immigration Canada (CIC), a national agency that oversees immigration to Canada.

To adopt a child from the United States—or any other foreign country— you must first obtain permission from the CIC to bring the child into Canada. To obtain that permission, you must have a home study done in your home province. Once you have done that, you should apply to the CIC to sponsor the child for permanent resident status in Canada. Under no circumstances should you bring a child into Canada without CIC approval. Once the CIC receives your application it will contact authorities in your province for a letter of consent for you to pursue adoption. If the CIC approves your application to sponsor a child from another country, it will require you to sign a binding commitment to support the child for ten years or until the child reaches age twenty-five, whichever comes first.

Once you clear the CIC hurdle and comply with the laws of the child's country of residence—some countries require you to finalize the adoption with local judges before you remove the child from their jurisdiction—all of your subsequent efforts will be directed toward the public agency in your home province. Since adoption laws vary from province to province, we will examine the adoption requirements in each province as they relate to both domestic and international adoptions.

ALBERTA ADOPTIONS

Each year Alberta Children's Services, a division of the Children's Ministry, places about a dozen infants and nearly two hundred special needs children into adoptive homes. It also oversees about one hundred and fifty placements arranged by the five private agencies licensed to do adoptions in Alberta. The private agencies approve adoptive families using the same screening and home assessment requirements used by Children's Services, and they see the process through to finalization. Unlike Children's Services, the private agencies charge a fee for their services.

For adoptions through Children's Services, it is not a "first come, first served" process since the ministry gives priority to applicants who can accept the following:

- A child with major physical, emotional, medical, or developmental challenges (Down's syndrome, fetal alcohol syndrome, spina bifida, seizure disorders, and so on)
- A child seven years of age or older
- A sibling group of three or more children
- A child who has been featured in the media
- A foster child who has been in your home at least six months

To be approved for adoption, you have to undergo a home study. What happens to your application depends on whether you request an infant or an older child with special needs. If you request an infant, the child's birth mother may select the adoptive family for her child from nonidentifying profiles. If you request a child older than two years of age, your caseworker will make the final decision about which child you are offered. If the child is twelve or older, it will have to consent to the placement in advance.

Alberta prohibits any contact between the adoptive parents and the birth parents until the ministry is satisfied that the adoptive parents are eligible to adopt a child. It is against the law for anyone to give or receive money to birth or adoptive parents unless the payment is authorized by Children's Services.

Before the court issues an adoption order finalizing the placement, the applicant is required to give notice, no less than thirty days before the hearing, to the ministry, the child (if he or she is age twelve or older), and the birth parents. Upon reaching the age of eighteen, the child and adoptive parents have the right of access to the adoption records.

If you want to adopt a child from another country, you have two options: you can adopt a child privately or you can adopt through the system set up by the government of the other country. Although you cannot adopt directly through Alberta Children's Services, the ministry has established an adoption services bureau that coordinates international adoptions from several countries, including Russia, Guatemala, Vietnam, and China. Alberta officials will review the home study done by the private agency handling your adoption and, if everything is in order, will issue a letter to the CIC stating that it did not arrange your adoption but that it is willing to recognize the adoption as finalized by a foreign jurisdiction.

The important thing to keep in mind about international adoptions in Alberta is that they cannot be finalized in a Canadian court, only by a court in the child's country of origin. If the child's country has not implemented the Hague Convention, which stipulates how international adoptions should be processed, then it will not be able to process the application for a Canadian adoption.

Alberta residents who pursue international adoption are responsible for all the costs involved with the immigration fees, the child's medical expenses, the home assessment report, translation costs, and legal fees. Often those costs add up to $20,000 or more. The average length of time to complete an international adoption in Alberta is one to two years. With that in mind, Children's Services has issued the following warning:

> In international legal matters, there are no guarantees. You might begin the process to adopt a child, only to have the costs change or the program end without notice. Also, you need to allow reasonable time for each agency and department to complete its procedure and to forward documents

BRITISH COLUMBIA ADOPTIONS

Domestic adoptions in British Columbia follow the same procedural guidelines required in Alberta. You must fill out an application and then go through the home study process that requires interviews with adoption screeners, employment verification, references, a medical report, and so on. In any given year, public agencies in British Columbia will have about twelve hundred children available for adoption. Unfortunately, they will place only about one hundred and seventy-five of those children.

One of the things that sets British Columbia apart is its willingness to accept adoption applications from homosexuals (the only other provinces to accept same-gender couples are Ontario, New Brunswick, Newfoundland, and Nova Scotia). Like the other provinces, British Columbia requires its residents to begin the adoption process through either a public agency under the supervision of the Ministry for Children and Families or through one of the private agencies licensed by the ministry.

The Ministry of Children and Family Development has the following five core values that it uses for adoption placements:

- Children require permanence and the earlier this happens for children, the more beneficial it is for them.
- Every child needs a permanent legal family; therefore, adoption must be thoroughly considered for every child as an option for permanency.
- All types of families and parent compositions should be actively explored as potential adoptive placements.
- Children, birth parents, prospective adoptive parents, and caregivers should be provided with an understanding of the lifelong implications of adoption and with complete information to assist them in making informed decisions.
- Openness in adoption enables members of the adoption circle to maintain family and cultural connections and relationships and assists the child in developing a strong, healthy identity. The adoption circle is defined as birth patents, adoptive parents, adoptees, extended families, and other important people in the child's life.

Other areas of policy that distinguish public agencies in British Columbia from public agencies in the other provinces and in the United States include the following elements.

Parental and Child Consent

Birth parents or legal guardians, and children over twelve years of age, must consent to adoption and any name changes. Once that consent has been given, the birth parents or legal guardians have the right to revoke it by giving written notice, even if the child has been placed in an adoptive home. Mothers of newborns have the right to withdraw their consent within thirty days of the child's birth, even if the child has been placed with adoptive parents. In that situation the ministry is required to return the child to his or her birth mother.

In cases involving older children who have been made wards of the Crown, the child is returned to a foster home and not to the birth mother. A child who is twelve years of age or older has the right to revoke consent at any time before the adoption order is granted by a court. That right applies to all types of adoption in the province, including agency placements, private placements, and adoptions involving stepparents and relatives. It is a policy that is enforced even if the children consent to the adoption in another legal jurisdiction.

Openness

The belief that everyone affected by adoption is entitled to a maximum amount of openness is the foundation of British Columbia's public policy. The views of children affected by adoption and their birth parents must be taken into consideration by social workers formulating a permanent plan for them. The free flow of information is given a greater priority than the protection of privacy rights.

Cultural Identity

On the subject of cultural identity, public policy is clear. Social workers are instructed by the Ministry for Children and Families to conduct their duties with "understanding and respect for the cultural, racial and religious her- itage, place of origin, age and sexual orientation" of the child, the birth parents, and the adoptive parents. Adoption agencies are required to pre- serve the child's "unique cultural identity" while preparing an adoption plan. Guidelines admonish social workers: "When involving the Aboriginal child's family, Band or Aboriginal community in discussions about the child's permanence, which may include adoption, you must conduct your duties with understanding and respect for the importance of preserving their Aboriginal ancestry, culture and heritage.... It is in the child's best inter- ests to promote an understanding of the importance of the child's connec- tions with his or her whole life—past, present and future—as it relates to culture and heritage."

British Columbia's international adoption policies are structured so that public agencies have limited involvement. Social workers are required to provide information in response to inquiries from prospective adoptive par- ents who want to adopt children from outside the province, but they are not required to undertake home studies for that purpose. That is the sole responsibility of a private agency. However, the ministry is required to issue a statement of no objection after being informed by a private agency that the applicant has met all the requirements for adoption.

British Columbia residents pursuing international adoption are advised to satisfy the following requirements:

- You must have medical information and a social history of the child and the parents.
- You must prove that the birth parents have received informa- tion about adoption and alternatives to adoption from a licensed child welfare authority where the parents live.
- You must possess consent for the adoption obtained in a law- ful manner from the jurisdiction where the child is living.

- You must have a home study that approves you for adoption and makes the case that you are the right person to adopt this particular child.

- You must prove that you have given notice of the proposed adoption to anyone named by the birth mother as the child's birth father and to anyone who was named as the father on the birth certificate.

MANITOBA ADOPTIONS

In Manitoba, any resident who is eighteen years of age or older may apply for adoption with Child and Family Services. In an average year, about one hundred children are placed for adoption by the province, with almost as many children placed through private domestic placements and international placements.

Families who adopt through Child and Family Services are eligible for financial assistance if they adopt more than one child from the same family or if they adopt a child with special needs. The province identifies the following three types of assistance:

- One-time start-up costs for transportation, equipment, or necessary changes to the adoptive family's home

- Costs of special services for a child who has been diagnosed with special needs

- Ongoing maintenance payments to help with the daily care of a child with special needs or one who is in a sibling group; the amount is based on the applicants' income and family size.

Some families qualify for all three types of assistance. Once approved, the assistance may continue until the child reaches age eighteen. In some situations, it may continue if the family moves to another province

Manitoba allows private adoptions, but only through a handful of private agencies that it has licensed for that purpose. Birth parents are given the opportunity to select the adoptive parents for their child, but before an adoption can proceed they must engage the services of a lawyer and sign consents for the placement. The birth parents have twenty-one days after signing the consent forms to withdraw from the placement. No one can give or receive a payment or reward of any kind in connection with the adoption of a child, except for standard legal fees and fees to private agencies for specified services.

Residents of Manitoba interested in international adoption must notify Child and Family Services of their intention to adopt abroad. They can employ the services of any licensed agency in Canada, but the home study must be done by social workers who have been approved by Child and Family Services. You should be aware that it is illegal in Manitoba for individuals or private agencies to publish advertisements dealing with the adoption placement of specific children. Only in exceptional circumstances will the province allow an agency to advertise a specific child.

In adoptions completed before 1986, excerpted summaries of nonidentifying files are made available to adult adoptees, adoptees under the age of majority who have the permission of their adoptive parents, birth parents, and the siblings of deceased adoptees. In adoptions completed after 1999, full records will be made available for all involved in an adoption unless one of the interested parties has filed a written veto on the disclosure of any personal information that relates to them.

Manitoba has put a special emphasis in recent years on the adoption of Aboriginal children. In an effort to restructure its child welfare system, Manitoba has joined with the Assembly of Manitoba Chiefs, the Manitoba Keewatinook Ininew Okimowin, and the Manitoba Metis Federation for the purpose of establishing a province-wide Metis mandate. Because of those efforts, it is probably not a good time for a white, Asian, or black couple to apply to adopt a native child.

Manitoba does not solicit applications from homosexuals or same-gender couples.

NEW BRUNSWICK ADOPTIONS

New Brunswick places about forty-five children a year into adoptive homes, and pays subsidies to about one hundred adoptive families on an ongoing basis. International adoptions account for another thirty new cases per year. There are no international agencies that have been licensed to do business in the province, but there are a number of private practitioners who have been approved by the province to do home studies and postadoption progress reports.

Adults of any age, gender, sexual orientation, educational background, or financial status may apply to adopt in New Brunswick. Acceptance will depend on the applicants' ability to address the emotional, intellectual, and physical needs of the child. Decisions are made entirely on what is in the child's best interest.

The only major restrictions on adoption include the following:

- It is prohibited for anyone to give or receive money for adoption unless it has been authorized by the Department of Family and Community Services.
- Married applicants are required to have lived together as husband and wife for at least two years prior to the date a home study assessment begins.
- A birth parent may give consent to the adoption of his or her child at any time after the birth of the child, but if it is given during the first seven days of the child's life, it has no force until the eighth day after the birth.

NEWFOUNDLAND AND LABRADOR ADOPTIONS

In 2003, Newfoundland and Labrador completely overhauled their fifty-year-old adoption policies with legislation that gave them one of the least restrictive adoption programs in Canada. Among the highlights of the new policy are the following:

- Acceptance of single parents, along with same-sex and common-law couples
- Approval of self-help kits for relatives who arrange adoptions
- Approval of an ongoing exchange of information or contact by birth and adoptive parents
- Approval of an open records system of record keeping
- Acceptance of the rights of birth parents and children to block the government from releasing identifying information about them
- Acceptance of an individual's right to prevent the government from arranging contact with interested parties; violating a no-contact declaration can lead to jail terms of up to ninety days and fines up to $10,000
- Children twelve and older must give consent to their adoption; children under twelve must be informed of the adoption process and their views about adoption must be considered
- Prospective adoptive parents must be residents of the province for at least six months before applying for adoption.

Newfoundland and Labrador have no licensed international adoption agencies. Residents are not required by law to use a licensed agency to adopt from abroad. However, it is the policy of the Department of Health and Community Services not to issue letters of recommendation to adopting parents unless they use a Canadian adoption agency that has been licensed by a Canadian province.

NOVA SCOTIA ADOPTIONS

About one hundred and fifty children are adopted each year in Nova Scotia; two-thirds of them are placed by the province's Department of Community Services and the remaining one-third are placed by private agencies.

The following are things you should know about domestic agency adoptions:

- Applicants must be nineteen years of age or older. They must be Canadian citizens or have landed immigrant status and they must be residents of Nova Scotia.

- Birth mothers are given an opportunity to review applicants approved by the Department of Community Services for the purpose of selecting the best home for their child. Birth fathers may also be involved in that process.

- In some instances, a birth mother may chose an adoptive family for her child and then ask the Department of Community Services to have a home study completed on the family. If the department is able to approve the adoptive family, the placement will take place under department supervision.

- Birth parents are not allowed to participate in the selection process if their children have already been committed to the care of the Department of Community Services.

- It is illegal for anyone to publish information designed to recruit adoptive parents and it is illegal for anyone to publicly identify a child who is available for adoption.

What you should know about international adoptions:

- The first step is to apply at the Department of Community Services. After an initial screening, a list of private practitioners will be made available to you and you will be asked to arrange for the completion of a home study. You may use any international adoption agency in Canada to assist you in your adoption efforts. The Department of Community Services will supervise your application, but it will not be directly involved.

- There is a six-month probationary period that can be waived under special circumstances.

- If you adopt a child with special needs or a sibling group from abroad you may be eligible for financial assistance. The subsidy continues after the adoption is finalized and will be reviewed annually.

ONTARIO ADOPTIONS

Of the two thousand agency and private adoptions that take place each year in Canada, Ontario accounts for about seven hundred, and of the two thousand international adoptions that occur, Ontario accounts for about six hundred and fifty. As a result, Ontario processes about one-third of all the adoptions in Canada, a statistical distinction that is also indicative of the importance of its historical leadership role in child welfare issues.

Ontario's current system of providing for children in need of protection and assistance began in 1888 with the passage of legislation that allowed the courts to make children wards of institutions and charitable organizations. That led to the creation in 1893 of a network of children's aid societies that had the authority to remove abused children from their homes, support children in municipal shelters, and collect money from towns and cities to pay for the care of the children.

Today there are fifty-two Children's Aid Societies in Ontario (four of which are Aboriginal societies). Each society is based on a county jurisdiction, though some represent multiple counties, and governed by a board of directors that is selected from the community. The societies are funded by the Ministry of Community, Family and Children's Services, which also exerts an oversight role on professional standards. This system of operation is the strength of what is widely regarded as the best child welfare organization in the world. At the core of that strength are the local boards, which have the power to set policy and hire the professional staff, including the society's director. Board members are seldom involved in politics. They represent a cross-section of people in the community: teachers, business owners, doctors, lawyers, social workers in private practice, government employees, and so on.

Ontario's Children's Aid Societies are authorized to investigate suspected child abuse cases and to provide counseling in any situation that involves children. The staff are divided up into four main groups: Protection Workers who investigate child abuse allegations and counsel the parents with the goal of remedying the situation; *child care workers* who work with children who have been removed from their parents' home and placed in foster or group homes (when the children are infants, the caseworker may be a registered nurse); *foster home screeners* who do home studies on foster home applicants and make placement decisions when protection workers bring children into the society's care; and *adoption workers* who screen adoption applicants and supervise adoption placements. Some societies also have social workers who specialize in counseling mothers who want to place their unborn or recently born children up for adoption.

Under the Ontario system, adoption workers do not work in isolation. They are part of a social work team that is involved with myriad problems that affect children, including abuse and abandonment. That is one reason why adoption workers in Ontario are so well trained. They are cautious in approving adoption applications because they have seen, firsthand, the abuse that can occur to children at the hands of emotionally disturbed parents and relatives.

In Ontario there are four ways to pursue adoption:

- Through one of the province's fifty-two children's aid societies; since they are organized at the county level, you are required to apply in your county of residence

- Through private adoption agencies or individuals licensed by the Ministry

- Through international adoption agencies

- Through the courts in cases where a relative or stepparent applies to adopt children related to them by blood or through marriage

The same procedures are followed for all types of adoptions, with the exception of those in which relatives or stepparents file for guardianship of children related to them by blood or though marriage. In those instances, home studies are replaced by less-detailed reports that are prepared by a children's aid society or an officer of the court.

The following are things you should know about adoption in Ontario:

- Applications can be submitted by individuals, married couples, or same-sex couples that live together but are not married.

- You must be a resident to adopt in Ontario, though the law does not specify that you have to be a permanent resident.

- You cannot be discriminated against on the basis of race, religion, age, ethnic origin, gender, sexual orientation, or mental or physical disability.

- You can adopt more than one child at once as long as they are siblings.

- You must be eighteen years of age or older.

- Ontario stresses the importance of a child's emotional well-being and cultural background in relation to adoption. An emphasis is given to preserving the unique heritage and cultural ties of Aboriginal children and every effort is made to find adoptive homes for them within the Aboriginal communities. When such families cannot be found, parents outside that community may be considered as long as they agree to promote the child's awareness of his or her cultural heritage.

Children's Aid Society Adoptions

The children available for adoption come into care through one of two means. One way is through parents who voluntarily relinquish rights to the child—usually young, unmarried mothers who choose adoption over abortion. These children will typically be less than two years of age. The other is through the courts, which grant custody of the child to a Children's Aid Society as a result of parental abuse, neglect, or abandonment. This second group of children can range in age from infancy through fifteen years of age.

For various reasons, some children never find adoptive homes. In those situations, the law requires that Children's Aid Societies provide care until they reach sixteen years of age. That care is usually provided by foster homes. Since some children require care beyond the age of sixteen, Children's Aid Societies are authorized to provide for children until they reach the age of twenty-one, if they feel the child's situation merits extended care.

The availability of abortion and community acceptance of unmarried mothers have reduced the number of infants available for adoption. Most of the children who are available are older and are considered to be in the special needs category. This includes children who have had a history of painful experiences such as abuse or neglect, children who have developmental or physical challenges, and siblings who need parents to adopt them as a unit.

Since some Children's Aid Societies are located in rural areas with sparse populations, they sometimes have a difficult time finding adoptive homes for children with special needs. To assist those counties, the Ministry allows advertising in a newspaper column named "Today's Child," which features individual children who are in need of a permanent home. The Ministry also operates an adoption resource exchange in which adoption workers from all over the province travel to a central location twice a year to present videos and descriptions of their children and the kind of families they need. Adoption workers take that information back to their home counties and present it to adoption applicants they think would be appropriate for a particular child.

The important thing to remember about adopting a child from a Children's Aid Society is that the adoption worker's primary focus is on matching the family with the child—not the other way around. The child's needs always come first. That is sometimes difficult for adoptive parents to understand, especially if they have friends or relatives who applied at the agency after they did and received a child more quickly. Being approved for adoption by a Children's Aid Society does not mean that you will receive the next available child. You may wait months, or even years, before you are approached about a child.

Private Agency Adoptions

Private adoption agencies in Ontario are licensed and regulated by the Ministry of Children and Youth Services. Their standards and procedures are the same as those observed by the Children's Aid Societies, but with one main difference: since private agencies do not have guardianship of individual children, their focus is not so much on the children as it is on the adoptive applicants. Adoption workers at private agencies have little or no contact with available children prior to placement.

More often than not, private agencies look for children to place with their approved adoption applicants. Those children come their way in a variety of ways. Sometimes a birth parent will approach the agency and ask for help in locating a family for his or her child. There are many reasons why some parents choose private agencies over a Children's Aid Society for the placement of their children. It may be because they want an open adoption in which they can maintain contact with the child and the odds of doing that are better at a private agency. Or it may be because they live in an area where their family is well known and they prefer that the local Children's Aid Society not be privy to their family business. Most of the children placed in adoptive homes through private agencies are newborns or infants under six months of age. Private adoptions can only be done with the consent of the mother, with the consent of the father sometimes made a condition. Anyone who gives consent has twenty-one days to change his or her mind.

Private agencies are required to notify the Ministry of any proposed placements and then submit a home study for approval, along with a social and medical history of the child. The Ministry will review the placement and give its approval if it is felt to be in the best interest of the child.

A major difference between an adoption arranged by a Children's Aid Society and a private agency is cost. If you adopt privately, you will pay all the fees involved, including the cost of a home study and the cost of the private agency's services. Children's Aid Societies do not charge applicants for their services. It is illegal in Ontario for adoptive parents to provide or receive payment from birth parents.

International Adoptions

The professional standards required of international adoption agencies are the same as those required of agency and private adoptions. The main difference is that international adoption is more complicated from a logistical and legal standpoint—and, of course, it can be very expensive, with costs usually starting at $10,000.

In addition to the fees paid to the international adoption agency and to the authority in the child's country of origin, there are legal fees that have to be paid in both countries. For adoptions finalized out of Ontario, the Ministry charges a fee of $460 for relative adoptions and $925 for non-relative adoptions. There is no fee for international adoptions that are finalized in an Ontario court.

International adoption agencies in Ontario perform the following specific services:

- They accept applications from individuals or couples to adopt a child from a specific country (China, Russia, India, Vietnam, and so on).

- They complete a home study and send it to the Ministry for approval.

- They consider available children from the targeted country and present a particular child to approved applicants.

- They send the applicants' response to the appropriate adoption authority in the child's country of origin.

- If the country of origin agrees to the adoption, they assist the parents in applying for sponsorship of the child through a Canadian immigration center.

- If the adoption is not yet finalized in the country of origin, they send progress reports to the appropriate adoption authority in the child's country of origin until the adoption is finalized.

One important consideration to keep in mind is that Ontario residents are forbidden to leave the province for the purpose of arranging an international adoption without first doing three things. First, you must file an application with a licensed international adoption agency. Second, you must obtain a home study by an approved adoption practitioner. Last, you must obtain Ministry approval based on a review of the home study. If you disregard those restrictions, you may be convicted of a crime and pay a fine of up to $2,000, or serve up to two years in prison, or both. You will also end up losing the child you want to adopt.

PRINCE EDWARD ISLAND ADOPTIONS

The only adoption placements that can take place in Prince Edward Island are those undertaken by the director of child welfare, or someone the director has designated for that purpose. The province has no private international adoption agencies, but residents are free to use licensed, out-of-province adoption agencies.

Like Quebec and Nova Scotia, Prince Edward Island allows adoptive parents to claim parental leave of up to fifty-two weeks (the most allowed in Canada). In Prince Edward Island, only twelve weeks of that leave are eligible for compensation of up to 95 percent of the parent's salary. The remaining forty weeks are not eligible for compensation.

QUEBEC ADOPTIONS

Agency adoptions are provided in this province, but it is difficult to obtain information about them if you are not French speaking. The cultural tug-of-war between Quebec, which has a fiercely nationalistic leadership, and English-speaking Canada has gone on for decades and has affected every aspect of society, including adoption.

Quebec processes domestic adoptions through its department of children's services. It does not permit domestic private adoptions, but it encourages international adoptions. In an average year, Quebec's children's service agencies will place about two hundred children in adoptive homes. By contrast, Quebec residents pursue about twelve hundred international adoptions each year, with about nine hundred of those receiving letters of no-objection, or approval, by the province.

The following are things you should know about domestic adoptions:

- There is no minimum age other than a requirement that adoption applicants be at least eighteen years older than the person adopted, except when the person adopted is the child of the spouse of the adopter. However, if you have a good reason to adopt a child who is less than eighteen years younger than you are, you can petition the court to dispense with that requirement.

- No child aged ten or older can be adopted without the child's consent, unless the child is unable to express his or her will.

- Financial assistance is available for adoptive parents who have kept the child in a foster-parent situation for at least one year before an application for adoption was made.

- Adopted children fourteen years of age and older have the right to obtain the information necessary to locate their birth parents.

- Quebec residents who adopt are entitled to up to fifty-two weeks of parental leave. In some parts of the province, the leave is available to both parents, but in others it must be shared between the mother and father. The leave may also be shared between same-sex parents. Up to twelve weeks of that leave is compensated under Quebec's Parental Insurance Act. In addition, Quebec, unlike the other provinces, offers a five-week paternity leave.

The following are things you should know about international adoptions:

- Quebec residents may engage the services of private adoption agencies inside or outside the province. Residents may also initiate an independent adoption from countries that allow independent adoptions.

- Quebec has three main requirements for international adoptions: the applicants must be beyond the age of majority, they must be at least eighteen years older than the adopted child, and they must reside in Quebec.

- Adoption applicants must undergo a "psychosocial" assessment to determine if they are suitable parents. A psychosocial assessment is the same thing as a home study. Applicants can obtain the assessment from either a social worker or a psychologist in private practice, or from the province's department of children's services. The assessment must make one of three recommendations: acceptance of the adoption project, postponement of the adoption project, or rejection of the adoption project.

- Quebec was a pioneer in arranging for the adoption of children from China. As a result, Quebec residents have excellent access to available children in China. Over the past decade, several thousand Chinese children have been adopted and relocated to Quebec.

- Quebec residents who adopt are entitled to up to fifty-two weeks of paid parental leave. In some parts of the province, the leave is available to both parents, but in others it must be shared between the mother and father. The leave may also be shared between same-sex parents.

- Once the child arrives in Quebec, the adoptive parents must undergo six months of probation before the adoption can be finalized by a Quebec court. During that time, a professional appointed by the Centres Jeunesse (Youth Centers) meets with the adoptive applicants and prepares a report on the child's development in the home. In some cases, the countries of origin request progress reports on the placement.

- In the event that the adoption decree is issued in the country of origin, the adoptive parents must present the matter to a Quebec Youth Court to determine whether the child is eligible for adoption and that the proper consents have been obtained to meet Quebec standards.

SASKATCHEWAN ADOPTIONS

In Saskatchewan, the focus is on agency adoptions. Provincial child and family services agencies process about one hundred and fifty adoptions a year, which compares to about fifty private adoptions a year and less than ten international adoptions a year.

The following are things you should know about domestic adoptions:

- All adoptions must be processed through a provincial child and family services agency. Private adoptions are allowed, but there is only one approved private agency in the province.

- It is illegal to advertise that you are interested in adopting a child or that you have a child who is available for adoption.

- All adoptions require the consent of the birth parents.

- You must be a resident of Saskatchewan to qualify for adoption.

- All children aged twelve or older must give their consent to being adopted.

- Financial subsidies are available for the adoption of children with special needs.

- The majority of birth parents who put their children up for placement request some form of openness in the adoption. The level of openness varies from the exchange of identifying information to the child maintaining a direct relationship with the birth parents. Open adoptions are encouraged by the province.

- Adoptions must be completed within one year of placement of the child.

The following are things you should know about international adoptions:

- All applications must be processed through the province's children and family services department, but when it comes to the home study, residents have the option of going to licensed social workers approved by the province or private agencies located outside the province.
- Provincial authorities are required to confirm that counseling has been given to both the birth parents and the adoptive parents, that the child is authorized to enter Canada, and that consents for the adoption were freely given by the birth parents.

YUKON AND NORTHWEST TERRITORIES ADOPTIONS

These are two separate jurisdictional entities, but they are paired here for convenience since they both have small populations and share cultural identities. Most of the adoptions that take place in these provinces are what are known as Native Custom adoptions. Of the seventy-five or so adoptions that take place each year in the Northwest Territories, only about a dozen are agency or private adoptions.

The Native Custom adoptions that take place are a reflection of a long-standing practice among native groups to place children with the full cooperation of the birth parents and the adoptive parents in accordance with Aboriginal custom. These adoptions usually take place with relatives or other people in the same community.

Adoption policies in the Yukon and the Northwest Territories are similar in many areas. In the Yukon, any person who has reached the age of majority may adopt another person younger than the applicant; in the Northwest Territories a couple is allowed to adopt if at least one person is of the age of majority. In both provinces, it is illegal to advertise for a child or for adoptive parents.

ABORIGINAL ADOPTIONS

For the past several decades, passions have simmered among Canada's Aboriginal population, who feel that their opinions and wishes have been ignored by both the national government and the provinces. Among the many subjects under debate is adoption. Aboriginal sentiment regarding adoption is the result of the relocation, over a forty-year period, of an estimated twenty thousand native children who were placed into white adoptive homes.

In a "Statement of Reconciliation," the Government of Canada issued an apology that acknowledged the "mistakes and injustices of the past" and offered a framework for a new partnership. "Sadly, our history with respect to the treatment of Aboriginal people is not something in which we can take pride. Attitudes of racial and cultural superiority led to a suppression of Aboriginal culture and values. As a country, we are burdened by past actions that resulted in weakening the identity of Aboriginal peoples, suppressing their languages and cultures, and outlawing spiritual practices."

In 1982, a Canadian judge equated the Children's Aid Society practice of placing large numbers of native children with white foster and adoptive parents with "cultural genocide." In the years since then, various provinces have begun programs to reconnect those children with their birth families and culture. Decisions about how to proceed with Aboriginal adoptions have proved more problematic since child welfare agencies have been hesitant to make the social and emotional needs of adopted Aboriginal children secondary to their need for a strong cultural identity.

There are not enough Aboriginal adoptive homes for all the Aboriginal children who need permanent homes, but provincial social agencies are reluctant to place them with white families for fear of being accused of cultural genocide. As a result, the children sometimes are kept in an uncertain limbo. Some social workers see it as more of a political issue than a professional issue. Others, especially the native leaders, say the "political" issue cannot be separated from the professional issue.

Straight Talk about Aboriginal Children and Adoption
By Sandra Scarth, President of the Adoption Council of Canada

Let me start by saying that this is not an easy subject about which to have straight talk. Even beginning the dialogue makes us uneasy, because the word "adoption" is fraught with different emotions for all parties to any adoption. For adoptive parents, there is joy when a child is brought into their family that may be colored by feelings of loss related to infertility issues. For birth parents and their extended families, the sense of loss may never go away, even if they are involved in healthy open adoptions.

When Aboriginal people speak of their feelings about Aboriginal children placed in non-Aboriginal homes, it is clear that the sense of loss in the Aboriginal community is profound. The phrase "cultural genocide" used in a recent court case by an Aboriginal leader tells us just how strong those feelings are. These are difficult words for non-Aboriginal families who have adopted Aboriginal children with the best of intentions and want to raise their children to be comfortable with themselves and their cultural identity.

It would be wonderful if there was a simple solution to finding permanent family and cultural connections for the Aboriginal children currently caught up in the child welfare system and living for the most part with non-Aboriginal foster families. Recent court cases have highlighted the conflicting points of view. Opinions are polarized and ideological.

One point of view is that no Aboriginal child should ever be placed permanently in a non-Aboriginal family. An opposing perspective is that no child, Aboriginal or non-Aboriginal, should be moved from a family where there is an emotional attachment. Cultural and identity issues clash with attachment theory, and proponents of each approach believe ardently that they are acting in the child's best interests. As noted in an earlier editorial, "best interests" is a murky, subjective test that depends on the point of view of the person making the determination. That test will not solve our problem.

Before we even get to the question of adoption, we may need to step back and look at the underlying issues that have resulted in the overrepresentation of Aboriginal children in care of the child welfare system. Based on provincial data, it is estimated that 30 to 40 percent of all children in care are Aboriginal despite the fact that they represent only 5 percent of the child population in Canada.

A recent study by the Children's Bureau of the U.S. Department of Healthy and Human Services about the overrepresentation of children of color in the child welfare system concludes that there are several reasons, most notably, poverty, racism and lack of training in the area of cultural diversity for social workers and others involved. Canadian reports about Aboriginal children in the child welfare system have come to similar conclusions, but they also focus on colonization and assimilationist policies that have contributed to the problem. In addition, the National Policy Review outlines the inequity of funding for on- and off-reserve Aboriginal children that has not been adequately or comprehensively addressed at the federal, provincial or territorial levels.

The reality is that children in care are not only in care of non-Aboriginal agencies. There are many Aboriginal mandated agencies in Canada today, both First Nation and Metis, that have been driven by outdated funding mechanisms to adapt the old system of practice and delivery rather than developing more preventive services that conform more closely to Aboriginal values.

These issues raise a number of tough questions. The first and only one I can answer with any authority is why the Adoption Council of Canada, seen as primarily a non-Aboriginal organization, has identified the issue of Aboriginal children in the child welfare system as one of its highest priority areas for discussion and development of a position statement.

The directors of the Board feel strongly that every child in care of the child welfare system, whether Aboriginal or non-Aboriginal, has a fundamental right to a family with a lifelong commitment to that child. We further believe that children have a right to their identity and to maintain important connections to extended family and cultural community as outlined in the United Nations Convention on the Rights of the Child. We also believe that we share the responsibility for the overrepresentation of Aboriginal children in the child welfare system and should work collaboratively with our Aboriginal colleagues to help solve the problems in the system.

Source: This editorial was originally published in November 2004 in *Adoption Canada,* the newsletter of the Adoption Council of Canada. It is used with permission.

6 Raising an Adopted Child

Seldom have we come across young birth parents who really understood what they were getting into when they began the journey to parenthood. Adoptive parents are no different. Adopting a child is a learning experience that requires parents to educate themselves on the unique challenges and joys of parenthood.

Parenting an adopted child is similar to parenting a birth child, but it is not exactly the same, primarily because it involves an additional set of problems. Just because you know how to be a good birth parent does not mean that you know how to be a good adoptive parent. In addition to normal parenting challenges, the unique problems that parents may experience when raising an adopted child include the following:

- Teaching their child to deal with what is often a painful past
- Dealing with birth parents
- Resolving unexpected problems at school
- Dealing with the likelihood, in privacy-protected adoptions, that their child will one day want to locate the birth mother and father, and perhaps want to maintain a parent-child relationship with them
- Dealing with the deep sense of loss that children feel about their birth parents; it is not unusual to hear adopted children, especially teens, describe that feeling as a "hole in my soul." For many adoptive parents, this is a difficult issue to deal with because they cannot understand why the love they provide is not enough to fill that "hole."

IS IT IMPORTANT THAT I BOND WITH MY ADOPTED CHILD?

Adoptive parents typically experience more problems associated with bonding and attachment than do birth parents. That is the reason why adoption screeners pay so much attention during the home study process to their ability to deal with those problems.

Parent-infant bonding has always been held in high esteem, as it should be, but contrary to earlier belief, there appears to be no absolute "critical period for bonding" that will result in catastrophic results if not adhered to. Many adoptive parents have felt unfounded guilt when it was not possible for parents and babies to be physically together within minutes after birth. But parents should not be overly concerned that a good relationship is in jeopardy, or that they will be less able to form close attachments to the child, if they are unable to experience an immediate parent-infant bonding experience. How you bond is more important than when you bond.

After already adopting a beautiful daughter, Danny was as excited as any expectant father waiting for the birth of his first adopted son. When he and his wife, Chelsea, arrived at the hospital, they found the birth mother in the hospital room alone, having delivered a premature son named Josh. Chelsea found it hard to accept that Josh would have to stay in intensive care for a long time and she would not be able to take him home as expected.

"With Chelsea very depressed, baby Josh in intensive care, and a daughter at home, I learned about nurturing real fast," Danny later explained. "Up until then, Chelsea took the lead with that sort of thing. Now it was up to me to be there for her, the baby, and our daughter. I remember holding Chelsea as she cried, holding little Josh only a few minutes at a time, and then going home to hold our daughter, who was very scared for her baby brother. Each one needed me in a different way. They needed my arms around them, my smile—and they needed for my words to be gentle and comforting. It gave me a sense of oneness that I had never experienced. I now know what bonding is all about."

Danny and Chelsea did not get to take Josh home for several months after birth, but today the bond between baby Josh and both his parents is as strong and healthy as any parent-infant bond that follows a routine delivery.

Bonding—and the formation of strong emotional attachments—begins on day one. Josh's adoptive parents offered similar experiences to what he would have received from his birth mother if she had remained in his life. Chelsea cuddled and held him tight against her breast, while Danny tossed him around a bit before falling comfortably in a recliner to share a football game with him. Clearly, from the beginning, Josh enjoyed the warm, cuddly caresses of his adoptive mom, but he also benefited from facing the world of sports with his dad.

Touching, playing, smiling, and reading to your child should start on the first day of his or her life with you. Fathers often feel inadequate as care-givers, but with practice, they can build the same confidence that mothers develop from "just doing it!" Fathers will be pleasantly surprised if they take a few risks, like singing to their children, dancing with them, being silly to make them laugh, reading with expression, or making funny sounds. A father who plays imitation games or does what it takes to engage the baby will create a lasting connection.

Babies need stimulation, comfort, and a sense of security in order to learn to trust and to take risks with their emotions. Bonding doesn't just happen because you share the same house with them, nor do mothers have a monopoly on bonding. Both parents can form equal but different bonds with their children.

Before an older child can begin to form an emotional attachment to a new family, the child first must understand what happened to the birth family. Why did they stop being a family? Why was the child placed in fos-ter care? Why can't the child return to the birth family? Where is the birth family? Do they miss the child? The responsibility for helping to answer those questions lies with the caseworker to some extent, but it is a con-tinuing educational effort that must be picked up by the adoptive parents. The adoptive parents must give the child emotional support in order to facilitate adjustment to the new family.

In order for a child to become attached to the adoptive family, the child must learn how to give him- or herself permission to have more than one family, and must be provided with a vision of what that new family will look like. As an adoptive parent, you must convince the child that you are not threatened by the existence of the birth parents. If you are threatened, the child will pick up on that and it will delay or inhibit his or her ability to emotionally attach to your family.

WHAT SHOULD I EXPECT FROM MY ADOPTED CHILD?

Those precious years between the total dependency of infancy and the responsibility of elementary school are considered some of the most care-free years in a child's life. Unfortunately, most of us don't remember much about our preschool years. Family stories, photographs, and bits of memo-rabilia may offer fond reminders of this delightful time, but most of us are unable to recall many details of our own experiences.

It is a time of rapid growth and development, during which a child tran-sitions into a true contributing member of the family. Physical changes during the preschool years are less dramatic than in earlier years, as the child begins to take on more adultlike body proportions. The child seems to jump into a larger clothing size even before one season ends. The child becomes less chunky, and goes from a more gender-neutral appearance to one that is either masculine or feminine. Motor skills are used more effectively to walk, run, jump, and ride a tricycle.

Boys have more muscle and bone and less fat than girls do. For both, the growth process follows a predictable sequence. The toddler appears top-heavy because growth takes place from top to bottom. During this transition, its "pot-bellied" abdomen is considered normal for a while because it is holding almost full-grown internal organs. Shortly, the child's lower body will grow to catch up, causing it to grow taller and better proportioned, losing the "pot-belly." Upon entering school at age six, the child will resemble children in the upper grades more than younger siblings.

The following physical changes become more evident as motor skills develop:

- At about three years of age, the child can run in a straight line, jump with both feet, copy a circle, use simple utensils to eat, and stack a few blocks.

- By four years, the child is skipping, hopping, and catching a large ball. The child's fine motor skills now include buttoning large buttons, copying simple shapes, and drawing a simple figure.

- At age five, the child is ready to enter kindergarten and is usually using scissors, copying letters and numbers, balancing on one foot, running without falling, and building fairly complex structures with blocks.

Play is the primary activity of a preschooler. The child's play is usually designed to meet his or her own enjoyment needs. The child is more interested in the process of play than the outcomes of play. Psychologists use play as a means of observing a child's attempt to resolve conflict and gain power over the environment. The child initially watches others, only engaging in play for a minute or two at a time. The child then learns to play alone, avoiding interaction with others. Later, he or she tries to engage others in play, only slightly at first, but then moving into cooperative play.

Thinking Like a Four-Year-Old

Socially, preschoolers engage in conversations, play with siblings, and exhibit a sense of belonging. Emotionally, they exhibit complex feelings that sometimes vacillate from being witty and performing for anyone who will watch to being very absorbed in their private thoughts. Parents are sometimes embarrassed and at other times entertained—but continuously amazed—at their precious creations.

In their efforts to bring secret fantasies under control, children experience feelings of guilt. They seem to have an inner voice offering judgments concerning their behavior of right and wrong, and they fear punishment for fantasies that they label as "wrong." Preschoolers exhibit egocentric thinking, which means that they are unable to consider another person's point of view. They believe that nonliving objects are, in fact, alive and that all objects, whether living or nonliving, are made the same way. They learn to classify objects according to several categories. With practice they are able to sort according to color, size, and shape.

Preschoolers sometimes have difficulty retracing behavior, such as answering questions like, "What did you do with the ball this afternoon?" They also cannot understand that mass and volume remain the same when circumstances change. They have a difficult time believing that six ounces of juice in a large pitcher can remain the same when poured into a tall glass.

Matthew, who is four years old, loves to play with his mom's car keys. He will play with them any time he has a chance. When his mom couldn't find the keys one night, she became frustrated and insisted that he must find the keys he had played with earlier in the day. Mom tried to motivate Matthew by promising to take him to buy ice cream if he found the lost keys, but the bribe didn't work.

Unfortunately, Matthew was not capable of recalling details of previous events and retracing his actions from earlier in the day. He simply couldn't remember where he was playing with the keys, no matter how motivating the ice cream offer sounded. As an added incentive, his mom offered him his favorite juice while he tried to recall where the keys might be. Matthew loves juice, so as usual he whined and fretted until his mom poured the juice into his favorite tall glass. At age four, Matthew believes he gets more juice in the taller glass than in the wide-rimmed, shorter glass, even though his mom poured the juice from glass to glass to help him understand that the amount does not change.

Matthew has a very well-meaning mom who is simply uninformed about reasonable developmental expectations for a four-year-old. It would benefit both Matthew and his mom if she understood that Matthew should not play with anything of much value or any object that she might need in the near future. If adults allow children to play with such items, they should take responsibility for retrieving the valuables after playtime. As for the juice, only time will help Matthew understand that six ounces of juice is still six ounces of juice, no matter the size or shape of the container.

Preschool Gender Differences

Gender differences in preschool play may appear to be only slight, but what begins in preschool continues throughout life—boys prefer to play with other boys, girls with other girls. There seem to be visual cues as to who plays with whom: girls tend to walk in a straight line, arms at their side or folded across their midsection; boys shuffle back and forth in more of a sideways motion, their arms swinging. Boys are often larger and stronger than girls, and they may be able to hit, throw, and catch a ball better.

One of the most significant gender differences in preschoolers is how they choose to use their time. Boys tend to be more active and rough. Girls tend to prefer quieter play, such as drawing or playing with stuffed animals. Girls generally are more proficient at manual dexterity, hopping, and skipping; but boys generally can go up and down steps and jump better than girls. Boys usually prefer playing outdoors and girls usually enjoy indoor play more. Boys tend to enjoy playing in the sand, climbing, and playing with outdoor gadgets more than girls do.

The Middle Years (Ages Six through Twelve)

Many remember the middle years of life with greater fondness than any other time. Children in this stage have a good command of language. They can think clearly. And they can contribute to conversations with their opinions. Usually they have plenty of play time and start developing friendships that may continue the rest of their lives. Often neighbors and family members comment on "how big he's getting" and "how smart she is." The child is growing up, is learning daily, and should feel that "life is good."

On the first day of school, most first-graders are filled with excitement and anticipation. Some may be shy, some may be very outgoing, and some may be even a bit aggressive. They arrive in a variety of sizes and shapes. The largest may be six inches taller and sometimes twenty pounds heavier than the smallest in the class. These dramatic differences are only amplified during the next several years since children grow at different rates. Girls usually reach this growth spurt earlier than boys, so by late childhood, girls are sometimes standing head and shoulders above the boys.

The timing of all this is interesting since it often coincides with their initial interest in one another. Awkward as it may seem, boys cope fairly well with their height differences. It's when height, weight, or physical features fall outside the "accepted range" of tolerance that peers can be cruel and hurtful. Children who are obese, have large ears, wear glasses, or have other anomalies are often the target of ridicule by their peers.

The middle-to-late childhood years are full of physical challenges. Baseball, soccer, basketball, swimming, tennis, and football seem to be the sports of choice. Socially it's important to participate, whether it is in organized sports or with sandlot friends. Boys particularly feel the pressure to be part of a team activity.

Dramatic differences in abilities are evident in boys between the ages of six to ten. A major difference is noticed in the older boy's coordination and timing. He can now anticipate the baseball better, swing the bat in time to connect, and run, jump, and catch the ball in the outfield.

Although injury is always a possibility and fear of failure is ever present, participation in team sports seems to be beneficial for most children. It not only refines the child's motor and coordination skills but it also offers social contact and teaches the child to play by the rules. However, parents must be careful in their approach with children who are involved in sports. Encouragement is important, but constant pressure to excel may cause extreme harm. Participation in organized sports can be an opportunity for families to have fun together while providing the child with valuable life lessons.

The school age child learns at a remarkable rate. The child learns to read, spell, compute math, comprehend concepts, get along with others, follow directions, and work independently, all in the first year of formal education. During this time the child begins to perform mental operations that demonstrate an ability to focus on various aspects of a problem. The child can think beyond the present and begin to reason out issues. Soon the child will be able to challenge the adults in his or her life.

Learning to Learn Follows a Familiar Pattern

Daniel is nine years old and his brother Chase is five. Daniel doesn't mind that Chase chooses the allowance of ten dimes stretched wide across the table instead of the allowance of ten dimes placed very close together on the table. He understands that little Chase believes that the dimes far apart are more money than the dimes placed close together. He also understands that his mom always gives them equal amounts of milk each morning. So when little Chase insists on having the tall, slender glass because he wants more milk, Daniel gives in. He doesn't protest the dimes or milk because, at age nine, he is now able to comprehend the process of change.

Daniel was even able to help little Chase when he put twice as much chocolate powder in his glass as was needed. He was able to reverse the process and figure out that if he poured his milk into Chase's milk, stirred it up and then poured it back into his glass, both would have a good glass of chocolate milk. Although mom brags about Daniel's good-natured personality and generosity to little Chase, his behavior is probably better explained by his developmental maturity than his extraordinary kindness.

Some parents feel tempted to teach their children concepts they are not equipped to learn. It is a total waste of time. There is no learning advantage in offering training to children before they are capable of understanding it. You cannot hurry a child's mental processes along. Numerous researchers have tried to do just that, but with little success. As a result, educators have learned to provide students with activities that follow a developmental sequence that promotes a hands-on learning experience, moving students from what they can see to what they can imagine.

Numbers, letters, words, facts, and dates all bombard the youngster in the classroom. Increasing demands are placed on the child to memorize, retrieve facts, and process data in order to escape one grade and advance to the next. Early on, young children fail to use inferences—they can't "read between the lines," so to speak—and they are often easily distracted because they don't have much of an attention span. In new learning situations they seldom pay attention to details. Despite those roadblocks, children are able to formulate strategies for learning and find ways to use new material.

Memory is a necessary skill for successful academic achievement. Long-term memory develops more slowly than short-term memory. As a child learns to rehearse new information, repeat the information, and organize thoughts more efficiently, memory skills will improve. Likewise, as the child increases in general knowledge, memory skills will improve through the association of ideas.

The elementary school child is faced with making independent decisions almost daily. Many of these decisions have to do with "right and wrong." Moral development is fairly predictable. Parents must keep in mind that children cannot be expected to exercise good moral judgment until they are able to understand the concepts involved.

At the earliest stage of moral judgment, a child makes decisions based on self-interest, in order to avoid punishment or to get rewards. The child usually accepts the authority imposed on his or her life without distinction as to what it may believe. Throughout the middle years, children continue to make moral decisions based on their personal needs. They show no real loyalty to others, but they often agree with anyone who will return the favor and support their demands.

Navigating the Challenges

As children make their way through the middle years, they face many challenges. The child must learn self-discipline in order to conquer math, reading, spelling, and science. Facing homework nightly can create a family crisis if the child has trouble focusing on the work. The child begins to take on chores around the house, earn an allowance, and explore a world beyond the family backyard. Friends become increasingly more important and many children aspire to become a valued member of a sports team.

The years between six and twelve are ones in which a child begins to focus on building skills and developing a feeling of competency. The child is now ready to independently prove him- or herself worthy of notice. The child may concentrate efforts on sports, academics, music, or other activities. Few children dodge all the obstacles along this path; most do achieve a healthy sense of self-confidence, even if it is accompanied by the nagging voice of inferiority from time to time.

Gender differences may be noticed on the playground. Boys tend to show more achievement motivation by racing against one another, while girls often spend their time developing social relationships by chatting in small groups. Although most children during the middle years do not share intimate thoughts and feelings with their friends, they do show more self-confidence when playing with them. Developing friendships offers social feedback for the child and helps to slightly reduce his or her self-centered thinking.

Boys usually play in large groups with lots of tossing and tumbling around. They claim multiple "best friends," even when it is not a reciprocal relationship. Girls usually develop a much smaller circle of close friends and play games in which they can converse and share their feelings.

Friends can offer a different perspective on many issues for the child. On the positive side, they can offer feedback that fosters confidence in ways that parents cannot. They can even influence behavior. At times, the child at home appears totally different from the child known by his or her friends. Unfortunately, children with negative attitudes are the peer group's weakest link. They often bully and threaten smaller or weaker kids, ridicule underachievers, and tease or embarrass those who may be slightly different. Parents should take quick action in those situations. Try to help your child learn when teasing is acceptable and when those who tease should be avoided.

The concept of popularity becomes increasingly important during this time. Often popular children have a slight advantage over the others in school achievement, athletic abilities, confidence, physical attractiveness, or social skills. Girls seem to desire popularity slightly more than boys do.

The middle years consolidate a "sense of self" for boys. Less adult supervision is necessary and, if things are going well, parents feel confident of their parenting skills. Their child engages in conversations with them, expresses feelings, and will quickly protest any hint of unfairness. Parents begin to see their own behavior reflected in the behavior of their children. The affectionate parent is usually pleased to see his or her child be affectionate to a younger sibling. The angry parent has little reason to be surprised to hear foul language in a child who has been exposed to it in the home.

When all is said and done, it is sometimes helpful to remember poet William Wordsworth's observation that "the child is father of the man." The joy, frustration, laughter, and heartbreak that your children experience on the road to adulthood will combine, eventually, to make them into the adults that they will become.

HOW CAN I HELP MY CHILD ACCEPT HIS OR HER PAST?

Sometimes it is difficult for adoptive parents to understand that their child has a past. That's because, in the beginning, adoption was a joyful concept that seemed more about the parents than the child. It was all about what the child would do to make their life more meaningful. With the actual arrival of the child comes the realization that he or she had a previous life that did not include you.

If you adopted your child as an infant, you may not have to deal with a past until the child is of school age or older; but just because you have adopted an infant does not mean that there is no past. Because the child does have a past, there are questions you must ask during the selection process, the first being, "why is this child available for adoption?" Screeners vary greatly in the information they are willing to provide to adoptive parents. Some feel that the reason why the child was put up for adoption is not relevant. Others think it is relevant. If you are not told a specific reason why a child came into the agency's care, feel free to ask the screener.

Adopting an infant offers no guarantee that he or she does not have a past, unless the newborn is still in the hospital. We have seen infants come into the care of child welfare agencies who have been scalded by hot water, left outside in the cold, sexually molested, and spanked with wire coat hangers. Infants who have lived in war-torn countries abroad may have been exposed to exploding artillery shells or bombs, or may have been orphaned because of a terrorist attack that the child witnessed. An infant who has gone through abuse obviously will have different needs than one that has not.

An infant with a past has different needs than an older child with a past. It will need more holding, more baby talk, and more nurturing in general. It is important that both parents spend quality time with such a child. If you are a working parent, you need to take extended leave of at least one year. The last thing that an infant with a past needs is to be accepted by an adoptive parent who then turns the child over to a day-care center. If you have adopted an infant with a past, it needs you, and no one else.

If you adopt an older child, you must first understand his or her past before you can know what you should do to address the child's special needs. Did the child live in an orphanage or a foster home? Did the child have little human contact? Did the child suffer from physical or emotional deprivation while in the care of birth or foster parents?

Your efforts to help your child deal with the past will begin with questions about how much the child remembers about his or her previous life. If the child experienced moments of abuse, are those moments recalled in a matter-of-fact manner, without assigning blame, or does the child react with great emotion? Many children seem to automatically think that bad things happened to them because they are bad people.

A six-year-old boy was visiting relatives when he approached a couple of cocker spaniels that were kept in another room that was closed off with an expanding children's gate. When he gleefully approached the dogs with his hands outstretched, they barked at him. "Don't worry," said his uncle. "They only bite bad people."

"Oh," answered the boy.

Later the boy approached the dogs and whispered, "Please don't bite me—I'm a good boy!"

The uncle meant that the dogs would bite burglars and such, but the little boy assumed that the comment was directed toward him. That is very common for children that age. They see the world in black-and-white terms of good and bad. If adopted children remember bad things that happened to them, they feel certain that it was because they were bad. As an adoptive parent, you must be sensitive to those feelings. You must assure your child that bad things did not happen because the child is a bad person.

You must also resist the temptation to tell your child that his or her birth parents were bad. Shifting the blame may make you feel better but it will not help your child feel better. If you tell the child that his or her birth parents are bad, the child will eventually turn that blame back upon him- or herself by reasoning that the parents were bad because the child was bad.

If you are involved in an open adoption in which the birth parents have regular contact with your child, you must help the child understand that it is all right to have two sets of parents, even if his or her friends at school do not.

WHEN YOUR CHILD YEARNS FOR THE BIRTH PARENTS

If your adoption is one in which the identity of the parents was kept confidential, the odds are good that, sooner or later, your child will request information on how to find them. You may or may not know the identity of the birth parents. If you do know, you must decide whether to share that information. You must weigh the responsibility you feel to protect your child from the birth parents with the risks to your relationship if you do not. If you do not know the identity of the child's birth parents, you must decide whether to assist the child in any efforts to locate them.

Of course, the first thing you have to determine is whether you feel threatened by the prospect of your child locating the birth parents. If so, that is your problem, not the child's, and you should give a great deal of thought to whether you want to penalize your child because of your own insecurities.

The imagined phantom birth parents will reflect your child's own anger, confusion, and dreams. The imagined parents may be mean and cruel, or they may border on sainthood, or they may be seen as victims in need of protection. Unfortunately, the adoptive parent is usually the recipient of the child's displaced feelings. Since the birth parents are unavailable to the child, the child tends to shower the adoptive parents with a barrage of emotions, often vacillating from rage, hurt, and anger to depression and withdrawal.

When the child assumes a protective stance, it is usually not done to protect the parent, but rather to protect him- or herself. Feeling betrayed and unworthy of love, the child assumes that any negative comments about the birth parents are untrue, the result of a conspiracy. The child assumes that the adoptive parents distort information to make themselves look good and to foster ill will toward the birth parents.

We advise adoptive parents to give their children factual information about their birth, based on two "ifs": if it is known and if the child requests it. An adoptive parent may feel that he or she is sheltering the child from more hurt by withholding the truth, but as the child matures into adolescence and starts to ask questions, we recommend that parents share information in an honest, straightforward manner. This can be extremely difficult, but it is important that parents stay focused on separating their relationship with the child from that of the birth parents, and allow the child the opportunity to find the birth parents.

Without truthful information, the child may blame the adoptive parents for the birth parents' absence, and may suspect that there are underlying issues that the child doesn't know about. Facing the reality that the birth parents do not want to acknowledge the child, or acknowledge him or her as theirs, is a very difficult concept for a child to accept.

The bottom line for adoptive parents is that there is no place for them to hide. Their adopted child may grow into adulthood without ever wanting information about the birth parents. Then again, it may be the most important thing in the child's life. How you deal with this issue will be one of the major tests you will face as a parent. Don't run from it. Face it head on and do what you can to help your child cope with the past.

WHEN DO I TELL MY CHILD ABOUT THE ADOPTION?

In adoptions in which the birth parents' identities were kept secret, there will come a time when the child will want to know more about them. Not all children react in the same way. Some are satisfied with obtaining minor information, such as whether their birth parents were interested in sports or music. Others will want to know more details about their birth parents' family history in the hopes of discovering cousins, aunts, or uncles. Others feel such hostility toward their birth parents for placing them up for adoption that they avoid receiving any information about them.

Others still, such as Faith Hill, feel incomplete unless they meet with their birth parents and establish some sort of relationship with them. Hill's three-year search for her birth mother ended when the singer was twenty, when the two women met in a city park. "I found out she is a painter, an artist, and she has an incredible sense of style," Hill later told Jeanne Wolf in an article for *Redbook*. "She's very tall. She's a sweet, sweet woman. I have a lot of respect for her, and I had no feelings of anger or any of that.... I know she must have had a lot of love for me to want to give me what she felt was a better choice. Thank God she let me live."

One of the issues that will arise during the probationary period is how and when to tell the child, the family, and the community about the adoption. There is no point in telling an infant, of course, but it is recommended that you tell family and friends when the court finalizes the adoption. The best age to start discussing adoption with a child is around four or five years, before the child starts school. You start out saying simply, "You are adopted. That means that we loved you so much that we picked you to be our child."

That is not a concept that a four- or five-year-old will understand, but it will acquaint the child with the word "adoption" and lessen the shock value of being called such by older children or adults in the community. When you mention adoption, be careful not to pair it with words such as abandoned or rejected, and be especially careful not to criticize the birth parents. As the years go by, your child will want to understand more about adoption. The child will talk about adoption for several years before understanding what the word means. Generally speaking, the more a child understands about human reproduction, the more the child will understand the concept of adoption.

Telling a child that he or she is adopted is just the first step in a process that will continue well into adolescence. There will come a time when the child will want to understand why you chose him or her, why you were not able to have children of your own, and why the birth parents gave the child up for adoption. The child will want you to explain why adoption agencies and courts are able to decide where children live and will want to know more about the birth parents. Of course, if it is an open adoption, the child will want to know your opinion of the birth parents. Do you like them? Do you think they did the right thing by giving the child up for adoption?

When the child is older there will be lots of questions about your background and history. The child will examine your family albums and your childhood photographs in an effort to understand you better. It is at that point that you will be glad that you documented your child's arrival into your family with photographs and keepsakes. The child will understand that you had a history apart from him or her, just as the child had a history apart from you. The more details you can provide about the day that your lives came together, the more the child will cherish the stories of his or her childhood. One adopted child, after she became an adult, said:

> Adoption always made me feel special. Unlike my friends, I could remember the day that I met my Mom and Dad. That's because I was three when they adopted me. I don't remember anything about my foster home, but I have this image in my memory of Mom reaching out for me and Dad standing nearby smiling this big old smile that he still flashes when I walk into the room. I can remember the way the house smelled because Mom had made a special meal for me and I can remember how cold it was walking up to the house and then how warm I felt when I stepped inside. Today when Mom and I look through the adoption book she put together for me I can remember when individual pictures were taken. I talked about that album all the way through school and I think it made my friends jealous because they couldn't remember anything about their albums.

HOW DO I MAKE OPEN ADOPTION WORK FOR ME?

As an adoptive parent you have taken on a tremendous responsibility, without much information to help predict the child's personality, temperament, behavioral tendencies, and possibly inherited physical or mental health problems. In the last few years, with the arrival of "open" adoptions, more information has become available to adoptive parents and that has made the future seem a little bit more predictable.

Actually, the acceptance of open adoptions has paralleled acceptance of divorce in today's culture. Shared parenting is fairly common now with so many divorces. Trading weekends, holidays, and vacation time has become quite a juggling act for many divorced couples. We all know divorced parents who have had to learn how to share their children with their ex-spouses. As result, divorce has made open adoption seem like a familiar, if not reasonable, way to raise children.

As in divorce, open adoption does have its drawbacks. It is easy for you to have uneasy feelings and wonder if your child will see the biological parents as being more in charge. Will the child feel more attached to the biological parents, even if abuse occurred, or will the child play one set of parents against the other? The answer is possibly YES, YES, and YES. If allowed to, any child will try to work a situation to its advantage.

If shared parenting is an option you choose, it may be the right decision for your child but it could also be problematic for you. No two sets of parents have the same expectations or styles; in fact, usually there is some disagreement within an intact family on some aspects of raising a child. In an open adoption, we encourage adoptive parents to negotiate for the major decision making, rule making, and ultimate control of the child. That is not always possible, depending on the convictions of the birth parent, but it will be better for you if you can convince the birth parent that you need that leverage with the child to be an effective parent.

Adoptive shared parenting is usually not as equally divided as it is with divorce. We recommend that the biological parents be offered limited and casual contact with the child. This should be at your convenience and timed so that it will not disrupt your family. The arrangement should be similar to visitation you allow with extended family. From the beginning, you should make it clear to the biological parents that you expect them to respect your rules and support your efforts to discipline the child. Since family traditions and values vary greatly from family to family, your task is to persuade the biological parents that your traditions and values will provide the child with a better life than he or she otherwise would have had, using all the tact you can muster.

Evidence that the biological parents can be trusted is crucial and obtaining it may be a gradual process. You should not feel compelled to totally share your child. There are many levels of sharing and what is best for your child is a decision you should not be pressured into making to accommodate the whims of the biological parents. It is a decision that must be considered carefully and professional advice is highly recommended.

You do not want to erase your child's heritage, but neither do you want to feel as though your own is in second place either. Maintaining the balance can be tricky. Advice concerning types of sharing, levels of involvement, and frequency of contact will depend on many factors, including the following:

- *The biological parents' interest in sharing.* Some biological parents are more interested than others in sharing. Some actually prefer limited sharing. Know what you are getting yourself into before you agree on a final plan.

- *The psychological maturity of both sets of parents.* Take a close look at yourself; then take a close look at your co-parents. Are your maturity levels on the same page? Are you more alike than unalike?

- *Cultural impact issues.* Are you and the biological parents in agreement on whether explicit music videos, R-rated movies, violent video games, and so on are acceptable diversions for the child?

- *Personal and spiritual value systems.* Are you in agreement with the biological parents on what values should be instilled in the child? If you are a liberal Democrat and the biological parent is a conservative Republican, where do you see the common ground?

- *Stated goals of each set of parents.* It is very important for you to share your long-term goals for the child with the biological parent. Birth mothers and fathers are more likely to rise to the occasion and sacrifice some of their core beliefs if they are convinced that your plan will provide the child with a better life.

- *The child's past history with the biological parents.* If the child is old enough to remember hard times with the birth parents, the child is old enough to value that history, however negative it might have been.

- *The child's emotional readiness for shared parenting.* How you get along with the birth parents will depend to a great extent on how accepting the child is of shared parenting. For that reason, it is important to involve the child in as many discussions as possible. If you reach an agreement with the biological parents that you will make certain decisions in the shared-parent arrangement, it is important that the child be present when the biological parent agrees to allow you to set the rules for those situations.

- *The impact on other family members.* In addition to biological parents, adopted children may also have biological aunts, uncles, grandmothers, and grandfathers, thus providing the child with two sets of just about every family combination possible. The feelings and opinions of both sets of extended families must be taken into consideration if the adoption is going to go smoothly.

Adoptive parents must be aware that in some situations their efforts will not be appreciated and the biological parents may ultimately try to get their child back. It is extremely disruptive when biological parents try to "undo" what has legally been decided. This pursuit can foster false accusations, pulling the child in different directions, and totally disrupting the family. To minimize any potential conflicts, we recommend that shared parenting always be monitored by a professional mediator so that the decision to quickly modify or terminate the arrangement should it become harmful to the child is the responsibility of the professional.

Shared parenting can be very healing for an adopted child and can provide a wider range of experiences he or she would not otherwise obtain. Often in foreign adoptions, maintaining some relationship with the biological family or at least some individual in or from the home country is helpful to the child in developing an identity. Visiting the child's homeland on planned vacations has recently become popular for many families with children who were adopted from overseas.

HOW DO I DEAL WITH PROBLEMS AT SCHOOL?

Adopted children experience problems that other children do not have to face, such as pain-causing prejudice among other students and teachers—especially in biracial or gay and lesbian adoptions—or behavioral problems due to dysfunctional preadoption home situations with birth or foster parents.

Teachers are only human and many have biases about adoption. Difficulties can arise out of routine assignments. Writing an autobiography, for example, can be painful for an adopted child who does not know his or her family history.

If your child is having problems at school, it may be because of learning difficulties or an inability to get along with the other children. Both problems can be rooted in the fact that the child is adopted.

In high school, if the child is not as attractive, as talented in sports, or as academically successful as the other children, the child may wonder if it is because of the adoption. The child may blame everything that goes wrong in life on the adoption. If the child falls in love and the attraction is not mutual, the child may think it is because of the adoption. If classmates bully the child, he or she may believe it is because of the adoption, especially if the bully, sensing the child's greatest weakness, says, "You are not as good as I am because you are adopted." What seems silly or outrageous to you may be a serious matter to the child, so it is important that you treat all the child's questions with respect.

Adopted children have difficulty in school for many reasons. All of us have our strengths and weaknesses when it comes to learning new material. Over time, most of us learn strategies to use our strengths and minimize our weaknesses. Many very bright, successful people have learning deficits.

The diagnosis of a learning disability primarily has to do with the average expectation in the classroom. Performance significantly below the average in any academic area can be considered a deficit. The assumption that the child can't learn is often inaccurate. Learning styles vary across the general population. Some children learn better visually, some by listening to information, and others by tactile input. If a child is having problems in a particular academic area, it is important to analyze the problem. There are specialists who can assist in diagnosing learning problems.

As a parent you might need to remind yourself that most children's academic performance suffers in relationship to any emotional problems they may have. Do not be too quick to assume the child can't learn. If a learning disability is diagnosed, it is important to request special accommodation at school to assist the child in reaching his or her learning potential. Other resources such as tutorial assistance, structured homework assistance, and special remedial classes are usually beneficial.

WHEN THE LOVE YOU RECEIVE DOESN'T EQUAL THE LOVE YOU GIVE

Children receive love more easily than they give love. That characteristic is heightened in adoption for the simple reason that child-parent attachment fails in a higher percentage of cases involving adoptive children than it does with natural children.

Good adoptive parents will be able to accept the possibility that they may go through a lifetime in which they give more love than they receive. It takes a parent with a good self-image to be able to adjust to a one-way relationship with a child whom frustrated friends and relatives might depict as "unappreciative."

Trevor and June were devastated when they learned that they would never have children of their own. They were both from large families and they defined marriage in terms of children. It took them a year or two to adjust to what June called her "loss," time they spent dealing with their depression. They had thought about adoption, but not until their therapist suggested it to them did they feel they had permission to proceed.

The home study interviews were difficult for them because it required them to relive the painful emotions associated with their greatest disappointment in life. However, as the interviews progressed, they saw hope for the first time since they learned they would never have children of their own. The day that they learned they had been approved was the happiest day of their lives.

In the beginning, Trevor and June requested an infant of either sex. As the months went by, they modified their request to include a child of either sex up to two years of age. Two months later they received a telephone call from their adoption screener notifying them that he had a child he wanted to talk to them about.

Stephanie was twenty-three months of age. She had blonde hair, blue eyes, and a mischievous smile that seemed full of mystery. The adoption worker explained that Stephanie had been in a foster home for more than a year. Her mother had abandoned her immediately after giving birth to her in the hospital. The child's aunt took custody of Stephanie and attempted to raise her as a single parent. Unfortunately, the aunt died suddenly of a heart attack, making it necessary for Stephanie to be placed in a foster home.

When Trevor and June met Stephanie at a showing in the agency offices, they both instantly fell in love with her. She seemed perfect! The adoption worker explained to them that Stephanie had been unable to bond with her birth mother, due to the fact that the mother had abandoned her without ever holding her; but she had become attached to her aunt, who had spent a great deal of time with her. Stephanie took her aunt's death very hard. When she was placed in a foster home, she sometimes awakened at night and walked through the house, opening every closet door in an effort to find her aunt.

Trevor and June experienced behavior problems with Stephanie for the first couple of years, but as time went by, Stephanie settled into a routine and seemed to put her past behind her. The more time that Trevor and June spent with Stephanie, the more attached to her they became. On the surface, Stephanie seemed to be equally attached to them, but it eventually became obvious that she didn't feel the level of love for her parents that they felt for her. By the time Stephanie became a teenager, she routinely ended arguments with her mother with declarations of "I hate you—I always have!"

Stephanie's lack of closeness to them concerned Trevor, but June seemed more understanding. "She has no right not to love you," he protested, to which June usually responded, "She's just finding her own way. I know she loves me." June surprised herself with her understanding, for it was something she could not explain.

By the time Stephanie left home to enter college, June had become reconciled to her relationship with her daughter. "When she's ready to love me, she will let me know," she told Trevor each time he tried to make an issue out of it.

In the end, June was proved right. Stephanie married when she was twenty-two and had her first child when she was twenty-four. To June's surprise, she named the baby June. One day during one of their weekly visits,

Stephanie sat down next to June and put her arm around her in a loving way and said, "Mom, there's something I've been wanting to tell you for a long time."

June waited patiently, fearing the worst.

"I want to thank you for believing in me all those years. I love you so much—and I always have."

Those were words that June had waited twenty-five years to hear.

When June told Trevor, it made him angry. "Why didn't she say that ten or twenty years ago?"

"Because she wasn't ready."

Trevor and June's story is not as uncommon as you might think. Good adoptive parents need many parenting skills to succeed, but the one skill that the best of them always seem to have is an ability to postpone gratification. You should never enter adoption with the view that you are going to receive unqualified love and appreciation for your efforts. That is the way it usually works out in the end, but you have to be prepared for those occasions when the measure of the success of your adoption is the love you give, and not the love you take.

DEALING WITH SERIOUS CHILDHOOD PROBLEMS

Most of us want to know why things happen. Why am I suffering with this disease? Why does my son or daughter behave the way he or she does? Why does my child have trouble in school? Sometimes parents express an overwhelming desire to understand the "why" of their child's problem behavior, feeling that once they understand why, then they will be better able to deal with the problems.

Unfortunately, it's not that simple. It is difficult to pinpoint cause-and-effect relationships for many childhood problems. As a result, valuable time spent dwelling on the factors that contribute to some of life's tough problems for your child may be time wasted.

Parents tend to focus on cause too often, when assigning blame may be the actual objective. Casting blame seems to give comfort to some. Insisting that the hyperactive child is "just like his father" offers relief to the mother. Similarly, with adoptive children, it's easy to assume that blame lies with the biological parents or, at the very least, just from being adopted. To assume that adoption itself causes serious problems is totally inaccurate. More accurately, we can assume that many factors prior to the adoption may be major contributors in problem behaviors.

Research does suggest that adopted children are diagnosed with emotional problems at a slightly higher rate than their nonadopted peers.

Children who are available for adoption are more likely to have suffered physical and emotional abuse, neglect, multiple placements, and other traumas. Sadly, much of the reported suffering occurs while the child is part of a welfare system that is charged with caring for the child. These factors, along with the child's biological makeup, may be responsible for later behavior problems exhibited by the child.

There is indeed some association of cause and effect with adopted children, but choosing those notions to relieve parental guilt can be hurtful, if not a waste of time. Adoptive parents must understand that adopted children often have bedwetting, soiling, and learning problems, and an array of other behavioral problems. They may steal, run away, lie, withdraw, and have conflicts with authority. It's easy to think that early traumas may help explain, if not predict, serious behavior problems. The main thing is for parents to be aware and prepared for their adopted child to have behavior problems, which may be experienced at different times in the child's development.

Often parents report that their older adopted child tests the strength of the family bond early in the adjustment period. The child may act out, become aggressive, defy authority, or exhibit other problems that may be dangerous while trying to find where he or she fits in the family unit. This early adjustment period may be difficult for the whole family anyway, but particularly difficult if the adopted child is working against the bonding process. As the adoptive family tries to adjust to having another person around the house, managing different schedules, meeting the basic needs of the child, and learning likes and dislikes, the adopted child may be overwhelmed by the situation. Typically, the younger the adoptive child, the easier the transition. This assumes that the younger the child, the less trauma he or she has suffered.

Even when adoptive parents are well informed and expect some ups and downs, it can be difficult when disturbing behavior occurs. Often emotional and behavioral problems lack logic. They can indicate a seemingly self-destructive side to the child and occur at a time when the family seems to be adjusting well or considered happy. Some of the more frequently exhibited emotional and behavioral problems are discussed below.

Parents are cautioned never to try to diagnose their child based on a list of symptoms. Diagnosis of a mental or behavioral disorder requires a well-trained professional. Only an experienced mental health professional who is licensed or certified by a provincial or state credentialing board to diagnose and treat children should be trusted to provide services for your family. Although these professionals will want your input on specific symptoms, a diagnosis is far more complicated. An analysis of symptom duration, intensity, clusters of symptoms, family history, current life situations, intellectual and academic ability, peer relationships, age, and other factors are needed to make a diagnosis.

Depression

Adopted children are often described as having the right to be sad. This terminology seems strange for many of us, but well-meaning adults feel that it may explain or give the child an excuse for certain unwanted behaviors. In many cases, these children have endured pain from a variety of situations, beginning with being given away. This sadness is often expected and considered normal for an adopted child.

Childhood depression was not recognized as a diagnosis for children until fairly recently. Before 1980, many psychiatrists and psychologists believed that children did not possess the understanding and emotional maturity to feel depression as adults do. This may have been because childhood depression often does not present itself with the symptoms typical of adult depression. It is now diagnosed at an alarming rate and the consequences of depression are becoming well known.

Childhood depression is fairly common, but the exact numbers vary widely. Although reliable authorities disagree on the number of children who suffer from depression, they all estimate that a high number of children are at risk and do suffer depression. Each year, 8 to 9 percent of children from the age of ten to thirteen years suffer a major depressive episode, and between the ages of fourteen and sixteen years, as many as 16 percent of girls are affected by depression. Boys are diagnosed at about half the rate of girls. By age eighteen, as many as one out of every five teenagers has suffered at least one major depressive episode. This tremendous health problem is often misunderstood, misdiagnosed, or completely overlooked.

The number of children diagnosed with depression has increased over the past few years and the numbers continue to rise. Whatever the numbers, it is critical that children suffering from depression are appropriately treated. Without treatment, the likelihood of adult depression, along with other psychiatric problems, increases. Children who are depressed are often also diagnosed with other emotional or behavioral problems, which sometimes leads to confusion about childhood depression. It should be emphasized that early diagnosis and treatment are helpful in affecting the child's prognosis as an adult.

When a child is always sad, parents must be concerned and explore what is happening to their child. Unfortunately, many depressed children do not present the symptoms that indicate depression in adults. Children who are depressed often are described as irritable, not doing well in school, or have other, similar symptoms. They may have more physical complaints. They may have trouble concentrating. They may be argumentative. When parents sit and discuss these types of problems, few actually entertain the possibility that depression could be the culprit. That is why parents should consult with a mental health professional if they suspect that their child is depressed. A child psychologist or psychiatrist will want you to describe what behaviors are out of the normal range. Among the issues they will be looking for are specific symptoms and how long the child has had the symptoms. It is important for parents to be good informants.

Children have good and bad days. A child who gets upset and tearful over a disappointment but bounces back in a day or two is fine. if a child withdraws for weeks, is unresponsive, and lets pain for one situation bleed over into other parts of life, then those are signs that professional assistance is needed.

Early Warning Signs of Depression

Children may show the following signs of depression:

- The child sleeps late and has a hard time waking up. Depressed children may also wake up early and not be able to go back to sleep.

- The child becomes unusually irritable without apparent explanation and becomes angry over minor matters.

- The child complains of a loss of energy, and is not interested in the things that used to interest him or her. The child shows no interest in inviting friends over to play games, listen to music, or watch television; instead, he or she will do those activities alone.

- The child complains of a series of vague aches and pains for which there is no apparent cause (that is, no swelling, bruising, cuts, redness, signs of insect bites or stings, fever, bleeding, and so on).

- The child has a teacher who calls and says your child is falling behind or asks if anything is wrong.

- The child has mood swings, going back and forth between overexcitement and apparent sadness.

- The child loses interest in religious activities, or gains a sudden passion for them.

Parents should not be overly concerned if their child displays one or two of the above symptoms. However, if the child exhibits three or more symptoms, they should have the child evaluated by a professional.

Parents should be especially alert if depression runs in the child's biological family, or if one of the adoptive parents is being treated for depression. Most depressed children have mothers who suffer from the same illness. If parents are experiencing the symptoms of depression themselves, it is important they seek professional help—for their child's sake, if for no other reason. If they do not, their depression could contribute to the child's depression. The feelings of hopelessness and despair the parents experience do not mean that they are mentally ill and unfit to care for their children. Most people have feelings of depression at one time or another.

Therapists can make a major difference, so it is important to seek their help. If it turns out that there is a medical reason for the depression, such as a chemical imbalance, a physician who specializes in depression should treat it with medication. Medication and psychotherapy are usually very helpful in treating depression.

It may be hard to believe, but infants can show signs of depression. Their symptoms are not exactly the same, but they clearly show similar problems with mood. They may have decreased appetite with weight loss, sleep disturbance, fretfulness, withdrawal, crying, and apathy. Parents tend to describe these infants as having poor temperaments or as being difficult babies. Infants have even died due to depression during their very early years of life.

Depression in infants is usually related to the relationship with the caregiver. If an infant has lost a primary caregiver, the person with whom it has bonded, depression is a common response. Humans are capable of grieving only weeks after birth. In some cases, neglect or abuse can precipitate depression in infants and toddlers. Adopted babies are highly at risk for depressive symptoms. Parents need to be alert to the possibility and seek a professional opinion. As expected, many infants of foreign adoptions are highly at risk for depression also. As much as anything, they sense the numerous cultural differences such as language, habits, and interactions. New parents should be prepared for a very difficult flight home and a complicated adjustment period.

Preschoolers seem to act out more in response to their depressed feelings. Children aged three to five years old tend to cry a lot, be uncooperative, have tantrums, and have difficulty interacting with others, either withdrawing or being very aggressive. They can be very defensive and appear extremely selfish. Parents tend to describe these children as hard to deal with, stubborn, or challenging.

As with infants, preschoolers also become depressed after the loss of an attachment figure. Preschoolers are often the targets of abuse or neglect. In some cases, young parents may be overwhelmed with responsibilities and may unintentionally neglect the child. These small children are very aware of family problems such as fussing, fighting, or the effects of divorce. Some preschoolers become depressed when they must share attention with a new sibling.

Children in middle childhood tend to display depression by exhibiting low self-esteem, poor motivation, irritability, low frustration tolerance, extreme fears, withdrawal, aggression, and poor school performance. Physical complaints without organic causes are common. Parents may call them bad tempered, spoiled, lazy, angry, and whiney. Parents often disagree about how to deal with their child at this age. In some cases, parents become sidetracked by playing blame games when they should be addressing the real issues concerning the child's problems.

As a child grows up, it becomes increasingly difficult to explain the causes for depression. By eight to ten years of age, many adopted children have already suffered one trauma after another. They may have been in multiple placements, been abused or neglected, lost their caregivers over and over, and felt rejection and pain. They may have had poor nutrition, and experienced inconsistent rules and severe discipline. Some children available for adoption have extremely sad pasts and professionals actually marvel at how resilient they must have been in order to have survived all of it.

The depressed adolescent is even more difficult to deal with than depressed children at younger ages. The adolescent's behavior tends to escalate from restlessness and moodiness to sometimes running away, stealing, failing in school, sexual promiscuity, and all sorts of unacceptable behaviors. The depressed adolescent often withdraws and becomes isolated. Some turn to alcohol and drugs. Others develop eating disorders. Most refuse to interact with parents or other family members and make poor choices concerning friends. A depressed adolescent can be pushed into suicidal thoughts and gesturing with little provocation, including a breakup, conflict with peers, and feelings of failure. Not all depressed teenagers are suicidal, but depression increases the risk by about 25 percent.

Parents are often confused by a depressed adolescent. They have been warned that adolescence is a difficult time for their child, so they want to believe that the depressed symptoms are normal and the adolescent will eventually outgrow the problems. Sometimes parents will either give up or "wait for the kid to mature" or really bear down, giving parenting one last try by using some type of "tough love" concept. Unfortunately, neither approach is what a depressed adolescent needs.

If adoption occurs during adolescence, the adoptive parents should be well informed about the subtle signs and symptoms of depression and other emotional problems. Depending on the adolescent's adoptive journey, it may be inevitable that he or she will have to work through many complex emotional issues from the past. Professional assistance through the transition is highly recommended, even when no overt symptoms are noticed. It is likely that an adolescent having a depressive episode is not having a first bout with depression.

There are many factors that contribute to depression: heredity, family dysfunction, abuse, neglect, bonding and attachment issues, temperament, personality, traumatic events, stressors, brain functioning, and other physical disorders. These things, in different combinations, timeframes, duration, and intensity, are thought to contribute to the development of depression. A proper diagnosis will guide treatment for a child or adolescent of any age. For best results, treatment will involve all family members.

Reactive Attachment Disorder

Adopted children are a high-risk group for Reactive Attachment Disorder. These children have problems developing feelings of closeness or feeling in sync with another person. They have disturbances in their social behavior that begin before the age of five and are not due to a developmental delay. The child's difficulties are prevalent across all social situations, including interactions with parents. These children are described as either overly inhibited or overly disinhibited. Usually this condition is a response to parental or institutional abuse, neglect, or harsh treatment.

Children develop attachments based on bonding with another person who makes them feel protected and safe. Traumatized children can bond with abusers but they seldom feel attached to them. These "trauma bonds" can drive adopted children to respond negatively to loving adoptive parents and sometimes act out in very destructive ways. When children feel protected and understand that adoption is for life, they can then let their guard down and begin to confront their fears.

Symptoms associated with Reactive Attachment Disorder are rather scary to potential adoptive parents. Some children show symptoms of the disorder with a lack of eye contact, lack of affection, destructive behavior, cruelty to animals, stealing, abnormal eating patterns, preoccupation with fire, poor peer relationships, and abnormal speech patterns. Others have the same diagnosis, but they display the opposite behavior. They are outgoing and chatty, superficially engaging, and affectionate with strangers, and they make inappropriate demands and show a lack of impulse control. Children with reactive attachment disorder are consistently inconsistent!

If reactive attachment disorder is diagnosed, treatment can be slow and tedious. Therapy involves working with the child and parents to help the child process what was learned early in life about trust, protection, grief, and survival. The individual must re-experience conflicts from the past. Most therapists are typically not trained to provide treatment for these children. Parents should be very careful in selecting a qualified therapist.

DISRUPTIVE BEHAVIOR DISORDERS

There are several diagnoses that professionals use to describe similar behaviors. Children who have difficulty behaving at a generally acceptable level of mischievousness and noncompliance are often considered to have one of the disruptive behavior disorders. There are specific differences among the disorders, but generally they are used to describe children from early childhood through adolescence whose "naughtiness" exceeds any expected phase of growing up.

A description of several of these diagnoses is offered as a general discussion. It is not to be used to diagnose your child, but it may be helpful in understanding which of your child's behaviors exceed normal limits. The information may also assist you in knowing what specific behavior professionals will be asking you to describe.

Attention Deficit Hyperactive Disorder (ADHD)

Adopted children are not immune to any of the childhood disorders, so you can be certain that some adopted children will be identified by parents, school teachers, or a physician as having symptoms of ADHD. Often preschoolers are described as hyperactive by their parents. They describe them as being in constant motion, unable to sit still, except in front of the television.

Soon after entering kindergarten, the teacher agrees with the parents' opinion that a child is overactive. The teacher may add that the child doesn't finish work, is impulsive, can't seem to stay on task, and is disruptive to others in the classroom. However, sometimes by the time the child is in second grade, the father is convinced that the child is not trying, is a bit lazy, is not motivated, and is spoiled. The second-grade teacher may feel that the child is much smarter than the grades reflect, because the child makes numerous careless mistakes, doesn't finish homework, is easily distracted, and just won't pay attention. The mother insists on taking the child to the doctor to get medication for hyperactivity, but the father resists. Both are right in their own way. The child described needs to be evaluated for ADHD. A diagnosis based on a thorough evaluation is important prior to prescribing medication. Child psychologists are well trained to evaluate children with ADHD.

An ADHD evaluation is based on a comprehensive assessment of the child, including an analysis of information on prenatal history, birth and infant development, medical status, developmental history, strengths and weaknesses, temperament and learning style, peer relations, motor and coordination skills, comprehension, and school progress. Parents, teachers, other adults who interact with the child, the pediatrician, and the child him- or herself all need to provide information for the evaluation. It is imperative that the evaluation consider the child's inattentiveness, hyperactivity, and impulsivity across various situations and settings, and it is also imperative to be sure that the symptoms were present before the age of seven.

If a diagnosis of ADHD is made, it is recommended that a team approach be implemented to include the psychologist, parents, teacher, pediatrician, and child. The psychologist's responsibility is to be the team leader and help everyone gain a comprehensive understanding of ADHD and its effects. The school must be willing to provide accommodations as needed to assist the child's special challenges in the classroom. Parents must work closely with the school to develop and support an appropriate educational program for the child. They must also work with the psychologist to implement specific strategies for parenting and disciplining the ADHD child.

The child must know that it is a part of the team and has certain responsibilities in order to make progress. The child must understand that a diagnosis of ADHD helps explain his or her current situation, but is not an excuse for inappropriate behavior. The pediatrician must remain available for follow-up and to evaluate the need for medication as dictated by the team. Medication alone is seldom very effective, but it is helpful as part of the total team approach. Pills do not replace skills.

Oppositional Defiant Disorder

Another disruptive behavior disorder is Oppositional Defiant Disorder (ODD). Children who are diagnosed with Oppositional Defiant Disorder have parents from every walk of life. The diagnosis of this disorder has been argued for some time. It often overlaps or coexists with several other disorders and is often difficult to clearly differentiate. Children younger than thirty-six months will not be diagnosed with the disorder because the symptoms of ODD are still considered to be within the normal limits for that age range. ODD is considered after three years of age and when the child's negative pattern of behavior, persistent hostility, and defiance occur more frequently than expected for the age or developmental level.

Sometimes children at this age are in the midst of being taken into the welfare system, shuffled between foster homes, or adopted. These factors would be important considerations in making a diagnosis. Symptoms of ODD must persist for at least six months and not be accounted for by another childhood disorder such as depression or ADHD. Children who are diagnosed with ODD are usually described by their parents as angry, moody, argumentative, defiant to rules, resentful, and annoying. Such children often blame others for their own mistakes. When these behaviors occur one at a time and in isolation, they are considered normal, but when they are cumulative and chronic, they should cause concern.

Parents must be vigilant in pursuing professional assistance for these children. ODD is generally considered a precursor of more disturbing emotional problems. It can be easily ignored or excused when the child has been a product of dysfunction. It is important to seek assistance in learning how to effectively manage a child's chronic inappropriate behaviors. Parents who learn to calmly confront the behaviors and apply proper disciplinary strategies usually see positive results and may actually stop a downward spiral to more devastating behaviors.

Conduct Disorder

When a child's behavior escalates from being negative, defiant, and hostile at an early age to more major behavioral problems, including aggression, destruction, and serious violation of rules, parents are forced to confront the possibility of a conduct disorder diagnosis. Sometimes, while the parents are still trying to come to grips with the severity of the problem, the juvenile courts get involved because the child has been caught breaking the law. The parents, teachers, and school counselors often recall situations when the child has been cruel to animals, initiated fights, used weapons against others, set fires, deliberately destroyed the property of others, broken into someone's house, stolen property, or shoplifted.

Adoptive parents can feel betrayed, terribly hurt, and angry when their act of love and compassion for this child has been seemingly tossed aside. It appears particularly difficult for adoptive parents to reconcile their mixed emotions. Professional assistance can be helpful to both the parents and child in setting expectations and determining consequences. Of course, once a delinquent child has crossed the line and been caught breaking the law, the child must answer to the legal system.

Other Serious Behavior Disorders

Other serious adolescent disorders include the excessive use and abuse of drugs and alcohol, eating disorders, and suicidal urges. As parents, you should not overlook subtle signs such as slight changes in behavior, isolation, withdrawal from family activities, changes in sleep or eating patterns, weight change, and a decline in school performance. Parents should be in attendance at school functions, in close contact with school officials, and should know their child's friends and the friends' parents.

Parents should seek professional consultation at the first signs of abnormal changes. In general, parenting any child is challenging. For adoptive parents who may be dealing with their own grief and may let their empathy for their adopted child overshadow their wisdom, severe behavior problems can easily spin out of control before they realize it. We subscribe to ADHD expert Dr. Sam Goldstein's advice, "act, don't yak!" In other words, identify problems early, seek assistance, and develop a plan.

Early Warning Signs of Suicide

Suicidal children may exhibit the following behaviors:

- There are changes in eating and sleeping habits. The child may overeat or exhibit loss of appetite, may sleep too much or complain of not sleeping enough, or may decline to eat favorite foods.

- There are signs of a loss of energy (which may or may not be clearly related to sleep loss). For example, the child may claim to be "too tired" to go to the store.

- The child withdraws from family activities and time spent with friends. This is accompanied by an increase in time spent watching television or playing video games.

- The child uses drugs or alcohol.

- The child has an inexplicable drop-off of work habits at school (for example, an "A" student suddenly becomes a "D" student).

- The child has a series of physical complaints, such as headache, stomachache, and other things. Pay attention if the child "feels bad," but can't explain where it hurts.

- The child behaves aggressively to family members, friends, pets, or self.

- The child experiences a romance gone bad. Parents should not underestimate the emotional trauma their teenaged or pre-teenaged child can experience over unrequited "puppy love."

- The child makes mysterious comments, such as "what's the point?" or "I won't be a problem for you much longer."

WHEN ADOPTIVE PARENTS DIVORCE

It takes time for most of us to recover from a hurtful situation. It is when parents can't let go of the pain that damage is inevitable. We've seen many couples pretend that their arguments with each other are "for the children." It is not until the layers of hurt and anger can be peeled away that such individuals can see that they are merely hiding their hurt and anger behind their innocent children.

Children are often more resilient than adults. Depending on the age of the child, and the amount of parental support they receive, they can achieve a successful transition to a new family configuration. In most cases, children can forgive and then move on more quickly than their parents can. Just as parents move through certain stages after a divorce to achieve a healthy level of acceptance, so do children.

At each stage, the child must acknowledge the important facts of life. Once those facts are addressed, the child can move on to acceptance. Those stages are the following:

- *It's over.* The marriage has ended. Children must stop denying that their parents are just going through a phase or that things will get back to normal soon. To keep slight hope alive gives children unrealistic hope; once children understand "it's over," they can figuratively bury the fantasy.

- *You are powerless.* You didn't cause it and you can't fix it. Some children suffer extreme self-blame, feeling responsible for the family breakup. They may think, or actually say, "if only I had been a better student," or "if only I had behaved better," and so on. They may also feel that they have the power to reunite their parents.

- *You do not have to choose.* You can love both parents. It is important that children be allowed to remain close to both parents so they don't feel they have been divorced from either of them.

- *Believe that things will get better.* Children are full of hope and will believe in a better tomorrow with a little encouragement. Both parents should reassure their children that "things will get better," even if they themselves have not reached that level of acceptance.

We knew a twelve-year-old boy who devised an elaborate plan to "trick" his parents into getting back together after four long years of divorce-court battles. He believed he could conjure a scheme to reunite two people who no longer loved one another, even though both loved him. That child clearly is stuck in his path to readjustment. Although the parents continued to have conflicts, he offered ideas on how they could get back together, clinging to the unrealistic hope that they would work things out and reunite.

Not until a child has dealt with the facts can the permanence of the divorce finally be accepted. This is not a loss of hope evoked by depression, but rather a calm realization that the parents are no longer capable of having a happy life together. The child must learn to respect the parents' decision to dissolve the marriage and then turn to hopes for happiness in a different direction.

Children of divorce often have difficulty developing hope in future relationships. Some may progress through all the stages of acceptance of the parents' divorce, but then fail to ever advance to the point where they can believe that things will get better. Most children would benefit from psychotherapy when families break up. Professionals know how to assist a child through the crisis of a family breakup and can help the child confront the peripheral issues that often escape the attention of parents.

7 Single-Parent Adoptions

Once considered an oddity, single-parent adoptions are now commonplace among both men and women. In 1970, less than 1 percent of the adoptions in the United States involved single parents, but today that percentage varies from 8 to 33 percent, depending on the state (some states are friendlier than others).

Single-parent adoptions are legal in all fifty states, and single parents are seldom discriminated against by foreign governments that consent to adoptions in the United States. Even so, public and private adoption agencies still give a preference to couples, public agencies more so than private agencies. That is understandable since the mission of child welfare agencies is to take each child's long-term care into consideration. A child has better odds of surviving eighteen years of life with two parents than with one parent.

Single parents enter into the calculations when adoption agencies calculate the odds of survival for older children and children with special needs. When the decision is between temporary care in multiple foster homes versus permanent care with a single parent, the single parent offers better odds. As a result, almost all of the adoptions that take place with single parents are with older children and those with special needs who are in foster care. Single parents who adopt infants almost always obtain them from a foreign country.

WHAT KIND OF CHILD IS RIGHT FOR YOU?

Single-parent applicants are valued by adoption agencies because they are more likely to accept a child of color or one with special needs (defined as children with physical, emotional, or mental challenges, children with medical conditions, children with a history of abuse, or children who are members of a sibling group). The first thing you must decide before applying for adoption is what kind of child is right for you.

Can you accept a child of a different race? Or a child from a different culture who embraces a different set of religious beliefs? Just as important, can your family members support your decision? If you are not certain, it is crucial that you sit down with them, discuss your plans, and offer them an opportunity to provide feedback.

What if some family members are opposed to you introducing a different race or religion into the family, thereby transforming them into a multicultural extended family? Are you certain you want to cause a family rift among individuals who might have to support your child in the event of your death?

Adoption screeners will be happy to answer your questions, but you have a responsibility to do your own research before submitting an application. If you are considering a child of a different race or ethnic group, have you had any experience with people of that race or ethnic group? Do you have any friends who have adopted children of a different race? If not, do you know any multicultural families in your area that you can talk to about your plans?

The same sort of checklist should be followed if you are considering a child with special needs. Which "special needs" fit your comfort level and your personality? If a child has health problems, do you have the patience to deal with them—and will your employer be agreeable to you taking time off on a regular basis to tend to your child's medical needs? One way you can decide what kind of child is right for you is by looking back on your own childhood and early adulthood. Among your peers, what kind of people did you choose for your closest relationships? Consider the following questions:

- If you had friends with medical problems, were you supportive or did you resent the time they spent going to doctors?
- Did you have friends of different races and ethnic groups?
- Were you a leader or were you a follower? If you were a follower, were you led places you did not want to go? If you were a leader, did you ever resent the fact that some of your friends were dependent on you for leadership?

WHAT WILL AN ADOPTION SCREENER LOOK FOR?

The important thing to remember about the home study process is that the adoption screener is not there to be a stenographer, taking down your every thought on the subject of parenthood. He or she is there to do a *psycho-social* assessment of your life. In order to do that the screener must understand your past. You are the sum total of your past actions, not your current thoughts and opinions. It is your past that defines you.

Adoption screeners are always grateful when applicants spend time screening themselves before they come into the office. The screener will almost certainly ask you which method you used to decide what kind of child is best for you (refer to the above questions).

If you are white and want to adopt a black child, you will have a lot of explaining to do if you grew up in Alabama, attended private schools, and enrolled in a college that was only 10 percent black. The same thing would apply if you are black and want to adopt a white child, and grew up in Harlem, New York, attended all-black public schools, and a predominantly black university. The screener will be appropriately skeptical of your potential in either case.

The same line of thinking applies to the adoption of children with special needs. If you apply for a position as a bricklayer, shoe salesperson, or brain surgeon, the boss will want to know about your experience. The same thing applies to single applicants for special needs children. What is your experience? Think it through before you go into the office to apply. If you have no experience in a specific area, it would be to your advantage to delay your application until you obtain experience in the anticipated areas.

Adoption screeners will hold you to the same standard that they hold couples, but there are four areas where they will put special emphasis.

Past and Present Relationships

Be prepared to discuss your past and present romantic relationships. How long did each relationship last? How did each relationship end? Have you ever been arrested for harassing your significant other? What is the nature of your current relationship? Is it based on sex, love, companionship, or a combination of the three? Do you live together or separately? Do you ever plan to marry? The screener will want to meet your significant other to compare his assessment of your relationship with your own assessment. He or she will want to know what role the absence of children has played in the relationship.

The screener will want to know if your partner is enthusiastic about adoption or merely supportive of your efforts. He or she will want to know if you have ever received relationship counseling. The screener will want to know if you have ever separated as a couple and then reunited. If so, he or she will want to know why you separated.

Pet relationships may also be a subject of interest. If you have never had pets, the screener will want to know why. If you have a history of caring for dogs or cats, how did that work out for you? Did you ever "get rid" of pets because caring for them was too time consuming? Were you able to provide for your pets when you went out of town, or while you were at work? Did your need to take your pet to the vet ever cause friction at work? If so, how was that conflict resolved?

Finances

The most fundamental financial question is whether you earn enough money to care for a child without borrowing. Do you have money set aside for emergencies? Do you have health insurance and will you be able to add a child to your policy? Do you have life insurance? What are your plans to financially provide for the child in the event of your death? Do you have family members who will assume that responsibility? What are your spending habits? Are you in debt? Are your credit card balances at maximum limits? Have you ever filed for bankruptcy?

Health Issues

Couples with children have each other to fall back on in times of illness. Who do you have that you can fall back on? Do you have any serious illnesses such as cancer that will limit your longevity and put your child's long-term survival at risk? Do you have any diseases that might require you to be bedridden before the child is grown? Do you see an adopted child as someone who might provide care for you later in life?

Gender Awareness

Children must have male and female role models if they are to grow into healthy adults. What plans have you made to provide opposite-sex role models for your child? The screener will be extremely interested in your thoughts on this subject. Look at your application through the screener's eyes: He or she knows that single people can be every bit as good at being adoptive parents as married couples, and is on your side in that respect. But the screener also knows that successful single parenting requires a special effort, especially in areas such as gender awareness that come naturally to couples. The screener will want to be convinced that you have thought the matter through and devised a plan that will meet your child's needs.

THREE THINGS YOU ABSOLUTELY MUST DO

If you are considering applying for a child, or have already done so, you are dealing with a multitude of fears, doubts, and anxieties. That's entirely normal for a person who is committing two decades or more of life to the care and support of a child whom he or she may not have even met. People who commit to thirty-year home mortgages sometimes feel the same insecurities.

Once you get over the fear factor in adoption, and it generally goes away fairly quickly, you will have to face the practical reality of being responsible for another human's life. To get through that hurdle there are three things you absolutely must do.

Set Up a Support Network

The one thing you can count on is that things will go wrong. If you thought living alone was stressful, because of all the things that had to be fixed around the house or all the errands that had to be run, just wait until your beautiful child comes into your life. You can pretty much count on doubling the stress in your life.

It's true that there are now two of you in the home, but your new addition is not the type of roommate who can help you resolve problems. Now, instead of feeling overwhelmed on those days when you have a dental appointment, an important assignment at work, a driver's license renewal that must be done in person, and groceries to buy because the fridge is empty, you can add the babysitter who is sick with a cold and has to stay home in bed. What's a parent to do?

Even before your child arrives, it is important for you to set up a support network. You can take care of your problems—you always have, haven't you?—but your child is totally dependent on you to solve all problems on a daily basis. It is essential that you not only line up day care, but also a backup and a backup for the backup.

And that's only for starters. You also need a backup for emergencies. Who will keep your child if you have to be hospitalized overnight or for several days? Day care workers aren't in the habit of taking children home with them at the end of the day. You need someone you trust, preferably a family member who can step in and care for your child if you are incapacitated. This person must be someone you trust that you can empower to give life-saving medical consents should your child become ill. And what are your plans if you have to go out of town on business?

Setting up a support network is not the sort of thing you can do on a moment's notice. You should do it well in advance of your child's arrival.

Financial Planning

Children aren't cheap. You can figure a thousand dollars a month extra just to care for their basic needs—and that's if you are healthy and working. The purpose of financial planning is to prepare for when things go wrong.

Health insurance for you and your child is a must. Few things can send a family into bankruptcy faster than medical bills. Also, if your employer does not offer some kind of disability insurance that will give you sufficient income to provide for you and your child, you need to buy supplemental disability insurance.

Life insurance is another necessity. Depending on the age of your child, you have assumed responsibility for support for up to eighteen years. Heaven forbid that you drop dead the first year! But it happens and you need enough life insurance to support your child in your absence. Multiply the number of years until your child reaches eighteen by $30,000—and then add an additional $250,000 for college. If your child is five years of age—and you want the child to go to college—consider a life insurance policy in the range of $600,000 to $700,000.

As part of your financial planning you should have a will, though we prefer trusts for single parents since that will allow someone you trust to budget your assets, plus your insurance policy proceeds, until your child reaches the age of majority. If the trustee of your trust invests wisely—it could be the same person you choose to raise your child—the life insurance will not only take care of expenses, it will provide your child with a modest nest egg with which to begin life as an adult.

Locate Same-Sex Role Models for Your Child

If you are female and adopt a boy, it is important that you offer him strong male role models—and the same is true of males who adopt girls. Other than food and shelter, the most primary need that children have is for same-sex role models.

Making the right decisions in this area will do more to give your child a happy, productive life than anything else you can do. It will affect your child's health, academic performance, social development, and ability to maintain adult romantic relationships. The pool of available role models could include your family, your work associates, and your significant others.

WHAT SINGLE PARENTS SHOULD KNOW ABOUT RAISING BOYS

Children need attention, physical presence, affection, and guidance from both sexes. They need to feel protected and assured by the adults in their life that they are capable of taking control when necessary. A boy needs to be in the presence of a man who will be available to encourage him, take him places, talk to him, and guide him. The most qualified teacher for a boy is his male role model. Men can teach boys a value system, coping strategies, self-control, and self-reliance. Even when there is limited contact with a male, boys will find themselves becoming their male role models over time.

Mothers teach sons different skills. They teach them how to maintain relationships without exerting dominance. They teach them important social skills such as communication and self-expression. They teach them table manners. They teach them study habits. They teach them how to have sympathy for others, and they do that primarily by insisting that they display it when dealing with siblings, peers, and pets. Mothers are reservoirs of love and understanding that sons depend on for stability.

Most parents understand the need for children to have contact with both sexes, but many ignore that need. Children need both sexes to contribute equally, but differently, in their lives. Before a mother can know how to take the place of an absent father, she must first understand the role that males play in her child's life. Before a father can know how to take the place of an absent mother, he must understand the role that women play in his child's life. Most parents find the truth about gender responsibility surprising, which is why so many of them make the same mistakes over and over again.

Men teach male children things that often are not taught by women: self-control and empathy, math skills, and respect for women. If that latter trait—"respect for women"—comes as a surprise to you, you are not alone because the myth is that mothers teach sons to respect women. In truth, boys learn to respect women from other males.

Males who grow up in families with strong male role models do not have the same need to dominate women and create exclusionary, all-male activities, as do males who grow up in families with absent or uninvolved fathers. Statistically, the first group also leads happier lives. When happy and successful adult men are asked by researchers why they are happy and successful, they usually attribute it to happy and successful male role models. They seldom are able to explain the connection. It is just something that they seem to feel in their hearts.

It has long been understood that fathers teach their sons math and sports skills, but only recently have researchers learned that men are instrumental in teaching their sons self-control and empathy, two critical skills associated with success and happiness.

A twenty-six-year study that focused on the relationship between parenting and empathy levels in adults found that the most important correlation between parenting and empathy was a male's involvement in child care. That finding astonished mental health professionals, for in the absence of any existing research, they had assumed that empathy was a product of good mothering. To some people, empathy may sound like one of those throwaway concepts that have no bearing on the real world, but nothing could be further from the truth: empathy is what enables people to be law-abiding and compassionate citizens.

Women tend to think of self-control as something that they impose on their sons through discipline. Men tend to think of self-control as something that they can teach their sons; discipline is what they impose when boys do not learn self-control.

Males teach boys how to relate to both men and women. Mostly they do it by example, which is a good thing since little boys learn how to behave by watching other males, not by thinking about what is logical, proper, or acceptable. Mothers have difficulty teaching little boys how to behave around other males because they cannot do it by example without going to absurd lengths; they can only try to explain the concept to their sons with words, a communication that is doomed from the start. That approach works fine with daughters, who are more accustomed to talking things over with their mothers, but it doesn't work with sons—and mothers sometimes have a hard time understanding why. Just remember: fathers show; mothers tell.

You would think that sons raised by women would be more understanding of women's needs once they became adults, but it seldom works out that way. Statistically, a man who was raised by a woman is more likely to be abusive toward his spouse than a man who was raised by both sexes. There are exceptions, of course, but that is generally the case—and our experience supports that conclusion.

There are several reasons why mother-raised sons tend to be more abusive to spouses. They often blame their mothers for the fact that they grew up without fathers, even when blame is not justified. Adopted sons of single mothers sometimes feel anger toward their mothers for not getting married and providing them with a father. Later in life, that resentment often carries over to the spouse. Another reason for spousal abuse among men who did not have male role models as children is that they may never have learned how to argue with women. If a son never saw a male exert self-control when arguing with his mother, how could he possibly be expected to show self-control when arguing with his spouse?

Fatherless Boys Are at Greater Risk for Certain Ailments

Compared to children living with a father, fatherless children experience more accidental injuries, asthma, frequent headaches, and speech defects. Overall health also is affected by the absence of a father in the home. In a 1995 survey of children under seventeen, the U.S. Department of Health and Human Services found that 55 percent of the children found to be in good health lived with both biological parents, while only 42 percent lived with single mothers.

There is both a genetic and a cultural basis for how individuals react to pain. Boys and girls have different reactions. The genetic difference is based on estrogen, a chemical that increases the availability of pain-numbing endorphins in females and allows them to be more tolerant of the pain associated with illness than males. The cultural factor is the way in which males are taught from early childhood that "big boys don't cry" when they feel pain.

Even though they feel pain more acutely than their mothers and sisters, little boys are taught to "tough it out" by not complaining about their discomfort. In fatherless homes, mothers evaluate injuries to their sons in terms of their own pain threshold to similar injuries, which means that they tend to underestimate their sons' discomfort. Without meaning to do so, parents sometimes teach their sons to ignore the early symptoms of disease, for fear of being called "sissies," thus increasing the likelihood that their illnesses will require more extensive treatment.

Boys without male role models are at risk for depression—even without the presence of a family history of depression—but if that history is present, particularly in the mother, the odds of depression developing as a result of parental separation increase dramatically. Depression in boys is correlated with depression in mothers more so than with depression in fathers.

Information like this is helpful to both mothers and physicians. All too often, boys are blamed for having too many accidents that require first-aid attention. They are admonished to "be more careful" or they are told outright that they are "stupid" for having so many cuts and scrapes.

Mothers sometimes get angry with boys who display symptoms of depression because they think the children are hiding something from them, or because they interpret the child's behavior as a rejection of them as a parent. In those situations, parental anger only fuels the depression.

Imagine that you are a ten-year-old adopted boy being raised by a single mother. You feel sadness over not having a father, emotions that you cannot articulate to yourself, much less to another person. You feel powerless at a new school where you feel like an unwanted outsider. Yet your mother, who is twice your size, stands over you, angrily chastising you because of your sadness and threatening you with a loss of the very privileges that make you feel better unless you "straighten up" and show a better attitude. From that perspective, you can understand how a boy would perceive his mother's well-meant admonitions as veiled threats to deprive him of her love and attention. It is the type of parenting that could drive the child further into depression.

We aren't suggesting that single mothers lose sleep over fears that they are ruining their sons' health—most boys bypass or overcome the mental and physical ailments associated with not having a male role model in the home. But we think that an awareness of worst-case scenarios is helpful in reminding mothers that there is a cause-effect pattern at work in their parenting decisions. Usually, that awareness is enough to keep mothers alert to potential problems.

The most important thing a mother can do is to pay attention to her son's ailments. Is there a pattern? Is he spending too much time alone in his room? Does he become ill after conflicts at school or with his friends? You should look for patterns to his asthma attacks, headaches, speech problems, and injuries—and then stay on top of them. Sending your son to a physician is not enough. A physician can prescribe medications for most of the ailments we have mentioned, but unless he or she is aware of a behavioral pattern to your son's ailments, the physician is at a disadvantage. One of the worst mistakes that a mother can make is to assume that someone else, some good soul further down the road, will intervene to provide her son with a happy and successful life. If only real life were like that: in most cases, it is now or never.

The Little Man of the House

In a single-mother household, all the family responsibilities and decisions are thrust on one parent. Having to manage every aspect of family life alone is made worse when there is no contact with a partner.

Single mothers sometimes find themselves overwhelmed by financial pressures, maintaining the home, cooking, and cleaning, not to mention all the behavioral issues associated with the kids. In the midst of trying to carry the load of two parents, feeling isolated and uninterested in sharing with others, single mothers often turn to their children. Evidence indicates that children of single parents mature more quickly, are exposed to more adult situations, and participate more in family decisions.

In stressful times, single mothers tend to draw the family inward, sharing their pain and family responsibilities more. They may explain to the child that everyone has to help out more in a single-parent household. Depending on the level of dysfunction, the mother may turn to the child to assume the "other parent" role. In those situations, not only does the child help make family decisions, he often becomes the mother's closest companion.

On those occasions when the single mom initiates her son as the "other parent," that relationship is usually very different from a mother-daughter parenting pair. The son is vulnerable in a family where there is no father figure. He feels the tension of his mother's depression and her neediness. Sensing that his mother is emotionally fragile, he takes on a companionship role because he feels responsible for her. He may assume more and more household responsibilities. He may offer advice to his mother and check on her frequently. The son begins not only to take on extra duties to relieve his mother's load, but he may actually start guiding her through her life changes.

In these situations, the mother usually is too dysfunctional to comprehend how damaging this arrangement is for her son. Instead of caring for and protecting the son, she allows a role reversal so that it is she who is being cared for and protected. Over time, the mother's dependency can grow into a very problematic situation.

A mother who is dependent on her son can become very comfortable going to the movies with him, playing tennis with him, and attending community activities with him. He is encouraged to be strong, reliable, and responsible for the other family members. He feels needed and enjoys the power of his role, while feeling powerless in the overall world. His self-image is superficially enhanced by this leadership role. At times, he is expected to actually take control and tell his mother what to do. He is involved in the financial decisions and seems to have equal say in family decisions.

A boy who finds himself in that position typically builds up feelings of anger and resentment. Although he feels powerful in his new role, there is a part of him that feels hurt that he has been called upon to sacrifice his youth. At some point, he begins to realize that he is actually a replacement for an adult male. He slowly starts to understand that he is really his mother's second choice, and that causes anger toward her.

After serving as a pseudoparent—and sharing many of the important family decisions—sons do not return to the child role easily. Sometimes, when the mother starts dating and sharing decision-making tasks with an adult male, the son becomes very confused. After being forced to mature too quickly, he becomes alienated from his peers. If a mother sends him back to child status again, it often is more than he can handle.

We advise single mothers to resist the temptation to allow their sons to become surrogate husbands. There is basically no way that situation can have a happy ending for either the mother or the son. The best thing that a mother can do for her son is to be alert to the type and amount of family responsibility she allows him to assume. Encourage him to help out around the house, but draw the line at sharing family financial information or sharing personal fears that will make it necessary for him to be the comforter.

Lastly, single mothers should remember that being the "Little Man" of the house initially has a positive ring to a son who is flattered by being referred to as a man, but it eventually loses its appeal when the son realizes that the operative word in that phrase is "little." He will awaken one morning with the realization that he is being taken advantage of by the only parent in his life.

The same process occurs with male single parents raising daughters who sometimes find themselves backed into being the "little mothers" of the households. In those situations, daughters imitate the female roles they see when visiting friends who have opposite-sex parents. They pick up after their dad. They learn to cook. They ask him about his day at work. They laugh at grownup jokes they don't understand and hug dad every time he says something "cute." As with mothers and sons, it is a parenting relationship that usually leads to hurt feelings.

Games Play a Role in Discipline

Boys learn cause and effect from males. They learn that when they play games and break the rules, they are usually penalized, and that means they are at greater risk to *lose*. Little boys like to win. Moms sometimes have a difficult time disciplining boys because they are not the same people who have taught their sons about winning and losing.

Athletics are important for boys, not so much for the physical exercise (though with children today becoming increasingly obese, the importance of exercise has increased), or because of the teamwork or competition it engenders, but because of the gamesmanship involved. Nonathletic games, such as card or board games, or even computer games, accomplish the same function as sports.

What may appear frivolous to the mother is one of the most important building blocks in her son's development. When we describe a child as a "problem child," one who will not obey adults, what we are really saying is that he does not exhibit good self-control. No child wants to be punished for misbehavior. There is nothing about punishment that a child enjoys. He indulges in forbidden behavior because he does not have the self-control necessary to put on the brakes. Boys who are good at playing games with other people are usually good at accepting discipline.

Men and women sometimes have opposing approaches to discipline. Mothers soon learn that the best way to avoid the need for discipline is to allow their sons to watch television for hours at a time. The biggest problem with that, aside from subjecting them to programming of dubious value, is the fact that children who spend all their time watching television do not learn the play skills they need.

It never ceases to amaze us when we hear mothers complain that their sons, who have just spent four hours watching television, are suddenly difficult to discipline once they tire of that activity. Watching television is not a substitute for play activity; it teaches children nothing about self-control or negotiating with their playmates for what they want. If watching television is a good activity, why do parents invariably end up sending their children to their rooms for punishment for some misdeed once the television programming has ended?

Single mothers sometimes use television as a defense against discipline. When that doesn't work, they threaten to take away privileges. They spank as a last resort, primarily because it upsets them to strike their children. Single fathers are just the opposite. They urge the child to "go outside and play," instead of watching television. Admittedly, there may be selfish motivation involved, especially if there is a sports event that dad wants to watch on television, but they are more inclined to send children on "missions" of one kind or another, even if it is just to go outside and play.

Men seldom threaten to punish; they usually do it on the spot. That is what boys expect because that is what they have been taught while playing games. It's not three strikes, you're out *later*. It's three strikes, you're out *now*. Male parents spank their sons as a means of demonstrating physical dominance, something that becomes increasingly important as boys head into adolescence.

We refer to spanking here only to explain what happens in typical families. We don't recommend striking children at any age for any reason. Whatever advantages we are tempted to see in mothers and fathers paddling children for bad behavior are erased by our experience with parents who physically abuse their children. We've seen infants placed into foster homes because mothers spanked them, and we've seen children hospitalized because their fathers beat them so severely that they required medical care.

The reason so many parents spank their children is because it is often an effective short-term remedy to bad behavior. The problem is that, even when done lightly, the parent is also teaching lessons while administering punishment. They are teaching that violence is all right in some situations. They are teaching that one acceptable result of anger is violence. And they are associating violence with authority.

We will never forget the two boys, aged six and seven, who were given a sound spanking by their parents and abandoned on a city street corner. When we arrived at the police station, the boys were sitting on a wooden bench in the waiting area. There was a small wire cage on the bench between them. In the cage was a white mourning dove.

The sight of the brothers, paralyzed by fright and wide-eyed with uncertainty, while desperately clinging to their only possession, a solitary mourning dove, was heartbreaking, not just because of what had happened to them, but because of what we knew lay ahead for them. We placed them in a loving foster home, where the foster mother instinctively won them over by making a big fuss over their feathered traveling companion.

Within days, their parents were tracked down by the police and arrested. When they were interviewed, they said they had abandoned their two sons because they "did not mind." The father, who seemed surprised that abandoning children was against the law, explained that the more they spanked the boys, the worse their behavior became. "Finally, it just got to the point where they were bringing us down," he explained. "It was either them or us—you know, parents are people, too."

If you are spanking your child, you should stop, take a deep breath, and look for the source of the problem. If your child is misbehaving—and the disciplinary actions you administer are growing in frequency—increase the child's playtime with a same-sex role model. Children aren't born bad. They become what you allow them to become.

Recognize spankings for what they are: a failure of parenting. Also, consider that if your spankings are successful, they are successful only for specific behavior. What you are saying with a spanking is, "don't do that again or I'll hit you again!" The child associates the spanking only with the behavior in question. For that reason, spankings fail to teach children self-control. How can spanking teach self-control, especially if parents spank when they are angry? Self-control in children occurs when parents are successful in instilling a playtime mentality in them—break the rules and you lose! It is a lesson that applies to both parent and child. Try calmly saying, "I'm sorry you chose to misbehave. The consequence of your behavior is _____."

Empathy is the Key to Your Son's Success

Empathy is the most important survival skill a boy can possess. Some people consider empathy to be a "sissy" characteristic, one that makes boys too softhearted. Nothing could be further from the truth. Empathy is a survival skill that allows boys not only to care about what others are feeling, but to make accurate judgments in a wide range of social situations. Without empathy, boys would be unable to determine if people are uneasy, despondent, horrified, bored, cautious, playful, irritated, relieved, shy, hostile, dangerous, annoyed, or preoccupied. A boy without empathy is a disaster waiting to happen. Of all the skills that males teach boys, it is empathy that is the most important.

When three-time world heavyweight boxing champion Muhammad Ali (his birth name was Cassius Marcellus Clay Jr.) was born in 1942 in Louisville, Kentucky, America was still a good two decades away from accepting the fact that African Americans had the same rights as

Caucasian citizens. Racial segregation infected every segment of society, including the family unit, which was structured by white society in such a way as to minimize the contributions of male African Americans.

In the 1940s and 1950s, when Ali was coming of age, African American families were expected to be matriarchal, with fathers relegated to a secondary status. Not surprisingly, fathers tended to move from family to family, conceiving new children as they went, thus giving African Americans the largest percentage of fatherless children among the various racial and ethnic groups.

Ali's family was different. His mother, Odessa Clay, was the undisputed boss of the family insofar as the children were concerned, but his father, Cassius Clay Sr., took his parental responsibilities seriously and never abandoned his family. As a result, Ali beat the odds and grew up with his father in the home.

Cassius Sr. was not a perfect father by any means—he had an arrest record for disorderly conduct and reckless driving, and his wife had to call police for protection on three different occasions—but he did spend time with his children. "I made sure they were around good people; not people who would bring them into trouble," he told biographer Thomas Hauser in his book, *Muhammad Ali: His Life and Times*. "And I taught them values—always confront the things you fear, try to be the best at whatever you do. That's what my daddy taught me, and those are things that have to be taught. You don't learn those things by accident."

A sign painter by trade, Cassius Sr. sometimes took Ali with him when he went out on a job. He taught him how to draw letters and mix the paint, and he taught him how to interact with other men. As a result, from the age of twelve, Ali felt comfortable seeking out males who could teach him other things, such as boxing.

Ali's first male mentor was a white highway patrolman named Joe Martin, who had a television show called "Tomorrow's Champions." He arranged for Ali to work out at a local gym, where a black trainer named Fred Stoner taught him the mechanics of boxing. There is more to boxing than throwing and ducking punches. Stoner taught Ali how to read the faces of his opponents. It takes a great deal of empathy to be a championship boxer, for to be successful you must be able to determine your opponent's intentions and then counteract them with lightning speed.

As a result of all that positive male attention and instruction, Ali was able to grow into what many would consider a "man's man," all the while developing an uncommonly strong set of ethical and religious beliefs. Ali attributed those beliefs to his mother. "Every Sunday, she dressed me up, took me and my brother to church, and taught us the way she thought was right," Ali told Hauser. "She taught us to love people and treat everybody with kindness. She taught us it was wrong to be prejudiced or hate ... there's no one who's been better to me my whole life."

Ali displayed empathy toward others throughout his career, beginning with his refusal in 1966 to be drafted to fight in Vietnam (at the time, newspapers were filled with reports of violence against women and children at the hands of U.S. troops), by his involvement in the emerging civil rights movement (among African Americans, only Martin Luther King Jr. had a higher profile), and by his efforts to promote world peace. In 2000, the United Nations named Ali a Messenger of Peace, with a citation that read, "Through your contributions to sports and human rights, the message of peace, harmony and human dignity will resound throughout the nations."

As a child, Ali had everything in the world going against him: he was the wrong color for success in America; his family barely had enough money to get by; and he performed poorly in school. What he had going for him was a kind and compassionate mother, a father who never abandoned him despite several close calls, and male mentors who believed in him and taught him survival skills.

Ali is the best example we know of how empathy works as a survival skill.

Empathy as a Window on the World

Mom feels that she is being a bad mother if she ever frowns at her child, or shows displeasure. She wants her child to know only a friendly universe. Dad feels that he is being a bad father if he does not make it clear from the beginning that the world has quite a bite to it if certain rules are not followed.

Whether those attitudes are biological or cultural is really beside the point. Parents must raise children to live in the real world, not some vision of how the world should be. So as long as our culture supports and advocates gender differences in parenting, responsible parents have no choice but to address those differences.

Theological definitions aside, what we call morality is the ability to make decisions based on a judgment of whether our actions will help or hurt other people. Often our only clue is based on reading body language and facial expressions. If a boy does not have that ability, he will have a difficult time judging the appropriateness of his actions. One definition of a psychopath is someone who is without empathy for others. The masked gunman who robs a convenience store, puts his pistol in the face of the clerk, and then pulls the trigger, has no concept of what his victim is feeling. His emotions are focused entirely on himself.

A mother can possess a great deal of empathy. She can be the most loving, compassionate person in the world. But nature has wired her son so that she cannot transfer significant amounts of that empathy to him.

Again, there are exceptions: we can cite examples of empathetic mothers who have raised empathetic sons without a man's involvement, but they are in the minority.

Nature has decided that empathy is the responsibility of the male. If there is no male role model in the child's life to live up to that responsibility, the child suffers the consequences. He becomes aggressive, impulsive, and prone to risky behavior. In a report on violence, the National Research Council named several factors that their researchers found that correlated with aggressive behavior in children: "harsh and erratic discipline, lack of parental nurturance, physical abuse and neglect, poor supervision, and early separation of children from parents." It is that latter factor that we feel is the most important, for it directly affects other factors such as discipline and nurturance.

How Much Empathy Does Your Son Have?

Your son's empathy level should progress at a steady rate from early childhood, through school age, and into adolescence. Not sure where your son stands? Try this unscientific test to measure his development:

Preschool age: Clip photos from a magazine that you think demonstrate happiness, anger, and sadness—or make them yourself—then ask your son to tell you what the people in the photos are feeling. He should recognize all three expressions. If he does not, you have work to do. If he is unable to recognize anger, why then are you punishing him for not recognizing anger in your face?

School age: Clip four photos that show more complicated emotions such as annoyance, friendliness (this emotion will differ from happiness in that eye contact is a requirement for friendliness), and surprise. If he can correctly identify all three, you are on track; if not, spend time on the areas in which he is deficient. For example, if he misses "annoyance," explain to him that it is a level below anger.

Adolescence: This time, ask your son a series of questions. For example, ask him if he can tell the difference between when you are angry at him or simply frustrated over events that do not even involve him. Use specific examples of past situations to get him started. He should be able to describe the differences between those two emotions.

Another question to ask him is if he knows the difference between when you are preoccupied or when you are expressing disapproval of his actions. He should be able to discern that you are preoccupied if you say, "Can we talk about this later?" or if you respond to his questions with, "Uh-huh, uh-huh." If you are expressing disapproval, he should be able to recognize that by your critical comments.

If you go through a series of questions like this, you may discover that your conversation will open the door to better overall communication. You want to encourage your son to ask questions if he thinks he is misreading your feelings. In the process, you may learn that you have been misreading his feelings.

If you can't tell how much empathy your son possesses by observing him and talking to him, we have a pleasurable test that you can administer to him: give him a dog or a cat (if you don't want a pet in the household, take him to the house of a friend who has a pet). Simply hand the animal to him and watch his reaction. Does he hold it lovingly, or does he hold it too tightly?

If he holds it too tightly, and it protests with a cry for help, does he immediately release it and comfort it, or does he maintain his tight grip?

Boys of normal development are naturally very nurturing toward pets. They hold them like babies, cuddle them, talk "baby talk" to them, and proudly show them off to anyone who will pay attention. Boys who are lacking in empathy are less likely to hold pets and more likely to chase them, kick them, or throw things at them. They are also more likely to ridicule them and call them names such as "stupid" and "ugly."

Playtime: Dad's the "Main Man"

For infants, dad is the person who makes lots of noise coming into the room, the person who is always smiling and making eye contact because he has been away from his child all day. Sometimes he leans over and sticks his giant finger into the infant's tiny fist and stimulates the grasping reflex. Other times he lifts the infant into the air and swings him or her to and fro, taking the child's breath away. Dad is always fun.

By contrast, mom always seems to come quietly into the room, so as not to wake her sleeping child. She speaks in a soothing manner and tells baby how handsome he is. She makes eye contact when her purpose is non-nurturing in nature, but most of her time is spent feeding, bathing, and changing baby, tasks that usually require her to gaze someplace other than the infant's eyes.

For children of preschool age and older, dad is the parent who tosses balls with them, roughhouses with them, gets down on his hands and knees and pretends to be a horse, and the one who gleefully announces, "Everyone get ready—we're going for a ride in the car!" For boys, the play activities they experience with dad are crucial for their long-term emotional and social development.

For adolescent boys, playtime with dad takes on more of a competitive edge. The skills he learned from dad as a youngster are used during adolescence as weapons with which to be competitive with dad and his peers. Moms see competition as an event in which someone is hurt by being the loser; dads see competition as a means of solving problems while negotiating for dominance. Because moms don't want to see their sons get their feelings hurt, they try to protect them; dads understand that their sons' feelings will be hurt from time to time through competition, but they feel that the experience will prepare for a world in which winning is more important than avoiding hurt feelings.

In father-intact families, dads usually win the argument over whether a son should be exposed to hurt or failure. The father is not insensitive to his son's feelings; rather, he wants him to learn to live with pain instead of avoiding it.

Interestingly, dad's attitude toward his daughter will be exactly the opposite; he will fight to protect her from hurt or disappointment, while the mom takes a similar position to the one that he took with their son. Typically, mom and dad will see no inconsistency in their opposing positions.

Of course, not all fathers are good playtime teachers. If they grew up as sons without fathers—and had difficulty learning how to play because they didn't have a father in the home—they will find it difficult to give their sons proper instruction. Even if they did grow up with a father in the home, they may have had fathers who were overly critical of their efforts or prone to verbal abuse.

When fathers teach sons to play, hopefully it is to play fairly and to let their actions, not their tempers, speak for them. The nightly news offers frequent reminders of what happens when fathers teach their sons the wrong lessons. We have all seen video footage of fathers charging out onto the playing field, screaming obscenities, or even worse, fighting other adults over calls made by sports officials.

For better or worse, dads program their sons to be good players or bad players.

Men Usually Have Poor Self-Images as Parents

Sometimes it is difficult for fathers to appreciate the impact they have on their children because the cause-and-effect process of their actions is not as obvious as it is with mothers. It is helpful to remember that all fathers had mothers, and the natural tendency is for them to exalt the influence their mothers had on them, thereby exalting, by association, the influence their own children's mothers have on them.

Most men have poor self-images as fathers. Yes, it's true: they might "know it all" when it comes to home repairs or the car, but they feel downright stupid when it comes to their children. Dads just don't get it. They consider their major responsibilities to center around providing for the family and protecting it from harmful outside influences. Women who proclaim anything associated with child rearing to be exclusively their domain have helped perpetuate this myth.

Be Careful What You Say Around Infants

We have seen parents carry on serious, life-altering conversations in the presence of their children in the mistaken belief that they are focused on their toys. Parents should not assume that a child is not listening just because the child is playing and not making eye contact with them. On the contrary, parents should always assume that their children hear and understand everything they say in their presence.

Whether parents realize it or not, their children are learning serious lessons from them, even when that seems impossible. Within hours of birth, infants can respond to and in some cases imitate both parents' facial expressions. Sons pay particular attention to dad, not so much watching him, as absorbing his every facial response.

Sons learn how to deal with other people by watching their father. How does he treat the son's mother? How does he treat his own mother? How does he react to other males? How does he treat people whom he works with? Does he treat family members differently than he treats strangers? Those are the life lessons that fathers teach their sons, from infancy on, whether they realize it or not.

Faced with the loss of his father at an early age, Nobel Prize–winning French philosopher Jean-Paul Sartre pondered his uncertain fate:

> Whom would I obey? I am shown a young giantess, I am told she's my mother. I myself would take her rather for an elder sister. That virgin who is under surveillance, who is obedient to everyone, I can see very well that she's there to serve me. I love her, but how can

I respect her if no one else does? There are three bedrooms in our home: my grandfather's, my grandmother's, and the 'children's' .... A young girl's bed has been put into my room. The girl sleeps alone and awakens chastely. I am still sleeping when she hurries to the bathroom to take her 'tub.' She comes back all dressed. How could I have been born of her?

Sartre's insights, expressed in his autobiography *The Words*, [*] are those of a grown man, a literary giant who has come to terms with his childhood; but they are pertinent for all sons. When Sartre's father died, it was necessary for his mother to move into the house with her parents, where she was still treated as a child. Sartre saw what was happening, absorbing every nuance, as children are apt to do, but its significance was beyond his understanding at the time.

How could Sartre respect his mother when no one else did? How could he love her if she didn't love herself? How could he trust her if she seemed unsure of her own abilities? At the time, no one would ever have dreamed that a child of that age would have such thoughts. True, Sartre's intellect, even as a young child, was superior to that of other children his age, but the thought process he went through is comparable for all children.

When the father is in the home, the son witnesses him treating his mother with respect or disrespect, and he adopts similar attitudes toward his mother and women in general. If the father is not in the home, he observes how his mother is treated by her family and by strangers. If they don't respect her, then it is unlikely that he will either. Why would he? Remember, boys learn by example, not explanation. It would be nice if mothers were provided with guaranteed respect by their children, but boys aren't wired that way.

WHAT SINGLE PARENTS SHOULD KNOW ABOUT RAISING GIRLS

For the first year of life, daughters are more responsive to women than men. That is because during the first few months it is usually the mother who feeds her, talks to her the most, and holds her. At birth, daughters will recognize and prefer the sound of their female caregiver's voice to all others; but toward the end of the first year, daughters show a preference to being held by their primary male caregiver. That is because males hold them with more authority and tend to toss them around more aggressively during play, creating breath-taking sensations that are not soon forgotten by the daughter.

---

[*] Sartre, Jean-Paul. *The Words*. New York: Vintage, 1981.

When women speak of a man "taking my breath away," it is a throwback to infancy when males quite literally took her breath away while playing with her. It is especially important that males play with female children by the age of eighteen months because that is when children begin to figure out whether they are girls or boys.

A woman's ability to sustain a romantic or sexual relationship with a man depends on her relationship with the male role model in her life. Girls who have close relationships with their male role models grow up to have close relationships with the other men in their lives.

Girls who have bad relationships with their male role models invariably find it difficult as adults to sustain relationships with men. They are more likely to be divorced and have multiple marriages, and they are more likely to have difficulties with male employers. Girls who grow up without a male role model in the home are more likely to be promiscuous as teens and young adults. The adult entertainment industry is composed almost entirely of women who had absent or abusive fathers.

Reading and Arithmetic

When fathers spend time with their daughters on math problems, the daughters typically do well in math. When they do not spend time with their daughters, the daughters typically do poorly at math. It is possible for girls to do well in reading without a male's involvement, but when males are active participants, girls improve their reading skills and upgrade their verbal ability

Self-Image

Daughters cannot see themselves through their fathers' eyes, so they make judgments about themselves based on what they think their fathers think about them. When fathers do not spend time with their daughters, or when they are overly critical of the way they look, daughters grow up feeling inadequate. They look in the mirror and they hate what they see. They feel unlovable. It is not enough for a father to *know* that he loves his daughter; he must demonstrate that love to her on a regular basis by hugging her, paying attention to her opinions, and spending time with her.

Independence

Fathers teach daughters self-reliance. Women who are independent typically have male role models who spent time teaching them the practical aspects of life. Mardi Allen, one of this book's co-authors, recalls that her father taught her to always listen carefully to her car when she cranked it and drove away because it would tell her things she needed to know about its condition. That is the kind of practical advice that fathers can give daughters that will help them in the real world.

We recommend that single fathers teach daughters how to check the oil in the car, how to hang pictures, how to saw a piece of wood, how to use a hammer, how to play basketball and baseball, and how to make minor repairs around the house. That type of knowledge not only will make her more self-reliant as an adult, but it will carry over into other aspects of her life, such as employment.

Assertiveness

Parents who are overly protective of their daughters do a disservice to them. They should encourage them to be competitive and to be assertive in reaching their goals. Assertiveness and competitiveness are branches of the same limb. For whatever reason, parents often are hesitant to encourage their daughters to be competitive. Fathers are more likely to teach competitiveness to their sons than they are to their daughters, but when they teach the same skills to their daughters, it is usually with spectacular results. A competitive woman is an assertive woman, and that is always a plus, especially in the workplace.

The ages from eighteen months to five or six years are ones that parents both enjoy and fear the most. Daughters in this age group are prone to say and do cute things just about every day. The cuteness seems unending. The problem with cuteness that stems from assertiveness is that it is unpredictable.

Fathers are self-conscious with their pre-school age daughters when they are alone with them. They worry that the girls will ask questions that they cannot answer. They worry about public opinion because, in today's climate, they don't want strangers to think that they are attracted to children. They worry that they won't appear masculine in front of their male friends. They panic if their daughter says she has to go to the bathroom. They are likely to have a heart attack if she screams out from the other side of the bathroom door, "Daddy, would you bring me my dolly!" Mostly, fathers fear situations that might be misinterpreted by others.

Female-Female Relationships.

Just as fathers determine the nature of the relationships their daughters have with men, mothers determine the nature of the relationships that their daughters have with other women. Mothers who are warm and supportive produce daughters who are capable of forming strong friendships with other females. Mothers who are distant and cold produce daughters who avoid close friendships with other women. Women who have lots of same-sex friends usually have nurturing mothers. Women who have few or no close relationships with other females typically had mothers who offered limited nurturing.

For those reasons, it is important that single female parents with daughters make time for additional nurturing during their one-on-one time. If you are a working mother, you do not want to spend all your time at home barking orders about homework and household chores. You need to get down at eye level with your daughter and create situations in which you can praise her efforts and shower her with hugs.

The same rules apply to single male parents with daughters. You cannot possibly supply your daughter with the female nurturing that she craves, so it is imperative that you find her a female role model with a nurturing personality. If you aren't certain if the person you have selected has a nurturing personality, just ask her if she is close to her mother. If she is not, you might want to move on to number two on your list. You want a female role model who is close to her mother and her grandmother.

If you are thinking, "tTat's cold—I know a wonderful woman who had a dreadful childhood and she has lots of love to give," you are not being realistic. You cannot help a poorly nurtured woman by giving her someone to love. What she needs to feel better about herself is to be loved and that is not your daughter's role. If you want to save a lost soul, gamble with your emotions, not your daughter's.

Play, Play, Play

Parents can never play too much with their daughters. Not only does it teach them self-control and assertiveness, but it gives them self-confidence. For adults, play is a diversion from the realities of life. For children, play is the reality of life, the method by which they learn important survival lessons.

Since play is so important in child development, parents must learn what type of play is appropriate, and with whom. Play that is appropriate for a daughter—tickling her, for example, or squirting her with a water hose on a hot day, or tossing her around—would not be appropriate for the daughter's same-age friends.

Hug, Hug, Hug

Parents should not be afraid to display affection toward their daughters. They should hug them at every opportunity and tell them how proud they are of them. Whenever possible, parents should tuck their daughters in at night and give them a goodnight hug. Little girls thrive on intimacy because it makes them feel that they are an important part of the family. It is important that male single parents with daughters know the difference between verbal intimacy and physical intimacy. For example, it is not appropriate for a single father to kiss his daughter on the lips. Nor is it appropriate to bathe her once she is old enough to do it herself.

For single parents, both male and female, intimacy with a child can be seductive, especially if the parent has lived alone for a long time. Care must be taken to avoid isolation once the child comes into your life. You don't want to develop an "it's us against the world" mentality with your child. You adopted a child, not a partner.

Get Involved

Daughters of all ages enjoy private time with their fathers. It is important for fathers to drive their daughters to places, and take them on shopping expeditions to purchase "guy things" such as shoes or lawn equipment. Daughters benefit from seeing how their fathers react to strangers, how they talk to their guy friends, and how they react to misfortunes such as dropped grocery bags.

Protect, Protect, Protect

If there is one thing that fathers and daughters can agree on—at least until the daughters reach adolescence—it is the father's role as family protector. Little girls see their male parent as the High Sheriff in their lives: the person they can trust to protect them from things that go bump in the night; the person they can depend on to keep them out of danger while they go about the day-to-day business of living. Most fathers accept that responsibility with great pleasure.

Of course, there are things from which parents can and cannot protect their daughters. They can protect them from serious childhood illnesses, if they make certain that the girls receive their inoculations. They can protect their daughters from violent and sexual imagery on television, to some extent, if they monitor viewing habits and use care in what they watch when their children are in the room. And, if they know what to look for, they can protect their daughters from potentially abusive adults.

Parents cannot protect their daughters from getting their hearts broken by boys. They cannot protect them from teachers who don't recognize great intellect. They cannot protect their daughters from friends who do not want them in their groups. And they cannot protect them from a multitude of aches and pains.

Pigtails, Baseball, and Dance Recitals

Between six and twelve, girls develop lives outside the home. They start school, they join organizations, they play sports, and they form opinions about the differences between the sexes. Most likely, all boys will fall into the "icky" category. Daughters come home from school, after spending seven hours being chased by boys and having their pigtails pulled by them, only to look at their male role model with confusion over the fact that he is "one of them."

Parents who can remember being anxious while out in public with their three-year-old daughter, for fear of what she may say or do, may be surprised to discover that their twelve-year-old daughter is embarrassed to be seen in public with them. That has more to do with her friends, of course, than it does with her feelings about her parents. Regardless of how your daughter acts toward you—and sometimes she will be downright hateful—it is a good idea to remember that she still looks to you for love and understanding.

Talk, Talk, Talk

This is one of the most important things that you can do for your daughter. It doesn't matter if you had a rough day at work, good parents will find the time to talk to their daughters. You should turn off the television or step out of the kitchen or put down the newspaper and ask her about her day.

When she has had her say, you should tell her about your day at work and then answer her questions, however naïve they may seem. By talking to your daughter, you can boost her self-image by making her feel important. You make her feel safe and secure. And you teach her communication skills that will benefit her at school.

Discipline

Males discipline sons and daughters differently. They hold the sons to a different standard and they are more aggressive in their discipline. With daughters, fathers find that all they usually need to do is cast a look of disapproval; they seldom find the need for harsher methods of discipline.

Little girls quickly learn that they can "get away with murder" when dealing with their fathers, especially if they smile and show affection toward them while apologizing for their misbehavior. As long as they do not carry that little game into adulthood, it is of little consequence; unfortunately, some women never outgrow it. Grown women who engage in inappropriate actions, and then smile and say they are sorry, learned that behavior as children. Because they got away with it then, they expect that behavior to have the same results with their adult boyfriends or husbands.

For some reason, mothers are not nearly as likely to show favoritism when they discipline children of the opposite sex.

Private: Do Not Enter

Daughters can change almost overnight once they reach school age. The same daughter at six who asks her parent to bring something to her while she is in the bathtub will reel in horror at eight or ten if a parent should walk into her room unannounced. The exact time of that transformation varies from girl to girl, but there comes a time when they value privacy more than anything else.

It is important for parents to be alert to those changes. The first time that a daughter screams and slams the door in your face, you will be tempted to punish her. That would be the wrong thing to do. True, she over-reacted and showed disrespect to you, but under the circumstances it was understandable. You will know it is time to respect your daughter's privacy when she asks you to do so.

Just Say Cheese

It is essential for fathers to be photographed with their daughters. The tendency with most fathers is to be in portraits with the entire family, or to pose for photographs with their wife, or even to pose for "action" shots with their son. Rarely does a father pose for photographs with his daughter. But he should do this, because it contributes to her self-image, helps her feel love-worthy, and gives her something to cherish later in life.

Suffering through the Teenage Years

Parents seldom recall the years between thirteen and eighteen as the best years of their relationship with their daughter. Adolescence is a time during which girls transform into women; it a time is marked by rebellion, wide mood fluctuations, and parental confusion. The irony, of course, is that while adolescence is a time during which daughters work very hard to escape their parents' dominance, it is also the time during which they most need their love and guidance. It is not easy to love a child who is doing the emotional equivalent of kicking and screaming, but this is the challenge that parents with adolescent daughters face on a daily basis.

I Have Someone I Want You to Meet

What parent has not cringed upon first hearing those words? One of the hardest things for parents to accept is that their teenage daughters sometimes will be prone to date boys who are the opposites of their male role models. If the role model or father is a button-down-collar preppy type who wears his hair in a military brush cut, he can count on his daughter's boyfriends looking like his worst nightmare. Most likely they will all come from free-love families that attend nudist camps and live in vans down by the river.

Just the fact that a daughter has a boyfriend is often a difficult thing for a father to accept. For most of his daughter's life, he has been the only man in her life. Sharing that honor with a teenage boy is a challenge for all fathers who remember what it was like to *be* a teenage boy. How he handles that challenge will determine how rebellious his daughter will be for the remainder of her adolescence.

The Drug Wars

A generation ago, drugs were a problem, but they were limited to certain easily identifiable lifestyles. Today's parents may have heard warnings from their parents about pot-smoking hippies, but that was pretty much it. This is not so today. Drugs are prevalent throughout society. Parents have got to be experts on every type of illegal drug imaginable. Otherwise, how will they know it if they see it in their home?

I Hate You

There is a point in every adolescent girl's life when she positively hates her parents—or so she is likely to proclaim. She hates the way you dress. She hates the way you talk. She hates what you have done with your life. Unfortunately, this reaction is sometimes stronger in adopted children who know in their hearts that their *real* parents are super-cool trendsetters, perhaps even rock stars. There is not much you can do about that, except to ride out the storm.

When Daughters Become the Parents

When a mother turns to her daughter for emotional support, their relationship changes and they become friends. They talk long hours about the trials of life. The mother seems to regress somewhat as the daughter matures a bit. Often they spend time together as if they were the same age. Typically, the daughter neglects her needs in order to meet her mother's needs.

The end result can be less than amiable. A daughter may resent her mother's interference in her social circle; she may be jealous of her mom's ability to be the center of attention among her friends, and she may want her mother to seek her own friends. Other girls may mature quickly and begin to circulate more in adult social circles. Many actually compete with their mothers for male attention.

Once the mother accepts the daughter as an equal, it is difficult for the relationship to progress through traditional mother-daughter stages. There will come a point down the road when deep-seated resentments replace the coziness of being best friends. The daughter will enter adulthood and yearn for a mother figure in her life, and the mother will understand that her parental bond with her daughter has been replaced by a superficial friendship that is being eroded by the passage of time.

8 Gay and Lesbian Adoptions

For a very long time, adoption was the sole province of heterosexual married couples, but in recent years gay and lesbian couples have found increasing acceptance as adoptive couples. The initial shift in agency attitudes was essentially practical. Social service agencies, charged with the responsibility of placing children in safe and loving homes, have battled with the realization that heterosexual married couples have not responded to the thousands of older, special needs children in foster homes.

Until recently, any alternative family structure was automatically rejected as a possibility by adoption agencies. As same-sex couples began to openly demand more personal and legal rights, they also began trudging down the adoption road. The "Gayby Boom" was predicted during the 1990 American Psychological Association Convention as a future trend in the gay community—and it has come to pass.

Faced with much the same opposition encountered by singles who tried to adopt years earlier, gays and lesbians have witnessed a concerted effort to block them from adopting. In 1998, antihomosexual organizations turned their attention to developing a national campaign to ban homosexuals from being considered as foster parents or as adoptive parents. Since then, more and more legislation has been introduced throughout the country to keep gays and lesbians from adopting. The fight has recently become very visible with celebrities voicing opinions on both sides of the issue.

With so many children in need of loving homes—in 2003, there were about a half million children in the foster care system, with over one hundred and twenty-six thousand of them available for adoption—gay and lesbian couples stepped up and offered to give homes to the children whom heterosexual couples refused to adopt. Some of these children are considered "unadoptable" because of their ages, ethnic backgrounds, or health problems. Without available adoptive homes, these children are destined to remain in foster homes.

"So, what's the problem?" gay and lesbian applicants ask. "We'll take them."

The problem, of course, is that many people have a strong aversion to the gay lifestyle. Some adults who otherwise respect individual choice and refrain from casting aspersions on same-sex couples suddenly become very vocal when it comes to placing children into the homes of same-sex couples.

Ironically, some of the states that most vehemently fight the right of gay and lesbian couples to adopt are among the highest in percentage of children in need of homes. Pro-gay lawsuits against those states often cite dysfunctional family services systems and they question if the fight is really about "protecting the children." If protecting the children is the real issue, they argue, why don't states that are so strident in their opposition to gay adoptions spend as much time addressing that issue as they do fighting gay adoption?

There are six to nine million children in America with homosexual parents. Some of these children live with gay or lesbian parents; others have a range of relationships with the parents. The 2000 National Census revealed about six hundred thousand same-sex partner households (about 1 percent of the total), a fivefold increase since 1990.

Darin and his partner, Steve, adopted four children who were all considered high risk for one reason or another. Three-year-old Austin came to them with tangled hair, dirty fingernails, and a reluctance to speak. Warned that Austin was mentally challenged, Darin and Steve took him in and did their best to give him love, structure, attention, and the safety of a stable home. Within weeks of placement, Austin was hardly recognizable to the caseworker. He was outgoing, talkative, and happy. The other three children had similar backgrounds and also flourished in Darin and Steve's care.

Matthew was eleven and overcame a severe stuttering problem and some behavior problems. Debbie, five years old, made good progress in a special class for children with cerebral palsy. She mastered an augmented communication device and the other children in the house enjoy interacting with her using the large computer communication board. Brandon, the oldest, will always be teased by his peers about his mixed racial background, but he feels safe with Darin and Steve, maybe because he knows they have faced discrimination themselves and understand his hurt.

Critics of Darin's and Steve's family worry about how the children will fare in future months and years, when the men's lifestyle might become an issue for the children; but Darin and Steve, caught up in the day-to-day responsibility of parenting, don't live in the future. Caring for the present needs of the children is what matters the most to them.

With more children needing placement than there are placements available, and same-sex couples offering their homes, many lawmakers are now supporting the match. Long-standing ideas of the possible harm to children placed in these homes are being challenged in the courts. Using the standard of what is "in the best interest of the child," gay and lesbian activists are demanding that there be proof that there will be a negative effect on the child before they are disqualified from adoption.

WHERE IN THE UNITED STATES AND CANADA CAN GAYS ADOPT?

Ultimately, the decision of who can and cannot adopt is made by state or provincial government. There have been significant changes in recent years to the legal rights of same-sex couples. Some new laws work in favor of same-sex couples and others work against them.

There is widespread agreement that adoption options must always be based on what is "in the best interest of the child," but there is little agreement on how that "best interest" affects the definition of a family. In the United States, that definition is expressed state by state; in Canada, it is expressed province by province. Standards for international adoptions vary as well. Listings of jurisdictions and nuances of their statutes are moving targets and change from year to year.

Legislation concerning alternative family placement changes quickly and usually has idiosyncratic language unique to a particular jurisdiction. For gay and lesbian couples seeking to adopt, the best advice is to check the laws in their home state or province, even if the adoption is private or international. At this time, the following states allow gay and lesbian couples to adopt jointly:

California	Ohio
Massachusetts	Vermont
New Jersey	Washington
New Mexico	Wisconsin
New York	District of Columbia

Even in these states, couples must ensure that their sexual preference and behavior are not detrimental to the child. In other areas of the country, the feelings are quite the opposite. On page 5, Part II, Section G of the Florida Department of Children and Families adoption form, there are yes/no check boxes inquiring as to whether the applicant is homosexual or bisexual. If either of the two boxes is checked "yes," the applicant is deemed ineligible to adopt in Florida. The sad reality in Florida is that a gay or lesbian must lie in order to adopt a child. The adoption agency may suspect a lie, but it can often live with the "don't tell" philosophy.

Massachusetts enacted a policy to ban gays from being considered as foster or adoptive parents in the mid-1980s under the leadership of then-governor Michael Dukakis. After the ban, his administration removed a child from a gay foster home over the objection of the caseworker. Later the state supreme court overturned Dukakis's order, but unfortunately the child was sexually abused while living in a subsequent heterosexual foster home.

Currently, only Florida totally bans gays from being considered as foster or adoptive parents. In 1995, Nebraska banned gay foster parenting, and in 2000, Mississippi joined Utah in restricting adoption to only "married" couples. Without specifically naming same-sex couples, the laws are intended to keep them from adopting.

Most states have no specific law for or against gay adoption. Some states rely on indirect statutory barriers such as "marriage only" adoptions.

Things have changed since July 2003, when Texas's sodomy law was ruled to be in violation of the U.S. Constitution's due process and equal protection provision. The Supreme Court justices found, in a split decision, that the law was specifically aimed at homosexuals and violated the right of consenting adults to choose what they do in their bedrooms. This decision affected similar laws in thirteen other states.

One way that gays and lesbians have dealt with restrictive laws has been to be creative when applying the legal options available to them. Second-parent adoptions are viewed as a legal loophole by many gays and lesbians.

Second-parent adoptions occur when one parent adopts and then allows a second parent to adopt later, thus creating a second, legally recognized parent for the adopted child. After court battles in Vermont, Massachusetts, New York, and New Jersey, second-parent adoptions are now sanctioned by the highest courts. In twenty-one other states the courts have allowed second-parent adoptions for same-sex couples. Second-parent adoptions are allowed for gays and lesbians in London and Manchester, England; the Netherlands; and Ontario, Canada.

In July 2005, Canada became the fourth country in the world to allow same-sex marriage when Chief Justice Beverly McLachlin gave the Queen's consent to Bill C-28. However, the law does not directly affect same-sex adoptions, since that is determined by each individual province. Currently, gays and lesbians may legally adopt in British Columbia, Manitoba, Newfoundland, Labrador, Nova Scotia, Ontario, Quebec, Saskatchewan, and the Northwest Territories. Gay adoption is banned in New Brunswick and Prince Edward Island. The adoption of children by a same-sex partner has been allowed in Ontario since 1995 when the Honorable Justice J. P. Nevins struck down the provision of the Child and Family Act, which prevented four lesbian women from legally adopting their partners' children.

The Utah legislature sidestepped the gay adoption issue by passing a bill, drafted by Professor Lynn Wardle of Brigham Young University Law School, that prohibits any nonmarried, cohabiting adults from adopting. Since gay couples cannot legally marry in Utah, they are effectively shut out of the adoption process.

Conservatives seem to be making progress throughout the country in limiting same-sex couples' legal rights. Eighteen states have amended their constitutions to say that marriage is between one man and one woman.

Scotty and Lee moved their two adopted children to Kansas from California, where they were legally recognized as the boys' parents. They wanted the boys to enjoy the family atmosphere of their new community, but they soon began to live in fear that their children might be taken away from them. Kansas is silent on whether gays or lesbians can adopt, but it restricts unmarried couples from jointly adopting.

As Scotty and Lee explored their future in Kansas, they encountered comments that adoption should be limited to homes with a mother and a father. Key legislators claimed that they were not antigay or antichild. They just wanted to protect children from any possible harm. Scotty and Lee faced having what was already decided by California law undone by Kansas law. If that comes to fruition, they will have to move back to California to keep their family together.

The uncertainty has had a negative impact on their family because the time that they ordinarily would spend planning the boys' after-school activities is now spent having painful discussions about why they are no longer welcome in Kansas.

LIVING WITH A LIE

Children have been secretly adopted by gays and lesbians for many years; however, only recently has that become common knowledge. If you are a single homosexual, your options are dictated by state laws and agency policies. Depending on where you plan to adopt, you may be tempted to lie about your sexual orientation, or, at the very least, not volunteer information that would lead to your application being denied.

For years, gay and lesbian couples resorted to lies in order to form a family. One member of the couple would adopt as a single parent and pretend the partner was only a roommate or friend. Of course, lying on the application and in the interview could have ended the process completely if the truth became known to the screener; but desperate couples took the chance. Depending on where the family resided, the lies continued even after placement, making the couples fearful that once the lies were discovered, the child would be taken out of the home.

Some adoption screeners have a policy of "don't ask, don't tell." That might seem like a minor victory of sorts for gays and lesbians, but it is no guarantee that the placement caseworker, or the judge who must approve the adoption, will take the same "don't ask, don't tell" approach used by the screener. If you can't live with the uncertainty of being "outed," you should consider living in a state where gays and lesbians are allowed to adopt. There are several states, parts of Canada, and several foreign counties that sanction adoption for gays and lesbians.

Kevin and his partner Jody had been together for seven years. They lived in an upper-middle-class neighborhood in a Southern state. There was no question that their commitment to one another was as strong as that of any of their heterosexual friends and acquaintances. Both men were successful professionals who had done well. They had the respect of their peers at work, they were involved in community activities, and their home and yard were the envy of the neighborhood.

It was fairly apparent that Kevin and Jody were gay, but other than their immediate families and closest friends, almost no one spoke the words "gay" or "same-sex couple" aloud. Just like their heterosexual counterparts, they didn't make it a point to announce their sexual preference. Kevin and Jody were always seen together, but never publicly showed affection. Their state did not allow them to be married, but they shared their home, cars, budget, and future plans.

Kevin had a nephew, and Jody had a nephew and a niece. They loved to spend time with the children and they were often called on to babysit the children. They enjoyed the interaction and felt that they were effective with discipline. Somehow that wasn't enough, especially for Kevin. Jody felt that he would love having children in their home, but he had resolved that issue years ago when he made his lifestyle decision. Kevin was not able to let go of his desire to have children. He felt that he had love to give and he knew there were many children who needed a home.

Kevin and Jody made anonymous foster parent inquiries and quickly realized that their relationship would block them from receiving a child. After weighing the reality of the legal obstacles against their desire to raise a child, they decided to attempt to maneuver around the obstacles. It was illegal for gays to raise foster children in their state, but it was not illegal for single men to raise them.

Frustrated with a state that seemed to play semantic games with them, they used that loophole for Kevin to apply for foster children as a single man. After approval, he was informed that since he did not have a wife, he might have to wait a long time for a child unless he was willing to parent "special needs" children. Kevin's loving heart was open to any child who needed him. With such an accepting attitude, Kevin had two foster children to care for before very long.

Kevin and Jody didn't feel guilty about living a lie. They had wanted to be legally recognized as a loving couple through marriage, but they were denied that opportunity by the state. From the day the children came to live in their home, Jody was an equal parent to the boys, although the state considered him to only be a roommate. Kevin and Jody resented that they had to live a lie and it caused them pain to do so, but they felt that it was the only option that the system offered them.

WHY ARE SOME PEOPLE SO OPPOSED TO GAY ADOPTIONS?

Historically, public opinion has been firmly against gay and lesbian adoptions. In 1994, only 28 percent of those responding to opinion polls supported gay adoptions, while 65 percent opposed it. However, opinions may be changing as evidenced by a poll conducted in 2002 by ABC News. In the survey, supporters of allowing same-sex couples to adopt outnumbered those opposing it, with 47 percent in favor and 42 percent opposed.

The gay and lesbian community feels that the progress is significant, even if the split is very close. Actress and talk show host Rosie O'Donnell, who publicly acknowledged that she is a lesbian, fueled the fires of debate in 2002 when she shared her story of parenting her adopted children. Rosie's personal struggles to adopt brought particular attention to the 1977 Florida law prohibiting adoptions by homosexuals. The year before Rosie entered the debate, a federal judge in Miami upheld the 1977 law, which had been challenged by two gay fathers who sought to adopt two boys, ruling that since there is no right to adopt or be adopted, there is no right to apply for adoption. Despite ruling against the gay men, the judge voiced sympathy by recognizing that the emotional ties between the fathers and children were as close as those between biological parents.

How does America view the issue? The 2002 ABC News survey revealed that supporters are usually among younger adults, women, and the more educated adult population. Older adults, men, and less-educated individuals still oppose gay and lesbian adoptions. Regionally, the East and Midwest are much more supportive than the South, with the West in the middle. A large majority of Democrats and Independents support allowing same-sex couples to adopt, while Republicans overwhelmingly oppose it by a two to one margin.

Of course, no one can ignore the religious influence that follows these same geographic and demographic lines. Religious leaders have always condemned homosexual relationships, teaching that they are against nature and God. Many fundamentalist Christians teach that such relationships are "of the flesh" and sinful. Churches seldom open their doors to gay or lesbian couples except, of course, to try to talk them out of their "sinful ways." Many preachers proclaim that the proliferation of homosexuality is a sign of the end times. They feel that individuals who are attracted to the same sex willfully make a lifestyle choice and could change this choice if they tried. Same-sex couples are considered to be in conflict with biblical teachings that a man should be the head of a household with the woman and children functioning under his guidance. Pastors warn their followers that homosexuals are unstable, impulsive, and prone to be sexual predators. Homosexuality is considered to be against the traditional family, home, and Christian values.

Many stereotypical ideas about gays and lesbians cloud the debate, even among those who support gay and lesbian adoption. It is a common belief that all homosexuals seek indiscriminate sex with anyone available to them and should be considered emotionally disturbed due to a genetic mismatch: lesbians want to be men or look like men, and gay men want to be or look like women. They are accused of not being able to maintain or not wanting to maintain lasting relationships. It is believed that gays and lesbians are incapable of being faithful to another person. They are often described as self-indulgent, incompetent in crisis, and indecisive. In general, a large number of people believe gays and lesbians to be sinister, corrupt, and capable of exploiting and molesting children.

As a group, men are more negative about homosexuals than women. Those who have homosexual friends or are exposed to homosexuals in the workplace typically have a more accepting opinion. In communities where masculinity is highly valued and excellence in sports is almost mandatory, any male who doesn't fit that expectation is ridiculed and misunderstood. The individuals most likely to harbor negative feelings about gays and lesbians are highly traditional males who know few, if any, homosexuals, and are surrounded by people who share the same negative feelings.

Recent efforts to "protect children from gay parenting" continue to gain momentum. Politicians have spoken out against gay and lesbian adoptions by singles or same-sex couples. Texas State Representative Robert Talton, a Republican from Pasadena, has made it clear that he would rather have kids in orphanages than have gays and lesbians parent them. He justifies this stance by saying that at least in an orphanage, children would learn proper values.

Many liberal and conservative adults can accept the homosexual lifestyle as long as it doesn't affect children. Traditionalists have successfully maintained heightened concern about children being raised by same-sex couples. They argue that discriminatory laws against homosexual parenting are in the best interest of children. Gay rights opponents argue that gay men are disproportionately likely to molest children, although there is no evidence to support such claims. This highly charged claim is vehemently rejected by social scientists who maintain that sexual abusers overwhelmingly are either heterosexuals in adult relationships or lack any sexual response to adults. Rejecting those findings, gay rights opponents claim that adult males who target male children are by definition homosexual.

Pedophilia is usually considered an orientation of its own. Men who molest boys are almost never "gay" in the typical sense. A gay or homosexual is not defined simply by an attraction to another male (adult or child); in fact, there is very little overlap between men who are attracted to children and those who pursue romantic relationships with other males. It is the men who are involved in romantic relationships with other men who are most likely to apply to be adoptive parents. It would be a red flag to a screener if a gay man who had never had a significant adult companion in his life applied to be an adoptive parent.

There is a mistaken belief that children raised by same-sex parents will inevitably be gay or lesbian. Social conservatives argue that gays will either molest children under their care or recruit them to be homosexuals. The evidence doesn't support either claim. Molesters are more likely to be heterosexual and married. It is possible that some sons or daughters, in an effort to emulate their gay parent, might experiment with homosexuality, but there is no evidence that it occurs with great frequency, if at all.

WHAT IF MY SCREENER IS PREJUDICED?

There is enough prejudice to go around. Of course, if you are gay or lesbian, you will encounter caseworkers, psychologists, teachers, politicians, and a host of people in the community who are opposed to the adoption of children by homosexuals. You probably have no power to change their minds, but you do have the choice to work with an agency that is not prejudiced against you because of your sexual orientation.

Do some research before you choose an agency. Know the laws in your jurisdiction and understand the local policies. Seek out others in your situation for advice and recommendations. There are individual agencies that look favorably upon gays and lesbians, or at least not negatively. Remember that your goal is to adopt a child, not to make a political statement. Don't associate yourself with an agency that is known to be prejudiced. Much of the adoption process is subjective. An adoption screener can block your chances of being approved for adoption based on little factual information and a lot of personal bias.

How can you know if the screener is prejudiced? Chances are, you will not be able to make that determination based on the tone of the screener's voice. He or she is an experienced professional and is unlikely to allow tone of voice to reflect personal feelings. However, you can make this judgment based on the questions themselves.

If you are applying to an agency that does not have a stated policy on gay or lesbian adoptions and you tell the screener that you have a same-sex roommate, you can tell if the screener is prejudiced if he or she presses the issue of your sexual orientation. If the screener does not press the issue in the interviews, but requests an interview with your "roommate," do not be overly concerned unless he or she presses your partner about sexual orientation. It is the screener's job to interview every adult in the household and to make determinations about each adult's potential impact on an adopted child. A screener who is open-minded on the issue of gay and lesbian adoptions can gather the information needed without placing emphasis on your sexual orientation or the sexual orientation of your partner.

If you apply at an agency that has a stated policy of accepting gay applicants, then you have an obligation to be honest about every aspect of your personality makeup, including your sexuality. If you have a partner, both of you may want to go to the agency together to discuss your interest in adoption. At that point, the agency can tell you if it can help, and if it can work with both of you as adoptive parents. Local laws or policies may dictate that one of you adopt as a single parent and then try to seek second parent adoption status later. Discuss your options with the agency.

Next, you will need to be comfortable with the screener who conducts your home study. It is very important that you, as a client, feel comfortable with this person. The screener's job is to write a very detailed document describing you as a potential parent. It is unlikely that a screener who is prejudiced against gays would work for an agency that approves gay applicants. In a situation where you are honest about your sexuality, the screener will want to specifically address issues concerning the social aspects, community attitudes, and personal behavior as it relates to your sexual orientation.

It is to be expected that the screener will want to know your plans to address the negative opinions related to homosexuals adopting children. No matter how neutral the evaluator is personally, you must be questioned on how you plan to handle an adopted child's life with gay or lesbian parents. You also will need to be prepared to articulate that you understand that the normal pressures of parenting are exacerbated by being a part of a socially stigmatized group. You may not be welcome at ballgames, PTA meetings, or other events that involve your adopted child.

Many couples seeking to adopt feel that they must be perfect in order to be considered. For gay and lesbian couples, this feeling is magnified many times over. Not only must you be perfect, but you also must be able to overcome all the prejudice directed toward the gay community. You must prove that you're not a sexual predator, that you won't recruit your child to be homosexual, that your personal sexual behavior does not dominate your time, and that you won't deny your child opportunities to be around heterosexual families.

WHAT MUST I KNOW ABOUT GAY PARENTING?

Gay parents face the same challenges that single parents face, but there are important variations. If you applied for adoption in a state that allows gays to adopt—and you were honest with the screener about your sexual orientation—then you might have noticed that the agency was interested in your relationships with the opposite sex.

If you don't have a history of good relationships with the opposite sex, then it will be difficult for you to provide for your child's most basic needs. If you are male and you have adopted a child, that child, whether male or female, will need the influence of a female role model. If you are female and you have adopted a child, that child, whether male or female, will need the influence of a male role model. If you have been unable throughout your life to form close friendships with members of the opposite sex, you cannot hope to teach your child to have close relationships with the opposite sex.

If you are considering adoption, keep in mind that a promise to provide a child with an opposite-sex role model is not good enough by itself. You must have a history of successful relationships with the opposite sex. If that is not the case with you, we recommend that you postpone your adoption application until you can demonstrate that you can provide an opposite-sex role model for a child.

Children adopted by heterosexual parents may be teased for a variety of reasons when they start school. They may be physically or mentally challenged, or they may have mixed race heritage, or they may be grossly overweight. Or if they were adopted by a heterosexual single parent, they may be teased for not having a mother or a father.

Children adopted by gay parents face all of the same risks of being teased, but they also risk being teased and taunted for having a "queer" parent, a distinction that is invariably more difficult for a boy to accept than a girl. Children are not known for their understanding and tolerance of differences among their playmates.

A heavy burden for a child who is adopted is also having to take up for gay or lesbian parents. The adopted child may feel rejected by others and join those who find gay or lesbian parents disgusting. As a prospective gay adoptive parent, you should come to terms with those possibilities *before* adopting so that you can discuss them with the adoption screener at the time of your interview.

It's no secret that heterosexual parents often have a difficult time accepting homosexuality in their own children. As a gay parent, will you have the same reaction if your son or daughter informs you that he or she is heterosexual? This is a question that goes to the core of parenthood. The heterosexual father who goes ballistic when his son tells him that he is gay may not be reacting so much to the gay issue as to the realization that his son will not be a carbon copy of himself.

As a gay parent, you will feel the same disappointment, whether you care to admit it or not, if your child grows up to be straight. How you deal with that will determine, as much as anything, how successful an adoption placement will be in your home. This is your dilemma: If you encourage your child to explore a gay lifestyle—and therefore be like you—you provide ammunition to your harshest critics. If you do nothing—and allow your child to find his or her own way—the statistical odds are overwhelming that your child will not be gay. How you handle the realization that your child will not be like you will ultimately define you as a parent.

WHEN THERE IS ONE BIOLOGICAL PARENT

Some gay couples, desperate to be parents, turn to artificial insemination or surrogates to produce a biological offspring. After the birth of the baby, the nonbiological parent may face a battle to legally become the second parent. In some states, artificial insemination or surrogates may not be a legal option for singles. Even when those options are available, some states will not allow a same-sex partner to become the legal parent of the child.

If lying is the mechanism same-sex couples use to create a family, then additional lies usually follow. The couple must live a lie in front of their children and the children most likely will feel pressured to join them in their lies. Most same-sex couples feel that there is something very wrong with having to create and maintain a family through lies.

In states where lies are the only route to adoption, same-sex couples must have assistance and the cooperation of those around them to accomplish their goal of parenting. During the application process, the adoption agency asks probing questions about your personal life, activities, interests, background, and yes, sexual history. People involved in a gay or lesbian relationship may lie. They may deny their love for a same-sex partner and minimize their influence and contributions. Adoption screeners may probe even deeper if the lies are apparent. If the screener uncovers the lies during the home study, the adoption process ceases and the applicant is rejected.

To minimize the possibility of being caught in a web of lies, some couples solicit help from an opposite-sex friend to pose as the partner to create the "desirable heterosexual" facade. Elaborate stories are concocted; references are well versed in the story line and everyone involved denies or avoids acknowledging that the applicant actually is a partner in a same-sex couple.

The state agency sent Jennifer to Christy's home to conduct a home study. She had been on the job for about two years and knew the policy against approval of adoption by same-sex couples. As Jennifer interviewed Christy, she recorded vital information about her past and current relationships. Christy informed Jennifer that Richard was her current boyfriend and he was very supportive of her decision to adopt as a single parent. Jennifer was impressed by Christy's professional achievements, her well-kept house, and her circle of equally well-educated friends. All the references were extremely supportive of Christy's ability to be a good parent. Jennifer had no data to suggest there would be any negative impact on a child adopted by Christy.

During her interview with Richard, Jennifer found him less invested in the relationship than Christy had implied. Jennifer felt that the couple might not last too much longer; however, she was confident that Christy could handle a breakup with Richard and it would not affect her decision to adopt a child. During her interview, Christy reported a close friendship with a woman named Debbie. Christy indicated that Debbie was the person she confided in and turned to in times of trouble. There may have been some subtle signs of attraction to Debbie, but Jennifer had no solid evidence that the relationship was anything more than a close-knit friendship.

Several years after the adoption, Christy dropped the façade involving Richard and she admitted that her true desire was to be with Debbie in an intimate relationship. During the legal battle for Debbie to become the second parent, Jennifer was called on to testify. Although she realized that she had been hoodwinked several years before, she supported their desire to grant Debbie parental rights. Because she felt that Christy was one of her best adoptive parents, her testimony supported Christy and Debbie's request.

Other stories about same-sex couples do not have such a happy ending. A couple in Florida who had brought three children into their home through foster care lost all their children once their gay status was known. Shortly after the children were taken from their home of many years, the couple ironically saw pictures of them on the Internet listed as children in need of a home.

In some states that allow homosexual couples the opportunity to adopt, the opportunity is in no way equal to what their heterosexual counterparts enjoy. Singles and homosexuals are usually offered children with special needs or multiple children from the same family. If they prefer to wait for a child of a specific age or ethnic background, the wait may be very long or it may last forever. The children with special needs may include those considered mentally challenged, behaviorally disordered, hyperactive, or those who possess other physical or mental disorders. Often these children have been in abusive, neglectful home situations or have lived in multiple foster homes. They have learned that the world is unfair and cruel. They may have never felt much of a bond or attachment to anyone, and adults seem to be the cause of most of their problems.

Since homosexual couples know the pain of discrimination and abuse, they actually relate very well to these children and seldom hesitate to take children with special needs into their homes. Same-sex couples are well aware of how cruel the public can be and they seem to be eager to bond with children who have been cast away. In many instances, these children with special needs appear to have multiple disabilities upon arrival in the adoptive or foster home. With a lot of love and understanding, a strong bond develops. Sometimes these children overcome what once seemed to be overwhelming challenges. It is rewarding to see how quickly some children who have been tossed about from one foster home to another blossom and exceed all expectations once they are placed in an accepting environment.

IS THERE PROOF OF A NEGATIVE EFFECT ON CHILDREN?

The use of research studies to determine the impact on a child living in a homosexual household is a logical step in resolving the issue. However, studies vary from researcher to researcher. Unfortunately, the personal biases of researchers, pro and con, can influence the end results. The way the study is conducted, the subjects being studied, and many other factors help guide the final conclusions. Not surprisingly, the studies conducted or funded by religious groups report a negative impact and those conducted or funded by gay or lesbian groups report a positive impact.

The idea that the sexual habits of a parent should not be an issue unless it has a negative effect on the child has been upheld by the courts. In 1998, a New Jersey court enacted a policy that evaluates gay adoptive parents by the same criteria as married couples. New Hampshire repealed its ban on gays serving as adoptive or foster parents in 1999. Other states judge the best parent and the best home for each child in the foster and adoptive system on a case-by-case basis.

It is difficult to find scientific evidence of the specific negative effect on children adopted by same-sex couples. Those who argue that gay and lesbian adoption should be banned cite the liberal attitudes and over-tolerance of differences prevalent in gay households. Conservative religious leaders seem to prefer that children not be exposed to the homosexual lifestyle. They fear that children may come to consider an alternative life-style to be acceptable.

The religious leaders are at least partially right. There is evidence that children raised by gay and lesbian parents show a measurable difference in their tolerance toward those who are different. The accusation that gays either molest or recruit children under their care to homosexuality is not substantiated by proof. Further, there is no study that connects being gay or lesbian to having gay or lesbian parents. In fact, there is plenty of anec-dotal evidence that most gays have heterosexual parents.

The American Academy of Pediatrics endorsed gay adoption in the February 2002 issue of *Pediatrics* in a policy statement entitled "Technical Report: Coparent or Second-Parent Adoption by Same-Sex Parents," upset-ting conservatives who began to question the sexual orientation of their children's pediatricians. The report stated that in light of research that shows that children of gay and lesbian parents "function just as well emo-tionally, cognitively, and socially as children of heterosexual parents, courts should stop using sexual orientation as grounds to deny members of same-sex couples the right to adopt their partner's children." The report went on to identify that second-parent adoptions potentially do the following:

- Guarantee that the second parent's custody rights will be pro-tected if the couple separates
- Protect the second parent's rights to custody and visitation if the couple separates
- Ensure the child's eligibility for health benefits through both parents

WHEN DO WE TELL OUR CHILDREN THAT WE ARE GAY?

It is better to discuss parental sexual orientation during childhood instead of waiting until adolescence. The child's level of maturity, questions, and interest level should be considered. An excellent way to approach the issue is to explain it in terms of the diversity that exists within families, com-munities, and the world.

If your child refers to both parents as mom, mommy, or some name for "mother," or dad, daddy, and so on for father, then your child already knows that your family has two mommies or daddies. You may associate with other families that have two mommies or two daddies, but your child may also have friends that have one mommy and one daddy, or one daddy and no mommy, or one mommy and no daddy. Teaching your child that each family is unique is important. No matter what your family makeup might be, each person in the family is an important, valued member.

Children need to learn and appreciate early in life that there is diversity all around them. It may be the black boy in the choir, the adopted Chinese girl in science class, the child with cerebral palsy on the school bus, or the child with two dads; we all are different and come from different backgrounds and families. You may find that teaching your child to respect others for their uniqueness, rather than only embracing those who are similar, will be a blessing.

Your child's initial question of "why do I have two moms?" should not prompt you to provide a complete description of gay or lesbian sexual behavior. Rather, you should simply answer the question. In your discussion of uniqueness, you will also need to include the adoption issue. Your family is special because of the choice you, as parents, made to bring a child into your lives and home.

Explain that the love you shared for your partner was even made better by sharing that love with a child. Telling children that they have brought joy and happiness into your home helps create a very positive bond with them. Help your child understand that not everyone he or she associates with will be accepting of differences. Work with your child to learn ways to be respectful of everyone, even to those prejudiced people who may say hurtful things. You also might find it useful to practice role-playing situations that may prepare your child to be teased and taunted.

When it comes to describing sexual behavior, you should broach the subject in the same manner and time frame as any other parent. Most children neither need nor want details of your personal sexual behavior with your partner, heterosexual or homosexual.

You will need to discuss sexual development, functioning, and behavior before your child reaches puberty. Having changes occur in the body that are unexpected can be very scary for a young person. If you are single and have adopted a child of the opposite sex, you may ask a friend or relative who is the same sex as your child to have the "birds and bees" discussion.

Your family, friends at work, and those in your community may secretly be afraid that because you are homosexual, your influence will discourage your child from choosing a heterosexual lifestyle. It is your responsibility to ensure that you do not put pressure on your child to choose your lifestyle.

Of course, you will remember the pressure you felt to conform to a hetero-sexual society. Homophobic fears are still very strong in our society. Typically young, educated professionals will tolerate your sexual orientation better than older people, but even they may also voice fears for children in your care.

Current research is on your side. A number of studies have shown that children raised in gay or lesbian homes report that they are very happy with their gender and show no evidence that they suffer gender identity diffi-culties. Gender-role behavior studies suggest that there is no difference in the toy preferences, activities, interests, or occupational choices between children of homosexual parents and those of heterosexual parents. In gen-eral, the research reports that fears about gender identity, gender role behavior, and sexual orientation are unfounded.

PREPARING FOR THE FUTURE

When death interrupts life, families can be torn apart. Major life changes occur when a loved one dies, no matter how the family is structured. Your wishes are not guaranteed after your death, unless your will or trust is prop-erly written. Surprises can occur when a loved one dies without having made the proper arrangements. To exercise power after death, you must take care of the details prior to death.

Gay and lesbian couples are very aware of discrimination. From health benefits and retirement to custody of children, same-sex couples are treated very differently than their opposite-sex counterparts. When these couples choose to live in areas that do not legally acknowledge their rela-tionship, their future is in jeopardy. In crisis situations, hospitals, extended families, adoption agencies, and the courts may feel compassion for the couple and their wishes, but still will follow the community's discrimina-tory policies. A second parent who doesn't have the proper paperwork may be denied power to authorize care for a partner or for a child. In the event of death, the nonlegal parent has few, if any rights.

Same-sex couples sometimes take the risk of having only one partner adopt the child; the other partner never chooses to obtain "second parent" status. This is a risky situation and can lead to long legal battles if the legal parent dies or ends the relationship with the other. The nonlegal parent may not only lose the partner, but the child also.

If same-sex couples are not allowed to legally adopt where you live, it is important for you to have a written agreement with your partner. This doc-ument should clearly articulate what the two of you, a couple concerned about the welfare and future of your children, consider to be your relationship with the children. Having the assistance of an attorney will be helpful in recording your wishes.

If second-parent adoptions are not allowed where you live, write out exactly how you would want to handle certain situations. These documents are not always honored by the courts, but having a written document in place is always a good thing. The process will be far less complicated if you reside in an area that allows same-sex couples to adopt. The best scenario is for you to live where same-sex marriages are honored.

If you feel passionate about fighting for your rights, there may come a point when you may have to choose between living in a state that is hostile toward granting you and your child full rights, or relocating to a state in which those rights are guaranteed. Of course, there is no adoption screener on the planet that would not prefer to see you put the best interest of your child first.

9 Adoption Agencies in the United States and Canada

U. S. ADOPTION AGENCIES

This state-by-state listing of licensed adoption agencies is as comprehensive as the authors could make it, but despite their best efforts some agencies may have been overlooked. The authors do not endorse any of the agencies on this list; they are listed for reader convenience. Many of the agencies have web sites and readers are encouraged to search for those web sites to obtain more specific information.

ALABAMA

Alabama Department of
  Human Resources
Telephone 1-866-4AL-KIDS and
  request an application. You will
  be asked to return the application
  to a specific county office of the
  Department of Human Resources.
  Adoption applications are processed by the county of residence.

Private Agencies

AGAPE, Inc.
PO Box 3887

Huntsville, AL 35810
(256) 859-4481

Alabama Baptist Children's Homes
  and Family Ministries
PO Box 361767
Birmingham, AL 35236
(205) 982-1112

Catholic Family Services
733 37th Street, East
Tuscaloosa, AL 35405
(205) 533-9045

Catholic Family Services
2164 11th Avenue, South
Birmingham, AL 35205
(205) 324-6561

Catholic Family Services
PO Box 745
Huntsville, AL 35804
(256) 536-0041

Catholic Social Services
4455 Narrow Lane Road
Montgomery, AL 36116
(334) 288-8890

Catholic Social Services
PO Box 759
Mobile, AL 36601
(334) 434-1550

Family Adoption Services
529 Beacon Parkway West,
  Suite 108
Birmingham, AL 35209
(205) 290-0077

Lifeline Children's Services
2908 Pumphouse Road
Birmingham, AL 35243
(205) 967-0919

United Methodist Children's Home
  of Alabama
1712 Broad Street
Selma, AL 36701
(334) 875-7283

ALASKA

Anchorage Regional Office
The Office of Children's Services
550 West 8th Street, Suite 304
Anchorage, AK 99501
(907) 269-3900

Northern Regional Office
The Office of Children's Services
751 Old Richardson Highway,
  Suite 300
Fairbanks, AK 99501
(907) 451-2650

South-Central Regional Office
The Office of Children's Services
Unit 3
695 East Parks Highway
Wasilla, AK 99654
(907) 357-9780

Southeast Regional Office
The Office of Children's Services
Second Floor
3025 Clinton Drive
Juneau, AK 99801
(907) 465-3235

Private Agencies

Catholic Social Services
3710 East 20th Avenue, Suite 1
Anchorage, AK 99508
(907) 276-5590

Fairbanks Counseling and Adoption
912 Barnette Street
Fairbanks, AK 99701
(907) 456-4729

World Association for Children and
  Parents
4704 Kenai Avenue
Anchorage, AK 99508
(907) 345-7942

ARIZONA

The Division of Children, Youth and
  Families
Telephone (877) 543-7633 and
  request information about adoption. Based on where you live in
  Arizona, you will be referred to
  one of six districts that provide
  adoption services.

Private Agencies

Adoption Care Center
PO Box 5659
Scottsdale, AZ 85261
(480) 322-8838

Arizona Baptist Children's Services
PO Box 39239
Phoenix, AZ 85069
(602) 943-7760

Birth Hope Adoption Agency
3225 North Central Avenue, Suite
 1217
Phoenix, AZ 85012
(602) 277-2860

Catholic Community Services of
 Southeastern Arizona
PO Box 1777
Bisbee, AZ 85603
(800) 338-2474

Catholic Community Services of
 Western Arizona
690 East 32nd Street
Yuma, AZ 85365
(888) 514-3482

Catholic Social Services of Central
 and Northern Arizona
43 South San Francisco
Flagstaff, AZ 86001
(928) 774-9125

Christian Family Care Agency
1102 South Pantana Road
Tucson, AZ 85710
(520) 296-8255

Christian Family Care Agency
3603 North 7th Avenue
Phoenix, AZ 85013
(602) 234-1935

Commonwealth Adoptions
 International, Inc.
4601 East Ft. Lowell, Suite 200
Tucson, AZ 85712
(520) 327-7574

Dillon Southwest
3014 North Hayden Road,
 Suite 101
Scottsdale, AZ 85251
(480) 945-2221

Family Service Agency
1530 East Flower Street
Phoenix, AZ 85014
(601) 264-9891

Hand in Hand International
 Adoptions
931 East Southern Avenue, Suite
 103
Mesa, AZ 85204
(480) 892-5550

Home Builders for Children, Inc.
3014 North Hayden Road
Scottsdale, AZ 85251
(480) 429-5344

LDS Family Services
5049 East Broadway Boulevard,
 Suite 126
Tucson, AZ 85711
(520) 745-0459

MAPS Arizona
7000 North 16th Street, Suite
 120 #438
Phoenix, AZ 85020
(602) 277-9243

Oasis Adoption Services
4420 West Oasis Drive
Tucson, AZ 85742
(520) 579-5578

ARKANSAS

Adoption Advantage
1014 West 3rd Street
Little Rock, AR 72201
(501) 376-7778

Adoption Services Unit
Department of Children and Family
 Services
PO Box 1437 / Slot S565
Little Rock, AR 72203
(888) 736-2820

Private Agencies

Adoption Services, Inc.
2415 North Tyler
Little Rock, AR 72207
(501) 664-0340

Bethany Christian Services
320 North Rollston Street, Suite
 102-4
Fayetteville, AR 72701
(479) 442-8381

Bethany Christian Services
1100 North University, Suite 66
Little Rock, AR 72207
(501) 664-5729

Children's Home, Inc. Church of
 Christ
1502 East Kiehl Avenue, Suite B
Sherwood, AR 72120
(501) 835-1595

Children's Home, Inc.
 Church of Christ
5515 Old Walcott Road
Paragould, AR 72450
(870) 239-4031

Families Are Special
PO Box 5789

North Little Rock, AR 72119
(501) 758-9184

Integrity, Inc.
6124 North Moor Drive
Little Rock, AR 72204
(501) 614-7200

Searcy Children's Home Church
 of Christ
900 North Main Street
Searcy, AR 72143
(501) 268-5383

CALIFORNIA

Adoption Services Bureau
California Department of Social
 Services
744 P Street, MS 3-31
Sacramento, CA 95814
(916) 651-8089

Private Agencies

A Better Way, Inc.
3200 Adeline Street
Berkeley, CA 94703
(510) 601-0203

AASK (Adopt a Special Kid)
7700 Edgewater Drive, Suite 320
Oakland, CA 94621-3020
(510) 553-1748

ACCEPT (An Adoption and
 Counseling Center)
339 South San Antonio Road,
 Suite 1A
Los Altos, CA 94022
(650) 917-8090

Adopt A Child
2500-2504 West Manchester
 Boulevard

Inglewood, CA 90305
(323) 750-5855

Adopt International
121 Springdale Way
Redwood City, CA 94062
(650) 369-7300

Adopt International
160 Santa Clara Avenue
Oakland, CA 94610
(510) 653-8600

Adoption Network of Catholic
  Charities
San Francisco (211)
98 Bosworth Street, Third Floor
San Francisco, CA 94112-1002
(415) 406-2387

Adoption Options, Inc.
4025 Camino Del Rio South,
  Suite 300
San Diego, CA 92108-4108
(619) 542-7772

Adoption Options, Inc.
5353 Mission Center Road,
  Suite 303
San Diego, CA 92108
(619) 294-7772

Adoptions Unlimited, Inc.
4091 Riverside Drive, Suites 115
  and 116
Chino, CA 91710
(909) 902-1412

African Cradle
2601 Oakdale Rd, Suite C #138
Modesto, CA 95355
(209) 204-1927

Alternative Family Services
  Adoption
25 Division Street, Suite 201

San Francisco, CA 94103
(415) 626-2700

Angels' Haven Outreach
370 West Grand Blvd, Suite 207
Corona, CA 92882
(909) 735-5400

Angels' Haven Outreach
25134 Avenida Rotella
Santa Clarita, CA 91355-3006
(661) 259-2943

Aspira Foster & Family Services
  Adoption Agency
333 Gellery Boulevard, Suite 203
Daly City, CA 94015
(650) 758-0111

Bal Jagat Children's World, Inc.
9311 Farralone Avenue
Chatsworth, CA 91311
(818) 709-4737

Bay Area Adoption Services, Inc.
465 Fairchild Drive, Suite 215
Mountain View, CA 94043
(650) 964-3800

Bethany Christian Services -
  North (208)
3048 Hahn Drive
Modesto, CA 95350-6503
(209) 522-5121

Bethany Christian Services - South
16700 Valley View Avenue,
  Suite 210
La Mirada, CA 90638
(714) 994-0500

Better Life Children Services
1337 Howe Avenue, Suite 107
Sacramento, CA 95825
(916) 641-0661

Children's Bureau
3910 Oakwood Avenue

Los Angeles, CA 90004-3487
(323) 953-7356

East West Adoptions, Inc.
2 Parnassus Road
Berkeley, CA 94708
(510) 644-3996

Ettie Lee Youth and
  Family Services
13139 Ramona Boulevard, #C
Irwindale, CA 91706
(626) 960-8381

Family Connections Adoptions
Main Office
1120 Tully Road
Modesto, CA 95350
(209) 524-8844

The Family Network, Inc.
307 Webster Street
Monterey, CA 93940
(831) 663-5428
(800) 888-0242

Family Solutions
203 North Gold Circle Drive,
  Suite 101
Santa Ana, CA 92705
(714) 835-1333

God's Families International
  Adoption Services
19389 Live Oak Canyon Road
Trabuco Canyon, CA 92679
(714) 858-7621

God's Families International
  Adoption Services
PO Box 320
Trabuco Canyon, CA 92678
(949) 858-7621

Hand In Hand Foundation
200 Helen Court

Santa Cruz, CA 95065
(831) 476-1866

Hannah's Children's Home
1045 West Katella Avenue, #330
Orange, CA 92867-3550
(714) 516-1077

Heartsent Adoptions, Inc.
15 Altarinda Road, Suite 100
Orinda, CA 94563
(925) 254-8883

Holt International Children's
  Services
3807 Pasadena Avenue, Suite 115
Sacramento, CA 95821
(916) 487-4658

Holy Family Services - Counseling
  and Adoption
Pasadena Office
402 South Marengo Avenue
Pasadena, CA 91101-3113
(626) 432-5680

Holy Family Services - Counseling
  and Adoption
San Bernardino Office
1441 North D Street
San Bernardino, CA 92405-4738
(909) 885-4882

Holy Family Services - Counseling
  and Adoption
Santa Ana Office
1403 South Main Street
Santa Ana, CA 92707-1790
(714) 835-5551

Holy Family Services - Counseling
  and Adoption
Thousand Oaks Office
80 East Hillcrest Avenue
Thousand Oaks, CA 91360
(805) 464-2367

Independent Adoption Center
391 Taylor Boulevard, Suite 100
Pleasant Hill, CA 94523
(925) 827-2229

Indian Child and Family Services
1200 Nevada Street, Suite 202
Redlands, CA 92374
(909) 793-1709

Institute for Black Parenting
1299 East Artesia Boulevard,
 Suite 200
Carson, CA 90746
(310) 900-0930

International Christian Adoptions
41745 Rider Way, #2
Temecula, CA 92590
(909) 695-3336

Kern Bridges Adoption Agency
 (272)
1321 Stine Road, Suite 100
Bakersfield, CA 93309-7337
(661) 322–0421
Fax: (661) 322–8448

Kinship Center
595 East Colorado Boulevard,
 #810
Pasadena, CA 91101
(626) 744-9814

Latino Family Institute Inc.
1501 Cameron Avenue, Suite 240
West Covina, CA 91790
(626) 472-0123

Life Adoption Services
440 West Main Street
Tustin, CA 92780
(714) 838-5433

Lilliput Children's Services
130 East Magnolia

Stockton, CA 95202
(209) 943-0530

Nightlight Christian Adoptions
801 East Chapman Avenue,
 Suite 106
Fullerton, CA 92831
(714) 278-1020

North Bay Adoptions
444 10th Street, Third Floor
Santa Rosa, CA 95401-5267
(707) 570-2940

Olive Crest Adoption Services
2130 East Fourth Street,
 Suite 200
Santa Ana, CA 92705
(714) 543-5437

Optimist Adoption Agency
7330 North Fiogueroa Street
Los Angeles, CA 90041
(323) 341-5561

Share Homes
307 East Kettleman Lane
Lodi, CA 95240(209)
334-6376

Sierra Adoption Services
138 New Mohawk Road, Suite 200
Nevada City, CA 95959
(530) 478-0900

St. Patrick's Home for Children
6525 53rd Avenue
Sacramento, CA 95828
(916) 386-1603

The Sycamores Adoption Agency
625 Fair Oaks Avenue, Suite 300
South Pasadena, CA 91030
(626) 395-7100

True to Life Children's Services
1800 North Gravenstein Highway

Sebastopol, CA 95472
(707) 823–7300

Vista Del Mar Child Care Services
3200 Motor Avenue
Los Angeles, CA 89934
(310) 836-1223
(888) 228-4782

Westside Children's Center
12120 Wagner Street
Culver City, CA 90230
(310) 390-0551

Wings of Refuge
5777 West Century Boulevard,
  Suite 900
Los Angeles, CA 90045
(310) 670-6767

COLORADO

Colorado Adoption Services
333 Quebec, Suite 4030
Denver, CO 80207

Friends of Children of Various
  Nations, Inc.
1756 High Street
Denver, CO 80218

CONNECTICUT

Connecticut Department of
  Children and Families
Thomas Dematteo, Director of
  Administrative Law and Policy
505 Hudson Street
Hartford, CT 06106
(860) 550-6306

Private Agencies

Catholic Charities, Catholic Family
  Services Archdiocese of Hartford
467 Bloomfield Avenue

Bloomfield, CT 06002
(860) 242-9577

Catholic Charities, Hartford
  District Office
896 Asylum Avenue
Hartford, CT 06105-1991
(860) 522-8241

Catholic Charities, New Haven
  District Office
478 Orange Street
New Haven, CT 06502
(203) 787-2207

Catholic Charities, Waterbury
  District Office
56 Church Street
Waterbury, CT 06702
(203) 755-1196

Children's Center
1400 Whitney Avenue
Hamden, CT 06514
(203) 248-2116

Community Residences, Inc.
732 West Street, #2
Plainville, CT 06489
(860) 621-7600

Connection, Inc.
955 South Main Street
Middletown, CT 06457
(860) 343-5500

Curtis Home Foundation
380 Crown Street
Meriden, CT 06450
(203) 237-9526

Family Services, Inc.
92 Vine Street
New Britain, CT 06052
(860) 223-9291

Franciscan Family Care Center, Inc.
271 Finch Avenue

Meriden, CT 06450
(203) 237-8084

International Alliance for
  Children, Inc.
2 Ledge Lane
New Milford, CT 06776
(203) 354-3417

Jewish Family Service of New
  Haven
1440 Whalley Avenue
New Haven, CT 06515
(203) 389-5599

Jewish Family Services Infertility
  Center
740 North Main Street
West Hartford, CT 06117
(860) 236-1927

LDS Social Services
34 Jerome Street, Suite 319
PO Box 378
Bloomfield, CT 06004
(800) 735-0149

LDS Social Services
547 Amherst Street, Suite 404
Nashua, NH 03063-4000
(603) 889-0148
(800) 735-0419

Lutheran Social Services of
  New England
(800) 286-9889
http://www.adoptlss.org

New Opportunities for
  Waterbury, Inc.
232 North Elm Street
Waterbury, CT 06702
(203) 575-9799

North American Family Institute
10 Waterchase Drive

Rocky Hill, CT 06067
(860) 529-1522

Rainbow Adoptions
  International, Inc.
80 Garden Street
Wethersfield, CT 06109
(860) 721-0099

St. Francis Home for Children, Inc.
651 Prospect Street, Box 1224
New Haven, CT 06505
(203) 777-5513

Thursday's Child, Inc.
227 Tunxi Avenue
Bloomfield, CT 06002

Waterford Country School
78 Hunts Brook Road
PO Box 408
Quaker Hill, CT 06751
(860) 442-9454

Wellspring Foundation
21 Arch Bridge Road
PO Box 370
Bethlehem, CT 06751
(203) 266-7235

Wheeler Clinic, Inc.
91 Northwest Drive
Plainville, CT 06062
(860) 646-6801

DELAWARE

Department of Services for
  Children, Youth and Their
  Families
1825 Faulkland Road
Wilmington DE 19805
(302) 633-2655

Private Agencies

Catholic Charities
1155 Walker Road
Dover, DE 19904-6539
(302) 674-1600

Catholic Charities
PO Box 2610
Wilmington, DE 19805
(302) 655-9624

Child and Home Study Associates
242 North James Street,
  Suite 202
Wilmington, DE 19804-3168
(302) 475-5433

Children and Families First
2005 Baynard Boulevard
Wilmington, DE 19802
(302) 422-9013

Children's Choice of Delaware, Inc.
1151 Walker Road
Dover, DE 19904-6539
(302) 678-0404

Children's Choice of Delaware, Inc.
University Office Plaza, Bellevue
  Building, Suite 102
Newark, DE 19702
(302) 731-9512

LDS Family Services
500 West Chestnut Hill
Newark, DE 19713
(302) 456-3782

Madison Adoption Agency
1009 Woodstream Drive
Wilmington, DE 19810
(302) 475-8977

Tressler Adoption Services of
  Delaware
http://www.tressler.org

Welcome House, Inc.
910 Barley Drive
Wilmington, DE 19807
(302) 654-7683

DISTRICT OF COLUMBIA

Child and Family Services Agency
400 6th Street
Washington, DC 20024
(202) 727-5300

Private Agencies

Adoption Service Information
  Agency, Inc. (ASIA)
7720 Alaska Avenue NW
Washington, DC 20012

Adoptions Together
419 7th Street, NW, Suite 201
Washington, DC 20004
(202) 628-7420

The American Adoption Agency
1228 M. Street, Second Floor
Washington, DC 20005

Barker Foundation, Inc.
4400 MacArthur Boulevard NW,
  Suite 200
Washington, DC 20818
(202) 363-7511

Catholic Charities Archdiocese of
  Washington D.C.
1438 Rhode Island Avenue NE
Washington, DC 20018
(202) 526-4100

Catholic Charities Archdiocese of
  Washington D.C.
4914 Ayres Place SE
Washington, DC 20019
  (202) 581-3630

Catholic Charities Archdiocese of
  Washington D.C.
The James Cardinal Hickey Center
924 G Street NW
Washington, DC 20001
(202) 772-4327

Children's Adoption Resources
  Exchange
1039 Evarts Street, NE
Washington, DC 20017
(202) 726-7193

Family and Child Services, Inc.
929 L Street NW
Washington, DC 20001
(202) 289-1510

Holy Cross Child Placement
  Agency
1915 Street, Suite 500
Washington, DC 20006

Lutheran Social Services of the
  National Capital Area
4406 Georgia Avenue NW
Washington, DC 20011-7124
(202) 723-3000

Progressive Life Center
1123 11th Street NW
Washington, DC 20001
(202) 842-4570

FLORIDA

Florida Department of Children
  and Families
1317 Winewood Boulevard
Building 1, Room 202
Tallahassee, FL 32399
(850) 487-1111

Private Agencies

A Bond of Love Adoption
  Agency, Inc.
1800 Siesta Drive
Sarasota, FL 34239
(941) 957-0064

Adoption Advisory Associates
1111 East Boca Raton Road
Boca Raton, FL 33432
(561) 362-5222

Adoption Agency of Central Florida
1681 Maitland Avenue
Maitland, FL 32751
(407) 831-2154

Adoption By Choice
St. Andrew's Square
4102 West Linebaugh, Suite 200
Tampa, FL 33624
(813) 960-2229
(800) 421-2229

All About Adoptions, Inc.
505 East New Haven Avenue
Melbourne, FL 32901
(321) 723-0088

Catholic Charities
1111 South Federal Highway,
  Suite 119
Stuart, FL 34995
(561) 283-0541

Catholic Charities
1505 NE 26th Street
Wilton Manors, FL 33305
(954) 630-9404

Catholic Charities
1801 East Memorial Boulevard
Lakeland, FL 33801-2226
(941) 686-7153

Catholic Charities
PO Box 8246
West Palm Beach, FL 33407
(561) 842-2406

Catholic Charities Bureau
134 East Church Street, Suite 2
Jacksonville, FL 32202-3130
(904) 354-3416

Catholic Charities Bureau
225 West King Street
St. Augustine, FL 32095
(904) 829-6300

Catholic Charities Bureau
1717 NE 9th Street
Gainesville, FL 32609
(352) 372-0294

Catholic Charities of the Diocese of
   Venice, Inc.
4930 Fruitville Road
Sarasota, FL 34232-2206
(941) 484-9543

Catholic Charities of Tallahassee
855 West Carolina Street
Tallahassee, FL 32309
(850) 222-2180

Catholic Social Service of Bay
   County
3128 East 11th Street
Panama City, FL 32404
(850) 785-8935

Catholic Social Services
11 First Street SE
Ft. Walton Beach, FL 32548
(850) 244-2825

Catholic Social Services
817 Dixon Boulevard, #16
Cocoa, FL 32922
(407) 636-6144

Catholic Social Services
1771 North Semoran Boulevard
Orlando, FL 32807
(407) 658-1818

Catholic Social Services of
   Pensacola
222 East Government Street
Pensacola, FL 32501
(850) 436-6410

Children's Home, Inc.
10909 Memorial Highway
Tampa, FL 33615
(813) 855-4435

Children's Home Society of Florida
1485 South Semoran Boulevard,
   Suite 1448
Winter Park, FL 32792
(321) 397-3000

Christian Family Services
2720 SW 2nd Avenue
Gainesville, FL 32607
(352) 378-6202

Everyday Blessings
13129 St. Francis Lane
Thonotosassa, FL 33592
(813) 982-9226

Florida Baptist Children's Home
1000 Chemstrand Road
Cantonment, FL 32533-8916
(850) 494-9530

Florida Baptist Children's Home
7748 SW 95th Terrace
Miami, FL 33156
(305) 271-4121

Florida Baptist Children's Home
8415 Buck Lake Road
Tallahassee, FL 32311-9522
(850) 878-1458

Florida Baptist Family Ministries
1015 Sikes Boulevard
Lakeland, FL 33815
(941) 687-8811

Given in Love Adoptions
151 Mary Esther Boulevard,
  Suite 305
Mary Esther, FL 32569
(850) 243-3576

Gorman Family Life Center, Inc.
dba Life for Kids
315 North Wymore Road
Winter Park, FL 32789
(407) 628-5433

Jewish Family & Community
  Services, Inc.
First Coast Adoption Professionals
3601 Cardinal Point Drive
Jacksonville, FL 32257
(904) 448-1933

Jewish Family Services
300 41st Street, Suite 216
Miami Beach, FL 33145
(305) 672-8080

Jewish Family Services, Inc. of
  Broward County
100 South Pine Island Boulevard,
  Suite 130
Plantation, FL 33324
(954) 370-2140

LDS Family Services
10502 Satellite Boulevard, Suite D
Orlando, FL 32837
(407) 850-9141

One World Adoption Services, Inc.
1030 South Federal Highway,
  Suite 100
Hollywood, FL 33019
(954) 922-8400

Shepherd Care Ministries
dba Christian Adoption Services
5935 Taft Street
Hollywood, FL 33021
(954) 981-2060

The Southwest Florida Children's
  Home
4551 Camino Real Way
Fort Myers, FL 33912
(941) 275-7151

St. Vincent Adoption Center
18601 SW 97th Avenue
Miami, FL 33157
(305) 445-5714

Suncoast International
  Adoptions, Inc.
12651 Walsingham Road,
  Suite C
Largo, FL 33774
(727) 596-3135

GEORGIA

Office of Adoptions
Georgia Department of Human
  Resources
Two Peachtree NW, Suite 8-400
Atlanta, GA 30303
  Georgia residents should call:
  (877) 210-5437
  Non-Georgia residents should
  call: (800) 603-1322

Private Agencies

Adoption Services, Inc.
PO Box 155
Pavo, GA 31778
(912) 859-2654

All God's Children, Inc
1120 Athens Road

Winterville, GA 30683
(706) 742-7420

Catholic Social Services, Inc.
680 West Peachtree Street, NW
Atlanta, GA 30308
(404) 881-6571

Children's Services
  International, Inc.
1819 Peachtree Road NE,
  Suite 318
Atlanta, GA 30309

Edgewood Baptist Church, Inc.
New Beginning Adoption and
  Counseling Agency
1316 Wynnton Court, Suite A
Columbus, GA 31906
(706) 571-3346

Georgia Association for Guidance,
  Aid, Placement and Empathy
  (AGAPE), Inc.
3094 Mercer University Drive,
  Suite 200
Atlanta, GA 30341
(404) 452-9995

Georgia Baptist Children's Home
  and Family Ministries North Area
9250 Hutchison Ferry Road
Palmetto, GA 30268
(770) 463-334

Hope for Children, Inc.
1511 Johnson Ferry Road,
  Suite 100
Marietta, GA 30062

Jewish Family Services, Inc.
Cradle of Love Adoption
  Counseling and Services
4549 Chamblee-Dunwoody Road
Atlanta, GA 30338-6210
(770) 955-8550

LDS Family Services
4823 North Royal Atlanta Drive
Tucker, GA 30084
(404) 939-2121

HAWAII

Department of Human Services
Social Service Division, East
  Hawaii
75 Aupuni Street, Suite 112
Hilo, HI 96720
(808) 933-0689

Department of Human Services
Social Service Division, Kauai
3060 Eiwa Street, Room 104
Lihue, HI 96766-1890
(808) 274-3300

Department of Human Services
Social Service Division, Maui
1955 Main Street, Suite 300
Wailuku, HI 96793
(808) 243-5256

Department of Human Services
Social Service Division, Oahu
420 Waiakamilo Road, Suite 300B
Honolulu, HI 96817-4941
(808) 832-5451

Department of Human Services
Social Service Division,
  West Hawaii
Captain Cook State Civic Center
PO Box 230
Captain Cook, HI 96704
(808) 323-4581

Private Agencies

Catholic Services to Families
200 North Vineyard Boulevard,
  Suite 302

Honolulu, HI 96817
(808) 537-6321

Child and Family Services
200 North Vineyard Blvd,
 Building B
Honolulu, HI 96817
(808) 521-2377

Crown Child Placement
 International, Inc.
PO Box 26419
Honolulu, HI 96825-6419
(808) 946-0443

Hawaii International Child
 Placement and Family
 Services, Inc.
1168 Waimanu Street, Suite B
Honolulu, HI 96814
(808) 589-2367

LDS Family Services Hawaii
 Honolulu Agency
1500 South Beretania Street,
 Suite 403
Honolulu, HI 96826
(808) 945-3690

IDAHO

Idaho Department of Health and
 Welfare
450 West State Street
Boise, ID 83720
(208) 334-5500

Private Agencies

Casey Family Program
6441 Emerald
Boise, ID 83704
(208) 377-1771

CASI Foundation For Children
2308 North Cole Road, Suite E

Boise, ID 83704
(208) 376-0558
(800) 376-0558

Idaho Youth Ranch Adoption
 Services
7025 Emerald
PO Box 8538
Boise, ID 83707
(208) 377-2613

LDS Family Services
255 North Overland Avenue
Burley, ID 83318
(208) 678-8200

LDS Family Services
1070 Hiline, Suite 200
Pocatello, ID 83201
(208) 232-7780

LDS Family Services
1420 East 17th, Suite B
Idaho Falls, ID 83404
(208) 529-5276

LDS Family Services
10740 Fairview, Suite 100
Boise, ID 83704
(208) 376-0191

New Hope Child
 and Family Agency
700 West Riverview Drive
Idaho Falls, ID 83401
(208) 523-6930
(800) 574-7705

ILLINOIS

Illinois Department of Children and
 Family Services
100 West Randolph Street 6-200
Chicago, IL 60601

Illinois Department of Children and
Family Services
406 East Monroe
Springfield, IL 62701

Private Agencies

Adoption-Link, Inc.
1145 Westgate, Suite 104
Oak Park, IL 60301
(708) 524-1433

Aurora Catholic Social Services
1700 North Farnsworth Avenue,
  Suite 18
Aurora, IL 60505
(708) 892-4366

Bethany Christian Services
9718 South Halsted Street
Chicago, IL 60628-1007
(773) 233-7600

Catholic Charities, Joliet Diocese
203 North Ottawa Street,
  Second Floor, Suite A
Joliet, IL 60432
(815) 723-3053

Catholic Charities, Springfield
  Diocese
120 South 11th Street
Springfield, IL 62703
(217) 525-0500

Catholic Social Services, Belleville
  Diocese
8601 West Main Street, Suite 201
Belleville, IL 62220
(618) 394-5900

Catholic Social Services, Peoria
  Diocese
413 NE Monroe
Peoria, IL 61603
(309) 671-5720

Catholic Social Services, Rockford
  Diocese
921 West State Street
Rockford, IL 61102
(815) 965-0623

Center for Family Building, Inc.
1740 Ridge Avenue, Suite 208
Evanston, IL 60201
(847) 869-1518

Chicago Child Care Society
5467 South University Avenue
Chicago, IL 60615
(773) 643-0452

Children's Home and Aid Society
  of Illinois
910 Second Street
Rockford, IL 61104
(815) 962-1043

Children's Home and Aid Society
  of Illinois
1819 South Neil, Suite D
Champaign, IL 61820
(217) 359-8815

Cradle Society
2049 Ridge Avenue
Evanston, IL 60201
(847) 475-5800

Evangelical Child and Family
  Agency
1530 North Main Street
Wheaton, IL 60187
(630) 653-6400

Family Resource Center
5828 North Clark Street
Chicago, IL 60660
(773) 334-2300

Family Service Agency of Adams
  County
915 Vermont Street

Quincy, IL 62301
(217) 222-8254

Family Service Center of
  Sangamon County
1308 South Seventh Street
Springfield, IL 62703
(217) 528-8406

Finally Family
161 West Harrison, Suite C-102
Chicago, IL 60605
(312) 939-9399
(800) 917-1199

Glenkirk
2501 North Chestnut
Arlington Heights, IL 60004
(847) 998-8380

Hobby Horse House
PO Box 1102
Jacksonville, IL 62651-1102
(217) 243-7708

Hope for the Children
1530 Fairway Drive
Rantoul, IL 61866
(217) 893-4673

Illinois Baptist Children's Home
4243 Lincolnshire Drive
Mt. Vernon, IL 62864
(618) 242-4944

Illinois Children's Christian Home
PO Box 200
St. Joseph, IL 61873
(217) 469-7566

Jewish Children's Bureau of
  Chicago
1 South Franklin Street
Chicago, IL 60606
(312) 444-2090

Lifelink
Bensenville Home Society

331 South York Road
Bensenville, IL 60106
(630) 521-8262

Lutheran Child and Family
  Services
120 South Marion
Oak Park, IL 60302
(708) 763-0700

Lutheran Child and Family
  Services
431 South Grand Avenue, West
Springfield, IL 62704
(217) 544-4631

Lutheran Child and Family
  Services
800 South 45th Street, Wells
  Bypass
Mt. Vernon, IL 62864
(618) 242-3284

Lutheran Child and Family
  Services
2408 Lebanon Avenue
Belleville, IL 62221
(618) 234-8904

Lutheran Social Services of Illinois
1144 West Lake Street, Third
  Floor
Oak Park, IL 60301
(708) 445-8341

Lutheran Social Services of Illinois
Chicago South Office
11740 South Western Avenue
Chicago, IL 60643
(773) 371-2700

New Life Social Services
6316 North Lincoln Avenue
Chicago, IL 60659
(773) 478-4773

Saint Mary's Services
717 West Kirchoff Road
Arlington Heights, IL 60005
(847) 870-8181

Sunny Ridge Family Center, Inc.
2 South 426 Orchard Road
Wheaton, IL 60187
(630) 668-5117

United Methodist Children's Home
2023 Richview Road
Mt. Vernon, IL 62864
(618) 242-1070, Ext: 239

Uniting Families Foundation
95 West Grand Avenue, Suite 206
PO Box 755
Lake Villa, IL 60046
(847) 356-1452

Volunteers of America of Illinois
224 North Desplaines Street,
  Suite 500
Chicago, IL 60661
(312) 707-9477

Volunteers of America of Illinois
4700 State Street, #2
East St. Louis, IL 62205
(618) 271-9833

INDIANA

Indiana Division of Family
  and Children
Bureau of Family Protection
  and Preservation
402 West Washington Street, Third
  Floor, W-364
Indianapolis, IN 46204
(317) 232-4622
(888) 204-7466

State Adoption Exchange/State
  Photolisting Service
Indiana Adoption Initiative
Indiana Division of Family
  and Children
615 North Alabama Street,
  Room 426
Indianapolis, IN 46201
(317) 264-7793
(888) 252-3678

State Reunion Registry
Indiana Adoption History Registry
Indiana State Department of
  Health, Vital Statistics
2 North Meridian Street,
  Section B-4
Indianapolis, IN 46206-1964

Private Agencies

AD-IN (Adoption of Indiana, Inc.)
1980 East 116th Street,
  Suite 325
Carmel, IN 46032
(317) 574-8950

Adoption Resource Services, Inc.
218 South Third Street, #2
Elkhard, IN 46516
(800) 288-2499

Adoption Services, Inc.
3050 North Meridian Street
Indianapolis, IN 46208
(317) 926-6338

Adoption Support Center
6331 North Carrolton Avenue
Indianapolis, IN 46220
(317) 255-5916
(800) 274-1084

Americans for African
  Adoptions, Inc.
8910 Timberwood Drive

Indianapolis, IN 46234-1952
(317) 271-4567

Baptist Children's Home
354 West Street
Valparaiso, IN 46383
(219) 462-4111

Bethany Christian Services
830 Cedar Parkway
Schererville, IN 46375-1200
(219) 864-0800

Bethany Christian Services
6144 Hillside Avenue, Suite 10
Indianapolis, IN 46220-2474
(317) 254-8479

Catholic Charities
315 East Washington Boulevard
Fort Wayne, IN 46802
(260) 422-5625
(800) 686-7459

Catholic Charities
340 Columbia Street, #105
South Bend, IN 46601
(574) 234-3111
(800) 686-3111

Catholic Charities
973 West Sixth Avenue
Gary, IN 46402
(219) 882-2723

Catholic Charities Bureau
123 NW Fourth Street, Suite 603
Evansville, IN 47708
(812) 423-5456

Catholic Family Services of
  Michigan City
1501 Franklin Street
Michigan City, IN 46360-3709
(219) 879-9312

Center for Family Building, Inc.
8231 Hohman Avenue,
  Suite 200, #3
Munster, IN 46321
(219) 836-0163

Childplace, Inc.
2420 Highway 62
Jeffersonville, IN 47130
(812) 282-8248

Children Are the Future
504 Broadway, Suite 725
Gary, IN 46402
(219) 881-0750

Children's Bureau of Indianapolis
615 North Alabama Street,
  Suite 426
Indianapolis, IN 46204
(317) 264-2700

Coleman Adoption Agency
615 North Alabama Street,
  Suite 319
Indianapolis, IN 46204
(317) 638-0965
(800) 886-3434

Compassionate Care
Wilder Center
Highway 64 West
Route 3, Box 12B
Oakland City, IN 47660
(812) 749-4152
(800) 749-4153

G.L.A.D.
PO Box 9105
Evansville, IN 47724
(812) 424-4523

Independent Adoption Center
537 Turtle Creek Drive South,
  Suite 23
Indianapolis, IN 46227

(317) 788-1039
(800) 877-6736

Jeremiah Agency
3021 Stella Drive
Greenwood, IN 46142-0864
(317) 887-2434

LDS Family Services
Indiana Agency
3333 Founders Road, Suite 200
Indianapolis, IN 46268-1397
(317) 872-1749
(877) 872-1749

Loving Option
206 South Main Street
PO Box 172
Bluffton, IN 46714
(219) 824-9077

Lutheran Child and Family
  Services
1525 North Ritter Avenue
Indianapolis, IN 46219
(317) 359-5467

Lutheran Social Services
PO Box 11329
Fort Wayne, IN 46857-1329
(219) 426-3347

Lutheran Social Services,
  Northwest Regional Office
1400 North Broad Street
Griffith, IN 46319
(219) 838-0996
Fax: (219) 838-0999

Open Arms Christian Homes
Route 2, Box A
Bloomfield, IN 47424
(812) 659-2533

Pathways Child Placement
  Services, Inc.
4109 Sylvan Drive

Floyds Knobs, IN 47119-9603
(502) 459-2320

Specialized Alternatives for
  Families and Youth of America
  (SAFY)
661 West Superior Street,
  Suite 200
Ft. Wayne, IN 46802-1019
(260) 422-3672

St. Elizabeth's
2500 Churchman Avenue
Indianapolis, IN 46203
(317) 787-3412
(800) 499-9113

St. Elizabeth's of Southern Indiana
621 East Market
New Albany, IN 47150
(812) 949-7305

Sunny Ridge Family Center, Inc.
900 Ridge Road, Suite H
Munster, IN 46321
(219) 836-2117

Valley Children's Services
One Professional Center
1801 North Sixth Street,
  Suite 800
Terre Haute, IN 47804
(812) 234-0181

The Villages, Inc.
652 North Girl's School Road,
  Suite 240
Indianapolis, IN 46214-3662
(800) 874-6880

IOWA

Iowa Department of Human
  Services
Adult, Children, and Family
  Services

Hoover State Office Building,
  Fifth Floor
Des Moines, IA 50319
(515) 281-5358

State Reunion Registry
Iowa Mutual Consent Voluntary
  Adoption Registry
Iowa Department of Public Health,
  Bureau of Vital Records
Lucas State Office Building,
  First Floor
321 East 12th Street
Des Moines, IA 50319-0075
(515) 281-4944

Private Agencies

Bethany Christian Services
Cedar Rapids
1642 42nd Street NE
Cedar Rapids, IA 52402-3063
(319) 832-2321
(800) 238-4269

Bethany Christian Services
Des Moines
8525 Douglas Avenue, Suite 34
Des Moines, IA 50322-3300
(515) 270-0824
(800) 238-4269

Bethany Christian Services
Orange City
PO Box 143
Orange City, IA 51041-0143
(712) 737-4831
(800) 238-4269

Bethany Christian Services
Pella
617 Franklin Street, Suite 201
Pella, IA 50219-1522
(641) 628-3247

Catholic Charities of the
  Archdiocese of Dubuque
PO Box 1309
Dubuque, IA 52004-1309
(563) 588-0558
(800) 772-2758

Catholic Charities of Sioux City
1601 Military Road
Sioux City, IA 51103
(712) 252-4547

Children and Families of Iowa
1111 University Avenue
Des Moines, IA 50314
(515) 288-1981

Children's Square U.S.A.
  Child Connect
541 Sixth Avenue, Box 8-C
Council Bluffs, IA 51502-3008
(712) 322-3700

Families of North East Iowa
PO Box 806
Maquoketa, IA 52060
(319) 652-4958

Four Oaks, Inc.
5400 Kirkwood Boulevard
Cedar Rapids, IA 52406-5216
(319) 364-0259

Healing the Children
412 East Church Street
Marshalltown, IA 50158
(515) 753-7544

Hillcrest Family Services
4080 1st Avenue NE
Cedar Rapids, IA 52402
(319) 362-3149

Keys to Living
463 Northland Avenue
Cedar Rapids, IA 52402-6237

Lutheran Family Service
230 Ninth Avenue, North
Fort Dodge, IA 50501
(515) 573-3138

Lutheran Social Service of Iowa
3116 University Avenue
Des Moines, IA 50311
(515) 277-4476

Ralston Adoption Agency
2208 South Fifth Avenue
Marshalltown, IA 50158-4515
(800) 304-0219

Tanager Place
2309 C Street, SW
Cedar Rapids, IA 52601
(319) 365-9164

Young House, Inc.
PO Box 845
Burlington, IA 52601
(319) 752-4000

KANSAS

Kansas Department of Social and
  Rehabilitation Services
Children and Family Policy Division
915 SW Harrison, Fifth Floor
Topeka, KS 66612
(785) 296-0918

Private Agencies

A.C.T. (Adoption, Consultation and
  Training Services, Inc)
4717 McCormick Court
Lawrence, KS 66047
(913) 727-2288

Adoption of Babies and Children,
  Inc. (ABC Adoption)
9230 Pflumm
Lenexa, KS 66215

(913) 894-2223
(800) 406-2909

Adoption and Beyond, Inc.
10680 Barkley, Suite 230
Overland Park, KS 66323
(913) 381-6919

Adoption Centre of Kansas, Inc.
1831 Woodrow Avenue
Wichita, KS 67203
(316) 265-5289
(800) 804-3632

Adoption Option
7211 West 98th Terrace, #100
Overland Park, KS 66212
(913) 642-7900

American Adoptions
8676 West 96th Street, Suite 140
Overland Park, KS 66212
(913) 383-9804

Catholic Charities, Diocese of
  Dodge City
2546 20th Street
Great Bend, KS 67530
(316) 792-1393

Catholic Charities, Diocese of
  Salina
PO Box 1366
Salina, KS 67401
(785) 825-0208
(888) 468-6909

Catholic Community Services
2220 Central Avenue
Kansas City, KS 66102
(913) 621-1504

Catholic Social Service
425 North Topeka
Wichita, KS 67202
(316) 264-8344

Christian Family Services of the
Midwest, Inc.
10550 Barkley, Suite 100
Overland Park, KS 66212
(913) 383-3337

Family Life Services of
Southern Kansas
305 South Summit
Arkansas City, KS 67005-2848
(316) 442-1688

Heart of America Adoption Center
108 East Poplar
Olathe, KS 66061
(913) 342-1110

Kansas Children's Service League
Kansas City - Black Adoption
Program & Services
630 Minnesota Street, Suite 210
Box 17-1273
Kansas City, KS 66117
(913) 621-2016

Kansas Children's Service League
Manhattan
217 Southwind Place
Manhattan, KS 66503
(785) 539-3193

Kansas Children's Service League
Wichita
1365 North Custer
PO Box 517
Wichita, KS 67201
(316) 942-4261

Kaw Valley Center
4300 Brenner Road
Kansas City, KS 66104
(913) 334-0294

Lutheran Social Services
1855 North Hillside
Wichita, KS 67214-2399
(316) 686-6645

Lutheran Social Services of Kansas
2942 SW Wanamaker Drive,
Building B, Suite 1C
Topeka, KS 66614
(785) 272-7883
(800) 210-5387

Sunflower Family Services
1503 Vine Street, Suite E
Hays, KS 67601
(913) 625-4600
(800) 555-4614

The Villages, Inc.
2209 SW 29th Street
Topeka, KS 66611
(785) 267–5900

KENTUCKY

Commonwealth of Kentucky
Cabinet for Families & Children
275 East Main Street, 3CE
Franford, KY 40621
(502) 564-2147

State Reunion Registry
Program Specialist
Department for Social Services
275 East Main Street,
Sixth Floor, West
Frankfort, KY 40621
(502) 564-2147

Private Agencies

Adopt! Inc.
135 Lackawana Road
Lexington, KY 40503
(859) 276-6249

Adoptions of Kentucky
One Riverfront Plaza, Suite 1708
Louisville, KY 40202
(502) 585-3005

Bluegrass Christian Adoption
  Services
1517 Nicholasville Road,
  Suite 405
Lexington, KY 40503
(859) 276-2222

Catholic Social Service Bureau
1310 Leestown Road
Lexington, KY 40508
(859) 253-1993

Catholic Social Services of
  Northern Kentucky
3629 Church Street
Covington, KY 41015
(859) 781-8974

Children's Home of Northern
  Kentucky
200 Home Road
Covington, KY 41011
(859) 261-8768

Chosen Children Adoption
  Services, Inc.
5427 Bardstown Road, Suite One
Louisville, KY 40291
(502) 231-1336

A Helping Hand Adoption Agency
501 Darby Creek Road, Suite 17
Lexington, KY 40509
(859) 263-9964
(800) 525-0871

Holston United Methodist Home
  for Children
503 Maple Street
Murray, KY 42071
(270) 759-5007

Home of the Innocents
10936 Dixie Highway
Louisville, KY 40272
(502) 995-4402

Hope Hill Children's Home
10230 Hope Means Road
Hope, KY 40334
(859) 498-5230

Jewish Family and Vocational
  Service
3587 Dutchman's Lane
Louisville, KY 40205
(502) 452-6341

Kentucky Baptist Homes for
  Children
10801 Shelbyville Road
Louisville, KY 40243
(502) 568-9117
(800) 928-5242

Kentucky One Church One Child
  Adoption Agency
170 West Chestnut Street
Louisville, KY 40203
(502) 561-6827
(800) 248-8671

Kentucky United Methodist Homes
  for Children or Youth
Mary Kendall Campus
193 Phillips Court
Owensboro, KY 42303
(270) 683-3723
(877) 887-4481

LDS Social Services
1000 Hurstbourne Lane
Louisville, KY 40224
(502) 429-0077

Shoemakers Christian Homes for
  Children and Adolescents
1939 Goldsmith Lane, Suite 136
Louisville, KY 40218
(502) 485-0722

Specialized Alternatives for
  Families and Youth of America
3150 Custer Drive, Suite 103

Lexington, KY 40517
(859) 971-2585

St. Joseph's Children's Home
2823 Frankfort Avenue
Louisville, KY 40206
(502) 893-0241

The Villages
109 North Main Street
Henderson, KY 42420
(502) 827-9090

LOUISIANA

Louisiana Department of Social
  Services
Office of Community Services
5700 Florida Boulevard, Eighth
  Floor
PO Box 3318
Baton Rouge, LA 70821
(225) 216-6925

Private Agencies

Acorn Adoption, Inc.
3350 Ridgelake Drive, Suite 259
Metairie, LA 70002
(504) 838-0080
(888) 221-1370

Beacon House Adoption
  Services, Inc
15254 Old Hammond Highway,
  Suite C-2
Baton Rouge, LA 70816
(225) 272-3221
(888) 987-6300

Catholic Charities Archdiocese of
  New Orleans
1000 Howard Avenue, Suite 1200
New Orleans, LA 70113-1916
(504) 523-3755

Catholic Social Services of
  Houma - Thibodaux
PO Box 3894
Houma, LA 70361
(985) 876-0490

Catholic Social Services of
  Lafayette
1408 Carmel Avenue
Lafayette, LA 70501
(337) 261-5654
(800) 256-7222

Children's Bureau of New Orleans
210 Baronne Street, Suite 722
New Orleans, LA 70112
(504) 525-2366

Holy Cross Child Placement
  Agency, Inc.
910 Pierremont Road, Suite 356
Shreveport, LA 71106
(318) 865-3199

Jewish Family Service of Greater
  New Orleans
3330 West Esplanade Avenue S.,
  Suite 600
Metairie, LA 70002-3454
(504) 831-8475

LDS Social Services
2000 Old Spanish Trail, Pratt
  Center, Suite 115
Slidell, LA 70458
(504) 649-2774

Louisiana Baptist Children's Home
PO Box 4196
Monroe, LA 71211
(318) 343-2244

Mercy Ministries of America
804 Spell Street
PO Box 3028
West Monroe, LA 71210
(318) 388-2040

St. Elizabeth Foundation
8054 Summa Avenue, Suite A
Baton Rouge, LA 70809
(225) 769-8888

St. Gerard's Adoption Network, Inc.
PO Drawer 1260
Eunice, LA 70535
(318) 457-1111

Sunnybrook Children's Home, Inc.
2101 Forsythe Avenue
Monroe, LA 71201
(318) 329-8161

Volunteers of America
Greater Baton Rouge, Inc.
340 Kirby Street
Lake Charles, LA 70601
(318) 497-0034

Volunteers of America
Maternity/Adoption Services
3939 North Causeway Boulevard,
  Suite 203
Metairie, LA 70002
(504) 835-3005

Volunteers of America of North
  Louisiana
360 Jordan Street
Shreveport, LA 71101
(318) 221-2669

Volunteers of America of North
  Louisiana
3728 South MacArthur Drive
Alexandria, LA 71312
(318) 442-8026

MAINE

Maine Department of
  Human Services
Bureau of Child and Family
  Services

221 State Street, State House
  Station #111
Augusta, ME 04333-0011
(207) 287-5062

Maine Department of
  Human Services
Calais District Office
88A South Street
Calais, ME 04619
(207) 454-9000
(800) 622-1400

Maine Department of
  Human Services
Caribou District Office
14 Access Highway
Caribou, ME 04736
(207) 493-4050
(800) 432-7366

Maine Department of
  Human Services
Ellsworth District Office
17 Eastward Lane
Ellsworth, ME 04605
(207) 667-1656
(800) 432-7823

Maine Department of
  Human Services
Farmington District Office
114 Corn Shop Lane
Farmington, ME 04938
(207) 778-8440
(800) 442-6382

Maine Department of
  Human Services
Fort Kent District Office
92 Market Street
Fort Kent, ME 04743
(207) 834-7770
(800) 432-7340

Maine Department of
 Human Services
Houlton District Office
11 High Street
Houlton, ME 04730
(207) 532-5055
(800) 432-7338

Private Agencies

C.A.R.E. Development
PO Box 2356
Bangor, ME 04401
(207) 945-4240

Good Samaritan Agency
100 Ridgewood Drive
Bangor, ME 04401
(207) 942-7211

International Adoption Services
 Centre
432 Water Street
PO Box 56
Gardiner, ME 04345
(207) 582-8842

Maine Adoption Placement Service
 (MAPS)
306 Congress Street
Portland, ME 04101
(207) 772-3678

Maine Adoption Placement Service
 (MAPS)
Bangor Office
181 State Street
Bangor, ME 04401
(207) 941-9500

Maine Adoption Placement Service
 (MAPS)
International Office
277 Congress Street
Portland, ME 04101
(207) 775-4101

Maine Adoption Placement Service
 (MAPS)
Main Office
58 Pleasant Street
Houlton, ME 04730
(207) 532-9358

Maine Children's Home for Little
 Wanderers
11 Mulliken Court
Augusta, ME 04330
(207) 622-1552

Maine Children's Home for Little
 Wanderers
93 Silver Street
Waterville, ME 04901
(207) 872-0261

SMART
PO Box 547
Windham, ME 04062
(207) 893-0386

St. Andre Home, Inc.
283 Elm Street
Biddeford, ME 04005
(207) 282-3351

MARYLAND

Maryland Department of Human
 Resources
Social Services Administration
311 West Saratoga Street
Baltimore, MD 21201
(410) 767-7506

Private Agencies

Adoption Resource Center, Inc.
6630 Baltimore National Pike,
 Suite 205-A
Baltimore, MD 21228
(410) 744-6393

Adoption Service Information
  Agency, Inc. (ASIA)
7720 Alaska Avenue NW
Washington, DC 20012
(202) 726-7193

Adoption Service Information
  Agency, Inc. (ASIA)
8555 16th Street, Suite 600
Silver Spring, MD 20910
(301) 587-7068

Adoptions Forever
5830 Hubbard Drive
Rockville, MD 20852
(301) 468-1818

Adoptions Together Inc.
5750 Executive Drive, Suite 107
Baltimore, MD 21228
(410) 869-0620

Adoptions Together Inc.
10230 New Hampshire Avenue,
  Suite 200
Silver Spring, MD 20903
(301) 439-2900

America World Adoption
  Association
6723 Whittier Avenue, Suite 406
McLean, VA 22101
(703) 356-8447
(800) 429-3369

Associated Catholic Charities
Archdiocese of Baltimore
1 East Mt. Royal Avenue
Baltimore, MD 21202
(410) 659-4031

The Barker Foundation
7945 MacArthur Boulevard,
  Room 206
Cabin John, MD 20818
(301) 229-8300
(800) 673-8489

Bethany Christian Services
2130 Priest Bridge Drive, Suite 9
Crofton, MD 21114-2466
(410) 721-2835

Board of Child Care
3300 Gaither Road
Baltimore, MD 21244
(410) 922-2100

Catholic Charities Archdiocese
  of Washington DC
1438 Rhode Island Avenue NE
Washington, DC 20018
(202) 526-4100

Catholic Charities, Inc.
Delaware Diocese
1405 Wesley Drive
Salisbury, MD 21801
(410) 749-1121

Cradle of Hope Adoption
  Center, Inc.
8630 Fenton Street, Suite 310
Silver Spring, MD 20910
(301) 587-4400

Creative Adoptions, Inc.
10750 Hickory Ridge Road,
  Suite 108
Columbia, MD 21044
(301) 596-1521

Datz Foundation
16220 Frederick Road
Gaithersburg, MD 20877
(301) 258-0629

Family Building Center
409 Washington Avenue,
  Suite 920
Towson, MD 21204-4903
(410) 494-8112

Family and Child Services of
  Washington, DC, Inc.
5301 76th Avenue
Landover Hills, MD 20784
(301) 459-4121, Ext: 334

Family and Children's Society
204 West Lanvale Street
Baltimore, MD 21217
(410) 669-9000

Holy Cross Child Placement
  Agency, Inc.
St. John's Episcopal Church
6701 Wisconsin Avenue
Chevy Chase, MD 20815
(301) 907-6887

International Children's Alliance
7029 River Oak Court
Clarksville, MD 21029
(443) 535-9020

International Children's Alliance
8807 Colesville Road, Third Floor
Silver Spring, MD 20910
(301) 495-9710

International Families, Inc.
613 Hawkesburg Lane
Silver Spring, MD 20904
(301) 622-2406

International Social Service
American Branch, Inc.
700 Light Street
Baltimore, MD 21230-3850
(410) 230-2734

Jewish Family Services
6 Park Center Court, Suite 211
Owings Mills, MD 21117
(410) 466-9200

Jewish Social Services Agency of
  Metropolitan Washington
6123 Montrose Road

Rockville, MD 20852-4880
(301) 881-3700

The Kennedy Krieger Institute
2901 East Biddle Street
Baltimore, MD 21213
(410) 502-9533

Lutheran Social Services of the
  National Capital Area
4406 Georgia Avenue NW
Washington, DC 20011-7124
(202) 723-3000

Lutheran Social Services of the
  National Capital Area
7410 New Hampshire Avenue
Takoma Park, MD 20912
(301) 434-0080

New Family Foundation
5537 Twin Knolls Road, Suite 440
Columbia, MD 21045
(410) 715-4828

Rainbow Christian Services
6000 Davis Boulevard
Camp Springs, MD 20746
(301) 899-3200

Tressler Adoption Services of
  Maryland
2200 Broening Highway,
  Suite 110
Baltimore, MD 21224
(410) 633-6900

World Child International
207 Brooks Avenue
Gaithersburg, MD 20877
(301) 977-8339

World Child International
9300 Colombia Boulevard
Silver Spring, MD 20910
(301) 588-3000

MASSACHUSETTS

Massachusetts Department
of Social Services
24 Farnsworth Street
Boston, MA 02210
(617) 748-2267
(800) 543-7508

Private Agencies

Act of Love Adoptions
734 Massachusetts Avenue
Boston, MA 02476
(800) 277-5387

Adoption Resource Center at
Brightside
2112 Riverdale Street
West Springfield, MA 01089
(413) 827-4315

Adoption Resources
1340 Centre Street
Newton Centre, MA 02159
(617) 332-2218

Adoptions With Love, Inc.
188 Needham Street, Suite 250
Newton, MA 02164
(617) 965-2496
(800) 722-7731

Alliance for Children, Inc.
55 William Street, Suite G10
Wellesley, MA 02481-3902
(781) 431-7148

American-International Children's
Alliance (AICA)
PO Box 858
Marblehead, MA 01945
(866) 862-3678

Angel Adoptions, Inc.
11 Dix Street

Waltham, MA 02453
(781) 899-9222

Beacon Adoption Center, Inc.
66 Lake Buel Road
Great Barrington, MA 01230
(413) 528-2749

Berkshire Center for Families
and Children
480 West Street
Pittsfield, MA 01201
(413) 448-8281

Bethany Christian Services
1538 Turnpike Street
North Andover, MA 01845-6221
(978) 794-9800
(800) 941-4865

Boston Adoption Bureau, Inc.
14 Beacon Street, Suite 620
Boston, MA 02108
(617) 277-1336
(800) 338-2224

Bright Futures Adoption
Center, Inc.
5 Broadview Street
Acton, MA 01720
(978) 263-5400
(877) 652-6678

Cambridge Family and
Children's Services
929 Massachusetts Avenue
Cambridge, MA 02139
(617) 876-4210
(800) 906-4163

Catholic Charities of
Cambridge and Somerville
270 Washington Street
Somerville, MA 02143
(617) 625-1920

Catholic Charities Center of the
Old Colony Area
686 North Main Street
Brockton, MA 02301
(508) 587-0815

Catholic Charities of the Diocese
of Worcester
10 Hammond Street
Worcester, MA 01610-1513
(508) 798-0191

Catholic Charities of the Diocese
of Worcester, Inc.
53 Highland Avenue
Fitchburg, MA 01420
(978) 343-4879

Catholic Social Services of Fall
River, Inc.
783 Slade Street
Fall River, MA 02720
(508) 674-4681

Children's Aid and Family Services
of Hampshire County, Inc.
8 Trumbull Road
Northampton, MA 01060
(413) 584-5690

Children's Friend
21 Cedar Street
Worcester, MA 01609
(508) 753-5425

Children's Services of Roxbury, Inc.
504 Dudley Street
Roxbury, MA 02119
(617) 542-2366

China Adoption With Love, Inc
251 Harvard Street, Suite 17
Brookline, MA 02446
(800) 888-9812

Concord Family Service
Society, Inc.
111 Old Road to Nine Acre Corner,
Suite 2002
Concord, MA 01742-4174
(978) 369-4909

DARE Family Services
2 Electronics Avenue, Suite 7
Danvers, MA 01923
(978) 750-0751

DARE Family Services
17 Poplar Street
Roslindale, MA 02131
(617) 469-2311

Family and Children's Services
of Catholic Charities
53 Highland Avenue
Fitchburg, MA 01420
(978) 343-4879

Florence Crittenton League
119 Hall Street
Lowell, MA 01854-9671
(978) 452-9671

Full Circle Adoptions
39 Main Street
Northampton, MA 01060
(413) 587-0007
(888) 452-3678

Gift of Life Adoption Services, Inc.
1087 Newman Avenue
Seekonk, MA 02771
(508) 761-5661

Hope Adoptions, Inc.
21 Cedar Street
Worcester, MA 01609
(508) 753-5425

The Home for Little Wanderers
271 Huntington Avenue

Boston, MA 02115
(617) 267-3700

Interfaith Social Services
776 Hancock Street
Quincy, MA 02170
(617) 773-6203

Jewish Family and Children's
  Services Adoption Resources
1340 Centre Street
Newton, MA 02159
(617) 332-2218

Jewish Family Services of Greater
  Springfield, Inc.
15 Lenox Street
Springfield, MA 01108
(413) 737-2601

Jewish Family Services of
  Metrowest
475 Franklin Street, Suite 101
Framingham, MA 01702
(508) 875-3100

Jewish Family Services of
  Worcester
646 Salisbury Street
Worcester, MA 01609
(508) 755-3101

Love the Children of
  Massachusetts
2 Perry Drive
Duxbury, MA 02332
(781) 934-0063

Lutheran Social Services of New
  England
74 Elm Street, Second Floor
Worcester, MA 01609-2833
(508) 791-4488
(800) 286-9889

Maine Adoption Placement Service
  (MAPS)
Boston - International Office

400 Commonwealth Avenue
Boston, MA 02115
(617) 267-2222

Merrimack Valley Catholic Charities
439 South Union Street,
  Suite 4210
Lawrence, MA 01843
(978) 452-1421

New Bedford Child and Family
  Services
1061 Pleasant Street
New Bedford, MA 02740
(508) 996-8572

A Red Thread Adoption Services
681 Washington Street, Suite 12
Norwood, MA 02062
(781) 762-2428
(888) 871-9699

Special Adoption Family Services
A Program of Communities for
  People
418 Commonwealth Avenue
Boston, MA 02215-2801
(617) 572-3678

United Homes for Children
90 Cushing Avenue
Dorchester, MA 02125
(617) 825-3300

United Homes for Children
1147 Main Street, Suite 209-210
Tewksbury, MA 01876
(978) 640-0089
Fax: (978) 640-9652

Wide Horizons For Children
Main Office
38 Edge Hill Road
Waltham, MA 02451
(781) 894-5330

MICHIGAN

Michigan Family Independence
  Agency
Child and Family Services
  Administration
PO Box 30037
Lansing, MI 48909
(517) 373-3513

Private Agencies

Adoptees Help Adopt International
  5955 North Wayne Road
Westland, MI 48185
(734) 467-6222

Adoption Associates, Inc.
1338 Baldwin Street
Jenison, MI 49428
(616) 667-0677

Adoption Associates, Inc.
3609 Country Club Drive
St. Clair Shores, MI 48082-2952
(810) 294-1990

Adoption Associates, Inc.
13535 State Road
Grand Ledge, MI 48837-9626
(517) 627-0805

Adoptions of the Heart
4295 Summerwind Avenue, NE
Grand Rapids, MI 49525
(616) 365-3166

Alliance for Adoption
Jewish Family Service
24123 Greenfield Road
Southfield, MI 48075
(248) 559-0117

Alternatives for Children
  and Families
PO Box 3038

Flint, MI 48502
(810) 235-0683

Americans for International Aid
  and Adoption
2151 Livernois, Suite 200
Troy, MI 48083
(248) 362-1207

Anishnabek Community Family
  Services
2864 Ashmun Street
Sault Ste. Marie, MI 49783
(906) 632-5250

Bethany Christian Services
901 Eastern Avenue NE
PO Box 294
Grand Rapids, MI 49501-0294
(616) 224-7617
(800) 652-7082

Bethany Christian Services
919 East Michigan Avenue
PO Box 155
Paw Paw, MI 49079-0155
(616) 657-7096

Bethany Christian Services
1435 East 12-Mile Road
Madison Heights, MI 48071-2653
(248) 414-4080

Bethany Christian Services
2041 30th Street
Allegan, MI 49010-9514
(616) 686-0157

Bethany Christian Services
5030 North Wind Drive,
  Suite 108 E
East Lansing, MI 48823
(517) 336-0191

Bethany Christian Services
5985 West Main Street, Suite 104
Kalamazoo, MI 49009-8708
(616) 372-8800

Bethany Christian Services
6995 West 48th Street
PO Box 173
Fremont, MI 49412-0173
(231) 924-3390

Bethany Christian Services
12048 James Street
Holland, MI 49424-9556
(616) 396-0623

Binogii Placement Agency
2864 Ashmun Street, Third Floor
Sault Ste. Marie, MI 49783
(906) 632-5250

Catholic Family Services
1819 Gull Road
Kalamazoo, MI 49001
(616) 381-9800

Catholic Family Services of the
  Diocese of Saginaw
220 West Main
Midland, MI 48640
(517) 631-4711

Catholic Family Services of the
  Diocese of Saginaw
710 North Michigan Avenue
Saginaw, MI 48602
(517) 753-8446

Catholic Family Services of the
  Diocese of Saginaw
915 Columbus Avenue
Bay City, MI 48708
(517) 892-2504

Catholic Human Services
111 South Michigan Avenue
Gaylord, MI 49735
(517) 732-6761

Catholic Human Services
154 South Ripley Boulevard

Alpena, MI 49707
(517) 356-6385

Catholic Human Services
1000 Hastings Street
Traverse City, MI 49686
(231) 947-8110

Catholic Social Services of Flint
901 Chippewa Street
Flint, MI 48503
(810) 232-9950

Catholic Social Services of
  Kent County
1152 Scribner NW
Grand Rapids, MI 49504
(616) 456-1443

Catholic Social Services of
  Macomb County
15980 Nineteen Mile Road
Clinton Township, MI 48038
(810) 416-2311
(888) 422-2938

Catholic Social Services of
  Marquette, Upper Peninsula
347 Rock Street
Marquette, MI 49855
(906) 228-8630

Catholic Social Services of
  Monroe County
16 East Fifth Street
Monroe, MI 48161
(734) 242-3800

Catholic Social Services of
  Monroe County
8330 Lewis Avenue
Temperance, MI 48182
(734) 847-1523

Catholic Social Services of
  Muskegon
1095 Third Street, Suite 125

Muskegon, MI 49441
(231) 726-4735

Catholic Social Services of Oakland
  County
50 Wayne Street
Pontiac, MI 48342
(248) 333-3700

Catholic Social Services of St. Clair
2601 13th Street
Port Huron, MI 48060
(810) 987-9100

Catholic Social Services of Upper
  Michigan
500 South Stephenson Avenue,
  Suite 400
Iron Mountain, MI 49801
(906) 774-3323

Catholic Social Services of
  Washtenaw County
4925 Packard Road
Ann Arbor, MI 48108-1521
  (734) 971-9781

Catholic Social Services of Wayne
  County
9851 Hamilton Avenue
Detroit, MI 48202
(313) 883-2100

Catholic Social Services, St.
  Vincent Home
2800 West Willow Street
Lansing, MI 48917
(517) 323-4734

Child and Family Services
1352 Terrane Street
Muskeyon, MI 49442
(616) 726-3582

Child and Family Services of
  Michigan
2806 Davenport

Saginaw, MI 48602-3734
(517) 790-7500

Child and Parent Services
30600 Telegraph Road, Suite
  2215
Bingham Farms, MI 48025
(248) 646-7790
(800) 248-0106

Children's Center of Wayne County
100 West Alexandrine
Detroit, MI 48201
(313) 831-5520

Children's Hope Adoption Services
7823 South Whiteville Road
Shepherd, MI 48883
(517) 828-5842

Christ Child House
15751 Joy Road
Detroit, MI 48228
(313) 584-6077
Fax: (313) 584-1148

Christian Care Maternity Ministries
Baptist Children's Home
214 North Mill Street
St. Louis, MI 48880
(517) 681-2172

Christian Cradle
535 North Clippert, Suite 2
Lansing, MI 48912
(517) 351-7500

Christian Family Services
17105 West 12 Mile Road
Southfield, MI 48076
(248) 557-8390

Eagle Village Family Living
  Program
4507 170th Avenue
Hersey, MI 49639

(231) 832-2234
(800) 748-0061

Ennis Center for Children
91 South Telegraph Road
Pontiac, MI 48341
(248) 333-2520

Ennis Center for Children
129 East Third Street
Flint, MI 48502
(810) 233-4031

Ennis Center for Children
2051 Rosa Parks Boulevard
Detroit, MI 48216
(313) 963-7400

Ennis Center for Children
20100 Greenfield Road
Detroit, MI 48235
(313) 342-2699

Evergreen Children's Services
10421 West Seven Mile Road
Detroit, MI 48221
(313) 862-1000

Family MatchMakers
2544 Martin, SE
Grand Rapids, MI 49507
(616) 243-1803

Forever Families Inc.
42705 Grand River Avenue,
 Suite 201
Novi, MI 48375
(248) 344-9606

Hands Across the Water
2890 Carpenter Street, Suite 600
Ann Arbor, MI 48108
(734) 477-0135

HelpSource
201 North Wayne Road
Westland, MI 48185-3689
(734) 422-5401

Homes for Black Children
511 East Larned Street
Detroit, MI 48226
(313) 961-4777

Interact Family Services
1260 Woodkrest Drive
Flint, MI 48532

International Adoption Association
517 Baldwin Avenue
Jenison, MI 49428
(616) 457-6537
(888) 546-4046

Keane Center for Adoption
930 Mason
Dearborn, MI 48124
(313) 277-4664

LDS Social Services
37634 Enterprise Court
Farmington Hills, MI 48331
(248) 553-0902

Lula Belle Stewart Center
11000 West McNichols, Suite 116
Detroit, MI 48221
(313) 862-4600

Lutheran Adoption Service
21700 Northwestern Highway,
 Suite 1490
Southfield, MI 48075-4901
(248) 423-2770

Lutheran Adoption Service
Bay City Branch
6019 West Side
Bay City, MI 48706
(517) 686-3170

Lutheran Adoption Service
Grandville Branch
2976 Ivanrest, Suite 140
Grandville, MI 49418-1440
(616) 532-8286

Lutheran Adoption Service
Lansing Branch
801 South Waverly, Suite 103
Lansing, MI 48917
(517) 886-1380

Lutheran Social Service of
  Wisconsin and Upper Michigan
1009 West Ridge Street, Suite A
Marquette, MI 49855
(906) 226-7410

Methodist Children's Home Society
26645 West 6 Mile Road
Detroit, MI 48240
(313) 531-3140
Fax: (313) 531-1040

Michigan Indian Child
  Welfare Agency
405 East Easterday Avenue
Sault Ste. Marie, MI 49783
(906) 632-8062
(800) 562-4957

Michigan Indian Child Welfare
  Agency
1345 Monroe Avenue NW,
  Suite 220
Grand Rapids, MI 49505
(616) 454-9221

Michigan Indian Child Welfare
  Agency
6425 South Pennsylvania Avenue,
  Suite 3
Lansing, MI 48911
(517) 393-3256

Michigan Indian Child
  Welfare Agency
Baraga Office Tribal Center
Route #1
Baraga, MI 49908
(906) 353-6178

Michigan Indian Child
  Welfare Agency
Hannaville Office Tribal Center
N14911 B1 Road
Wilson, MI 49896
(906) 466-9221

Morning Star Adoption
  Resource, Inc.
3311 West Twelve Mile
Berkley, MI 48072
(248) 399-2740

Oakland Family Services
114 Orchard Lake Road
Pontiac, MI 48341
(248) 858-7766

Orchards Children's Services
30215 Southfield Road
Southfield, MI 48076
(248) 258-0440

Orchards Children's Services
42140 Van Dyke Road, Suite 206
Sterling Heights, MI 48314
(810) 997-3886

Sault Tribe Binogii
  Placement Agency
2864 Ashmun Street
Sault Ste. Marie, MI 49783
(906) 632-5250

Spaulding for Children
16250 Northland Drive, Suite 120
Southfield, MI 48075
(248) 443-7080

Spectrum Human Services
23077 Greenfield Road, Suite 500
Southfield, MI 48075
(248) 552-8020

Spectrum Human Services
28303 Joy Road

Westland, MI 48185
(734) 458-8736

Starfish Family Services
30000 Hivley Road
Inkster, MI 48141-1089
(734) 728-3400

St. Francis Family Services
17500 West 8 Mile Road
Southfield, MI 48075
(248) 552-0750

St. Vincent-Sarah Fisher Center
27400 West 12 Mile Road
Farmington Hills, MI 48334
(248) 626-7527

Teen Ranch Family Services
15565 Northland Drive,
  Suite 300, East
Southfield, MI 48075
(248) 443-2900

Whaley Children's Center
1201 North Grand Traverse
Flint, MI 48503
(810) 234-3603

MINNESOTA

Minnesota Department of
  Human Services
Children's Services
Human Services Building
444 Lafayette Road North
St. Paul, MN 55155-3831
(651) 296-3740

Private Agencies

Adoption Miracle
  International, Inc.
19108 Kingswood Terrace
Minnetonka, MN 55345
(952) 470-6141

Bethany Christian Services
3025 Harbor Lane, Suite 223
Plymouth, MN 55447-5138
(612) 553-0344

Caritas Family Services
305 Seventh Avenue North
St. Cloud, MN 56303
(320) 252-4121

Catholic Charities of the
  Archdiocese of Winona
111 Market Street
PO Box 3
Winona, MN 55987-0374
(507) 454-2270

Catholic Charities
Seton Services
1276 University Avenue
St. Paul, MN 55104-4101
(651) 603-0225

Child Link International
6508 Stevens Avenue S
Richfield, MN 55423
(612) 861-9048

Children's Home Society
  of Minnesota
1605 Eustis Street
St. Paul, MN 55108-1219
(651) 646-7771
(800) 952-9302

Chosen Ones Adoption Agency
1622 East Sandhurst Drive
Maplewood, MN 55109
(651) 770-5508

Christian Family Life Services
203 South 8th Street
Fargo, ND 58103
(701) 237-4473

Crossroads Adoption Services
4620 West 77th Street, Suite 105

Minneapolis, MN 55435
(612) 831-5707

Downey Side
400 Sibley Street, Suite 20
St. Paul, MN 55101
(651) 228-0117

Downey Side
606 25th Avenue South, #103
St. Cloud, MN 56301
(320) 240-1433

European Children's Adoption
  Services
6050 Cheshire Lane North
Plymouth, MN 55446
(763) 694-6131

Family Alternatives
416 East Hennepin Avenue
Minneapolis, MN 55414
(612) 379-5341

Family Resources
2903 Euclid Avenue
Anoka, MN 55303
(763) 323-8050

Hand in Hand International
  Adoptions
1076 Charles Avenue
St. Paul, MN 55104
(651) 917-0384

Holy Family Adoption Agency
525 Thomas Avenue
St. Paul, MN 55103
(651) 220-0090

HOPE Adoption & Family Services
  International, Inc.
5850 Omaha Avenue North
Oak Park Heights, MN 55082
(651) 439-2446

International Adoption Services
4940 Viking Drive, Suite 388

Minneapolis, MN 55435
(952) 893-1343

LDS Social Services
3120 Earl Brown Drive, Suite 210
Brooklyn Center, MN 55430
(763) 560-0900

Love Basket, Inc.
3902 Minnesota Avenue
Duluth, MN 55802
(218) 720-3097

Lutheran Home Christian
  Family Services
611 West Main Street
Belle Plain, MN 56011
(612) 873-2215

Lutheran Social Services
26 North 7th Avenue, #100
St. Cloud, MN 56303
(320) 251-7700

Lutheran Social Services
424 West Superior Street, #500
Duluth, MN 55802
(218) 726-4888

Lutheran Social Services
715 11th Street North, Suite 401
Moorhead, MN 56560
(218) 236-1494

Lutheran Social Services
2485 Como Avenue
St. Paul, MN 55108
(651) 642-5990

Lutheran Social Services of
  Minnesota
2414 Park Avenue
Minneapolis, MN 55404
(612) 879-5334

New Horizons Adoption
  Agency, Inc.
Frost Benco Building

Highway 254
Frost, MN 56033
(507) 878-3200

New Life Family Services
902 North Broadway
Rochester, MN 55904
(507) 282-3377

New Life Family Services
1515 East 66th Street
Richfield, MN 55423-2674
(612) 866–7643

Permanent Family Resource Center
1220 Tower Road
Fergus Falls, MN 56537
(218) 998-3400

Reaching Arms International, Inc.
3701 Winnetka Avenue North
New Hope, MN 55427
(763) 591-0791

Upper Midwest American
 Indian Center
1035 West Broadway
Minneapolis, MN 55411
(612) 522-4436

Village Family Services Center
715 11th Street, Suite 302
Moorhead, MN 56560
(218) 291-1214

Wellspring Adoption Agency
1219 University Avenue, SE
Minneapolis, MN 55414
(612) 379-0980

MISSISSIPPI

Mississippi Department of
 Human Services
Division of Family and
 Child Services
750 North State Street

Jackson, MS 39202
(601) 359-4981

Private Agencies

Acorn Adoptions, Inc.
113 South Beach Boulevard,
 Suite D
Bay St. Louis, MS 39520
(888) 221-1370

Bethany Christian Services
7 Professional Parkway, #103
Hattiesburg, MS 39402-2637
(601) 264-4984
(800) 331-5876

Bethany Christian Services
116 Lawrence Drive, #3
Columbus, MS 39702-5319
(662) 327-6740
(800) 331-5876

Bethany Christian Services
2618 Southerland Street
Jackson, MS 39216-4825
(601) 366-4282
(800) 331-5876

Catholic Charities, Inc.
PO Box 2248
Jackson, MS 39226-2248
(601) 355-8634

Catholic Social and
 Community Services
PO Box 1457
Biloxi, MS 39533-1457
(228) 374-8316

Harden House Adoption Agency
110 North Gaither Street
Fulton, MS 38843
(601) 862-7318

Jewish Family Services, Inc.
6560 Poplar Avenue

Memphis, TN 38138
(901) 767-8511

Mississippi Children's
  Home Society
1900 North West Street
PO Box 1078
Jackson, MS 39215
(601) 352-7784
(800) 388-6247

New Beginnings of Tupelo
1445 East Main Street
Tupelo, MS 38804
(662) 842-6752

Southern Adoption
12511 Marty Stuart Drive
Philadelphia, MS 39350
(800) 499-6862

MISSOURI

Missouri Department of
  Social Services
Division of Family Services
PO Box 88
Jefferson City, MO 65103
(573) 751-0311

Private Agencies

Action for Adoption
  1015 Locust Street
St. Louis, MO 63101
(816) 490-0198

Adopt Kids, Incorporated
109 West Jefferson
Kirkwood, MO 63122
(314) 725-1917

Adoption of Babies and Children
4330 Bellview, Suite 200
Kansas City, MO 64111
(800) 406-2909

Adoption and Beyond, Inc.
401 West 89th Street
Kansas City, MO 64114
(816) 822-2800

Adoption Counseling, Inc.
1420 West Lexington Avenue
Independence, MO 64052
(816) 507-0822

Adoption and Counseling
  Services for Families
7611 State Line, Suite 140
Kansas City, MO 64111
(816) 942-8440

Adoption and Fertility Resources
144 Westwoods Drive
Liberty, MO 64068
(816) 781-8550

Adoption and Fertility Resources
Seaport Professional Complex
Liberty, MO 64068
(816) 781-8550

Adoption By Family Therapy
  of the Ozarks, Inc.
Stoneridge Center
Kimberling, MO 65686
(417) 882-7700

Adoption Option
1124 Main
Blue Springs, MO 64015
(816) 224-1525

American Adoptions
306 East 12th Street, Suite 908
Kansas City, MO 64106
(800) 875-2229

Americans Adopting Orphans
8045 Big Bend Boulevard
Webster Groves, MO 63119
(314) 963-7100

Annie Malone Children & Family
  Service Center
2612 Annie Malone Drive
St. Louis, MO 63113
(314) 531-0120

Bethany Christian Services
1 McBride & Son Corporate
  Center Drive
Chesterfield, MO 63005-1406
(636) 536-6363

Boys and Girls Town of Missouri
13160 County Road 3610
St. James, MO 65559
(573) 265-3251

Butterfield Youth Services
11 West Eastwood
Marshall, MO 65340
(660) 886-2253

Catholic Charities of Kansas City
1112 Broadway
Kansas City, MO 64111
(816) 221-4377

Catholic Services for Children
  and Youth
#20 Archbishop May Drive
St. Louis, MO 63119
(314) 792-7400

Central Baptist Family Services
1015 Locust Street, Suite 900
St. Louis, MO 63101
(314) 241-4345
Fax: (314) 241-4330

Children of the World, Inc.
16 North Central
  Clayton, MO 63105
(314) 721-2130

Children's Home Society of
  Missouri
9445 Litzsinger Road

Brentwood, MO 63144
(314) 968-2350

Children's Hope International dba
  China's Children
9229 Lackland Road
St. Louis, MO 63114
(314) 890-0086

Christian Family Life Center
141 North Meremec, Suite 201
Clayton, MO 63105
(314) 862-6300

Christian Family Services, Inc.
7955 Big Bend Boulevard
Webster Groves, MO 63119
(314) 968-2216

Christian Family Services of
  the Midwest, Inc.
5703 North Flora
Gladstone, MO 64118
(816) 452-2077

Christian Salvation Services
4390 Lindell Boulevard
St. Louis, MO 63108
(314) 535-5919

Creative Families, Inc.
9378 Olive Boulevard, Suite 320
St. Louis, MO 63122
(314) 567-0707

Crittenton St. Luke's Health
  Care System
10918 Elm Avenue
Kansas City, MO 64134
(816) 765-6600

Dillon International, Inc.
1 First Missouri Center, Suite 115
St. Louis, MO 63141
(314) 576-4100

Downey Side Families for Youth
6500 Chippewa, Suite 324

St. Louis, MO 63109
(314) 457-1358

Echo
3033 North Euclid Avenue
St. Louis, MO 63115
(314) 381-3100

Edgewood Children's Home
330 North Gore Avenue
Webster Groves, MO 63119
(314) 968-2060

Faith House
5355 Page Avenue
St. Louis, MO 63112
(314) 367-5400

Family Builders, Inc.
203 Huntington Road
Kansas City, MO 64113
(816) 822-2169

Family Care Center
14377 Woodlake Drive, Suite 308
Chesterfield, MO 63017
(314) 576-6493

The Family Network, Inc.
9378 Olice Street, Suite 320
St. Louis, MO 63132

Family Resource Center
3309 South Kingshighway
St. Louis, MO 63116
(314) 534-9350

Farmington Children's Home
608 Pine Street
Farmington, MO 63640
(573) 756-6744

Friends of African-American
  Families and Children
  Service Center
3920 Lindell Boulevard, Suite 102
St. Louis, MO 63108
(314) 535-2453

Heart of America Adoption
  Center, Inc.
306 East 12th Street, Suite 908
Kansas City, MO 64106
(636) 625-2266

Highlands Child Placement
  Services
5506 Cambridge
PO Box 300198
Kansas City, MO 64130-0198
(816) 924-6565

Kansas Children's Service League
3200 Wayne, Suite W-104
Kansas City, MO 64109
(816) 921-0654

LDS Family Services
517 West Walnut
Independence, MO 63044
(816) 461-5512

Love Basket, Inc.
10306 State Highway 21
Hillsboro, MO 63050
(636) 797-4100

Lutheran Family and
  Children's Services
8631 Delmar Boulevard
University City, MO 63124
(314) 534-1515

Mattie Rhodes Memorial Society
5001 Independence Avenue
Kansas City, MO 64124
(816) 471-2536

Missouri Baptist Children's Home
MBCH Children & Family
  Ministries
11300 St. Charles Rock Road
Bridgeton, MO 63044
(314) 739-6811

New Family Connection
201 North Kingshighway
St. Charles, MO 63301
(636) 949-0577

Niles Home for Children
1911 East 23rd Street
Kansas City, MO 64127
(816) 241-3448

Our Little Haven
4326 Lindell Boulevard
St. Louis, MO 63108
(314) 533-2229

Reaching Out Thru International
  Adoption, Inc.
11715 Administration Drive,
  Suite 101
St. Louis, MO 63146
(314) 971-3073

Salvation Army Children's Shelter
101 West Linwood
Kansas City, MO 64111
(816) 756-2769

Salvation Army Hope Center
3740 Marine Avenue
St. Louis, MO 63118
(314) 773-0980

Seek International
4583 Chestnut Park Plaza,
  Suite 205
St. Louis, MO 63129-3100
(314) 416-9723

Small World Adoption
  Foundation, Inc.
15480 Clayton Road, Suite 101
Ballwin, MO 63011
(636) 207-9229

Special Additions, Inc.
701 Berkshire Drive

Belton, MO 64012
(816) 421-3737

MONTANA

Montana Department of Public
  Health and Human Services
Child and Family Services Division
PO Box 8005
Helena, MT 59604-8005
(406) 444-5919

Private Agencies

Catholic Social Services for
  Montana
Box 907
25 South Ewing
Helena, MT 59624
(406) 442-4130

Lutheran Social Services
PO Box 1345
Great Falls, MT 59403
(406) 761-4341

Montana Intercountry
  Adoption, Inc.
26 West Babcock
Bozeman, MT 59715

A New Arrival
804 Bayers Lane
Silver Star, MT 59751
(406) 287-2114

NEBRASKA

Nebraska Department of Health
  and Human Services
PO Box 95044
Lincoln, NE 68509-5044
(402) 471-9331

Private Agencies

Adoption Links Worldwide
6901 Dodge Street, Suite 101
Omaha, NE 68132
(402) 556-2367

American Adoptions
National Offices
8676 West 96th Street, Suite 140
Overland Park, KS 66212
(800) 236-7846

Catholic Charities
3300 North 60th Street
Omaha, NE 68104
(402) 554-0520

Child Saving Institute
115 South 46th Street
Omaha, NE 68132
(402) 553-6000
(888) 588-6003

Holt International Children's
  Services
10685 Bedford Avenue, Suite 300
Omaha, NE 68134
(402) 934-5031

Jewish Family Services
333 South 132nd Street
Omaha, NE 68154
(402) 330-2024

LDS Family Services
517 West Walnut
Independence, MO 63044
(816) 461-5512

Lutheran Family Services
120 South 24th Street
Omaha, NE 68102
(402) 342-7007

Nebraska Children's Home Society
3549 Fontenelle Boulevard

Omaha, NE 68104
(402) 451-0787

Nebraska Christian Services, Inc.
2600 South 124th Street
Omaha, NE 68144
(402) 334-3278

NEVADA

Nevada Department of
  Human Resources
Division of Child and
  Family Services
6171 West Charleston Boulevard,
  Building 15
Las Vegas, NV 89102
(702) 486-7633

Private Agencies

Catholic Charities of
  Southern Nevada
808 South Main Street
Las Vegas, NV 89101
(702) 385-2662

Catholic Community Services
  of Northern Nevada
500 East 4th Street
PO Box 5099
Reno, NV 89512
(775) 322-7073

LDS Social Services
513 South Ninth Street
Las Vegas, NV 89101
(702) 385-1072

NEW HAMPSHIRE

New Hampshire Department of
  Health and Human Services
Division for Children, Youth and
  Families

129 Pleasant Street
Concord, NH 03301
(603) 271-4707

Private Agencies

Adoptive Families for Children
26 Fairview Street
Keene, NH 03431
(603) 357-4456

Bethany Christian Services of New
  England
PO Box 320
Candia, NH 03034-0320
(603) 483-2886

Casey Family Services
105 Loudon Road
Building 2
Concord, NH 03301
(603) 224-8909

Child and Family Services of New
  Hampshire
99 Hanover Street
Manchester, NH 03105
(603) 668-1920
(800) 640-6486

LDS Social Services
547 Amherst Street, Suite 404
Nashua, NH 03063-4000
(603) 889-0148

Lutheran Social Services of New
  England
261 Sheep Davis Road, Suite A-1
Concord, NH 03301
(603) 224-8111
(800) 286-9889

New Hampshire Catholic
  Charities, Inc.
215 Myrtle Street
PO Box 686

Manchester, NH 03105-0686
(603) 669-3030
(800) 562-5249

New Hope Christian Services
210 Silk Farm Road
Concord, NH 03301
(603) 225-0992

Wide Horizons for Children
11 Powers Street
PO Box 176
Milford, NH 03055
(603) 672-3000

NEW JERSEY

New Jersey Department
  of Human Services
Division of Youth and Family
  Services
50 East State Street, Fifth Floor,
  CN 717
Trenton, NJ 08625-0717
(609) 984-2380

Private Agencies

Adoptions From the Heart
451 Woodland Avenue
Cherry Hill, NJ 08002
(609) 665-5655

Bethany Christian Services
445 Godwin Avenue
Midland Park, NJ 07432
(201) 444-7775

Better Living Services
560 Springfield Avenue, Suite C
PO Box 2969
Westfield, NJ 07090-2969
(908) 654-0277

Brookwood Child Care
25 Washington Street

Brooklyn, NY 11201
(718) 596-5555, Ext: 510

Catholic Charities
Diocese of Metuchen
PO Box 191
Metuchen, NJ 08840
(732) 562-1990

Catholic Charities
Diocese of Trenton
70 Lawrenceville Road
PO Box 5147
Trenton, NJ 08638
(609) 406-7400

Catholic Community Services of
 Newark
499 Belgrove Drive, Suite 2
Kearny, NJ 07032
(201) 991-3770

Catholic Family and Community
 Services
476 17th Avenue
Paterson, NJ 07501
(973) 523-9595

Catholic Social Services of the
 Diocese of Camden
810 Montrose Street
Vineland, NJ 08360
(856) 691-1841
Fax: (856) 692-6575

Children of the World
685 Bloomfield Avenue, Suite 201
Verona, NJ 07044
(973) 239-0100

Children's Aid and Family
 Services, Inc.
60 Evergreen Place
East Orange, NJ 07019
(973) 673-6454

Children's Aid and Family
 Services, Inc.
200 Robin Road
Paramus, NJ 07652
(201) 261-2800

Children's Choice, Inc.
151 Fries Mill Road,
 Suite 205-206
Turnersville, NJ 08012
(856) 228-5223

Children's Home Society
 of New Jersey
21 Main Street
Clinton, NJ 08809
(908) 735-9458

Children's Home Society
 of New Jersey
635 South Clinton Avenue
Trenton, NJ 08611-1831
(609) 695-6274

Christian Homes for Children
275 State Street
Hackensack, NJ 07601
(201) 342-4235

Downey Side Families for Youth
146 U.S. Route 130
Bordentown, NJ 08505
(609) 291-2784

Family and Children's Services
40 North Avenue
Elizabeth, NJ 07207
(908) 352-7474

Family Options
19 Bridge Avenue
Red Bank, NJ 07701
(732) 936-0770

The Gladney Center
257 West Broad Street

Palmyra, NJ 08065
(609) 829-2769

Golden Cradle
1050 North Kings Highway,
  Suite 201
Cherry Hill, NJ 08034
(856) 667-2229

Growing Families Worldwide
  Adoption Agency, Inc.
178 South Street
Freehold, NJ 07728
(732) 431-4330

Holt International Children's
  Services
340 Scotch Road, Second Floor
Trenton, NJ 08628
(609) 882-4972

Homestudies and Adoption
  Placement Services (HAPS), Inc.
668 American Legion Drive
Teaneck, NJ 07666
(201) 836-5554

Jewish Family and Children's
  Services of Southern New Jersey
1301 Springdale Road, Suite 150
Cherry Hill, NJ 08003-2729
(856) 424-1333

Jewish Family Services of Central
  New Jersey
655 Westfield Avenue
Elizabeth, NJ 07208
(908) 352-8375

Jewish Family Services of
  Metro West
256 Columbia Turnpike, Suite 105
Florham Park, NJ 07932-0825
(973) 674-4210

Jewish Family Services of
  Monmouth County
705 Summerfield Avenue
Asbury Park, NJ 07712
(732) 774-6886

Lutheran Social Ministries
  of New Jersey
6 Terri Lane, Suite 300
Burlington, NJ 08016-4905
(609) 386-7171

NU-Roots and International Ties
  (NURIT, Inc.)
17 Blackhawk Court
Medford, NJ 08055
(609) 654-2052

Reaching Out Thru International
  Adoption
312 South Lincoln Avenue
Cherry Hill, NJ 08002
(856) 321-0777

Seedlings, Inc.
375 Route 10 East
Whippany, NJ 07981
(973) 884-7488

Small World Agency
New Jersey Branch Office
257 West Broad Street
Palmyra, NJ 08065-1463
(609) 829-2769

Spence-Chapin Services to
  Families and Children
Branch Office
57 Union Place
Summit, NJ 07901
(908) 522-0043

United Family and
  Children's Society
305 West Seventh Street
Plainfield, NJ 07060
(908) 755-4848

NEW MEXICO

New Mexico Department of
  Children, Youth and Families
Central Adoption Unit
PO Drawer 5160
Santa Fe, NM 87502-5160
(505) 841-7949
(800) 432-2075

Private Agencies

A.M.O.R. Adoptions, Inc.
3700 Coors Boulevard NW, Suite F
Albuquerque, NM 87120
(505) 831-0888
(877) 712-2667

Adoption Assistance Agency
2800 Eubank, NE
Alburquerque, NM 87122
(505) 821-7779
(888) 422-3678

Adoption Plus
11811 Menaul NE, Suite 5
Albuquerque, NM 87112
(505) 262-0446

Catholic Social Services, Inc.
4985 Airport Road
Santa Fe, NM 87505-0443
(505) 424-9789

Child-Rite/AASK
126 Cavalry Road
Taos, NM 87571
(505) 758-0343

Child Rite/AASK
4801 Indian School Road,
  Suite 204
Albuquerque, NM 87106
(505) 797-4191

Choices Adoption and Counseling
2811 Indian School Road, NE
Albuquerque, NM 87106
(505) 266-0456

Christian Child Placement Services
1356 NM 236
Portales, NM 88130
(505) 356-4232

Families for Children
6209 Hendrex NE
Alburquerque, NM 87110
(505) 881-4200

Family Matters
3301-R Coors NW, #286
Albuquerque, NM 87120
(505) 344-8811

La Familia Placement Services
707 Broadway NE
Suite 103
Alburquerque, NM 87102
(505) 766-9361

LDS Family Services
3811 Atrisco Drive NW, Suite A
Albuquerque, NM 87120
(505) 836-5947

LDS Social Services
925 Cannery Court
Farmington, NM 87401
(505) 327-6123

New Mexico Parent &
  Child Resources
3500 Indian School NE
Albuquerque, NM 87106
(505) 268-4973

Rainbow House International
19676 Highway 314
Belen, NM 87002
(505) 861-1234

NEW YORK

New York State Adoption Services
New York City Metropolitan
  Regional Office
80 Maiden Lane, Sixth Floor
New York, NY 10038
(212) 383-1805

New York State Adoption Services
Rochester Regional Office
259 Monroe Avenue, Monroe
  Square
Rochester, NY 14607
(716) 238-8201

New York State Adoption Services
Yonkers Regional Office
525 Nepperhan Avenue
Yonkers, NY 10703
(914) 377-2079

New York State Department
  of Family Assistance
Office of Children and Family
  Services
40 North Pearl Street
Riverview Center, Sixth Floor
Albany, NY 12243
(518) 474-9406
(800) 345-5437

Private Agencies

Abbott House
100 North Broadway
Irvington, NY 10533
(914) 591-3200, Ext: 224

The ABSW Child Adoption,
  Counseling and Referral Service
1969 Madison Avenue
New York, NY 10035
(212) 831-5181

Adoption and Counseling
  Services, Inc.
1 Fayette Park
Syracuse, NY 13202
(315) 471-0109

Adoption S.T.A.R. (Support,
  Training, Advocacy and
  Resources), Inc.
2001 Niagara Falls Boulevard,
  Suite 5
West Amherst, NY 14228
(716) 691-3300

Advocates for Adoption, Inc.
362 West 46th Street
New York, NY 10036
(212) 957-3938

Angel Guardian Home
6301 12th Avenue
Brooklyn, NY 11219
(718) 232-1500, Ext: 267

ARISE Child and Family Services
1065 James Street
Syracuse, NY 13203
(315) 477-4291

Association to Benefit Children
419 East 86 Street
New York, NY 10028
(212) 831-1322, Ext: 340

Astor Home for Children
6339 Mill Street
PO Box 5005
Rhinebeck, NY 12572
(914) 876-4081

Baker Victory Services
790 Ridge Road
Lackawanna, NY 14218
(716) 828-9510

Bethany Christian Services
Warwick Reformed Church

16 Maple Avenue
Warwick, NY 10990
(914) 987-1453

Brookwood Child Care
25 Washington Street
Brooklyn, NY 11201
(718) 596-5555, Ext: 510

Cardinal McCloskey School
 and Home
2 Holland Avenue
White Plains, NY 10603
(914) 997-8000, Ext: 134

Catholic Charities of Buffalo
525 Washington Street
Buffalo, NY 14203
(716) 856-4494

Catholic Charities of Cortland
33-35 Central Avenue
Cortland, NY 13045
(607) 756-5992

Catholic Charities of Ogdensburg
716 Caroline Street
PO Box 296
Ogdensburg, NY 13669-0296
(315) 393-2660

Catholic Charities of Oswego
181 West 2nd Street
Oswego, NY 13126
(315) 343-9540

Catholic Charities of Plattsburgh
151 South Catherine Street
Plattsburgh, NY 12901
(518) 561-0470

Catholic Charities of Rome
212 West Liberty Street
Rome, NY 13440
(315) 337-8600

Catholic Charities of Syracuse
1654 West Onondaga Street

Syracuse, NY 13204
(315) 424-1871

Catholic Family Center
25 Franklin Street
Rochester, NY 14604
(716) 262-7134

Catholic Guardian Society
 of New York
1011 First Avenue
New York, NY 10022
(212) 371-1000

Catholic Home Bureau for
 Dependent Children
1011 First Avenue, Twelfth Floor
New York, NY 10022
(212) 371-1000

Catholic Social Services
 of Broome County
232 Main Street
Binghamton, NY 13905
(607) 729-9166

Catholic Social Services of Oneida
 and Madison Counties
1408 Genesee Street
Utica, NY 13502
(315) 724-2158

Child and Family Services of Erie
844 Delaware Avenue
Buffalo, NY 14209-2008
(716) 882-0555, Ext: 106

Child Development Support
 Corporation
352-358 Classon Avenue
Brooklyn, NY 11238
(718) 230-0056

Children At Heart Adoption
 Services, Inc.
145 North Main Street

Mechanicville, NY 12118
(518) 664-5988

Children of the World
27 Hillvale Road
Syosset, NY 11791-6916
(516) 935-1235

Children's Aid Society
Adoption and Foster Home Division
150 East 45th Street
New York, NY 10017
(212) 949-4961

Children's Home of Poughkeepsie
91 Fulton Street
Poughkeepsie, NY 12601
(914) 452-1420

Children's Village
Echo Hills
Dobbs Ferry, NY 10522
(914) 693-0600, Ext: 1223

Coalition for Hispanic Family
  Services
315 Wyckoff Avenue, Fourth Floor
Brooklyn, NY 11237
(718) 497-6090

Community Maternity Services
27 North Main Avenue
Albany, NY 12203
(518) 482-8836

Downey Side Families for Youth
371 Seventh Avenue
PO Box 2139
New York, NY 10116-2139
(212) 714-2200

Dunbar Association, Inc.
1453 South State Street
Syracuse, NY 13205
(315) 476-4269

Edwin Gould Services for Children
41 East 11th Street

New York, NY 10003
(212) 598-0051, Ext: 279

Episcopal Mission Society
305 Seventh Avenue, Third Floor
New York, NY 10001-6008
(212) 675-1000

Family and Children's Services
  of Broome County
257 Main Street
Binghamton, NY 13905
(607) 729-6206

Family and Children's Services
  of Ithaca
204 North Cayuga Street
Ithaca, NY 14850
(607) 273-7494

Family and Children's Services
  of Schenectady
246 Union Street
Schenectady, NY 12305
(518) 393-1369

Family Connections
20 Hyatt Street
Cortland, NY 13045
(607) 756-6574

Family Service of Utica
401 Columbia Street, Suite 201
Utica, NY 13502
(315) 735-2236

Family Service of Westchester
1 Summit Avenue
White Plains, NY 10606
(914) 948-8004

Family Support Systems Unlimited
2530 Grand Concourse
Bronx, NY 10458
(718) 220-5400, Ext: 403

Family Tree
2 Crestmont Drive

Clifton Park, NY 12065
(518) 371-1336

Forestdale, Inc.
67-35 112th Street
Forest Hills, NY 11375
(718) 263-0740

Gateway-Longview
605 Niagara Street
Buffalo, NY 14201
(716) 882-8468, Ext: 3884

Graham-Windham Child Care
33 Irving Place
New York, NY 10003
(212) 529-6445, Ext: 386

Green Chimneys
Doansburg Road, Box 719
Brewster, NY 10509-0719
(914) 279-2996, Ext: 149

Hale House Center, Inc.
155 West 122nd Street
New York, NY 10027

Happy Families International
  Center, Inc.
3 Stone Street
Cold Spring, NY 10516
(914) 265-9272

Harlem-Dowling Children Services
2090 7th Avenue
New York, NY 10027
(212) 749-3656

Heartshare Human Services
191 Joralemon Street
Brooklyn, NY 11201
(718) 422-4219

Hillside Children's Center
1337 East Main Street
Rochester, NY 14609
(716) 654-4528

Ibero American Action League Inc.
817 East Main Street
Rochester, NY 14605
(716) 256-8900

Jewish Board of Family and
  Children Services
120 West 57th Street
New York, NY 10019
(212) 582-9100

Jewish Child Care Association
120 Wall Street, Twelfth Floor
New York, NY 10005-3904
(212) 425-3333

Jewish Family Services
  of Erie County
70 Barker Street
Buffalo, NY 14209
(716) 883-1914

Jewish Family Services of
  Rochester
441 East Avenue
Rochester, NY 14607
(716) 461-0110

Lakeside Family and
  Children's Services
185 Montague Street
Brooklyn, NY 11201
(718) 237-9700

LDS Social Services of New York
22 IBM Road, Suite 205-B
Poughkeepsie, NY 12601
(914) 462-1288

Leake and Watts Children's Home
463 Hawthorne Avenue
Yonkers, NY 10705
(914) 375-8700

Little Flower Children's Services
186 Joralemon Street

Brooklyn, NY 11201
(718) 875-3500, Ext: 367

Lutheran Social Services, Inc.
83 Christopher Street
New York, NY 10014
(212) 784-8904

McMahon Services for Children
305 Seventh Avenue
New York, NY 10001
(212) 243-7070, Ext: 259

Miracle Makers, Inc.
510 Gates Avenue
Brooklyn, NY 11216
(718) 483-3000

New Beginnings Family and
  Children's Services, Inc.
141 Willis Avenue
Mineola, NY 11501
(516) 747-2204

New Hope Family Services
3519 James Street
Syracuse, NY 13206
(315) 437-8300

New Life Adoption Agency
711 East Genesee Street,
  Suite 210
Syracuse, NY 13210
(315) 422-7300

The New York Foundling Hospital
590 Avenue of the Americas
New York, NY 10011
(212) 727-6828

Ohel Children's Home and Family
  Services
4510 16th Avenue, Fourth Floor
Brooklyn, NY 11204
(718) 851-6300

Parsons Child and Family Center
60 Academy Road

Albany, NY 12208
(518) 426-2600
Fax: (518) 447-5234

Pius XII Youth/Family Services
188 West 230 Street
Bronx, NY 10463
(718) 562-7855

Salvation Army
Hearts and Homes
677 South Salina Street
Syracuse, NY 13202
(315) 479-1324

Seamen's Society for Children
  and Families
25 Hyatt Street, Fifth Floor
Staten Island, NY 10301
(718) 447-7740, Ext: 302

Sheltering Arms
  Children's Services
122 East 29th Street
New York, NY 10016
(212) 679-4242, Ext: 300

Spence-Chapin Services to
  Families and Children
6 East 94th Street
New York, NY 10128
(212) 369-0300

St. Augustine Center
1600 Filmore Avenue
Buffalo, NY 14211
(716) 897-4110

St. Cabrini
Route 9W
West Park, NY 12493
(914) 384-6500

St. Christopher Ottilie
90-04 161st Street
Jamaica, NY 11432
(718) 526-7533

St. Christopher Ottilie
175 Seacliff Avenue
Glenn Cove, NY 11542
(516) 759-1844

St. Christopher Ottilie
570 Fulton Street
Brooklyn, NY 11217
(718) 935-9466

St. Christopher Ottilie
Third Avenue and Eighth Street
PO Box Y
Brentwood, NY 11717
(516) 273-2733

St. Christopher's, Inc.
881 Gerard Avenue
Bronx, NY 10452
(718) 537-5301, Ext: 120

St. Dominics
343 East 137th Street
Bronx, NY 10454
(718) 993-5765

St. Joseph's Children's Services
540 Atlantic Avenue
Brooklyn, NY 11217-1982
(718) 858-8700

St. Mary's Child and Family
 Services
525 Convent Road
Syosset, NY 11791
(516) 921-0808

St. Vincent's Services
66 Boerum Place
PO Box 174
Brooklyn, NY 11202
(718) 522-3700, Ext: 251

Talbot-Perkins Children Services
116 West 32nd Street,
 Twelfth Floor

New York, NY 10001
(212) 736-2510, Ext: 291

Urban League of Rochester,
 Minority Adoption Program
265 North Clinton Avenue
Rochester, NY 14605
(716) 325-6530

Voice for International
 Development and Adoption
 (VIDA)
354 Allen Street
Hudson, NY 12534
(518) 828-4527

You Gotta Believe
1220 Neptune Avenue
Brooklyn, NY 11224
(718) 372-3003

NORTH CAROLINA

North Carolina Department of
 Health and Human Services
Division of Social Services,
 Children's Services Section
325 North Salisbury Street
2408 Mail Service Center
Raleigh, NC 27699-2408
(919) 733-4622

State Adoption Exchange/State
 Photolisting Service
North Carolina Adoption Resource
 Exchange
325 North Salisbury Street
2411 Mail Service Center
Raleigh, NC 27699-2411
(919) 733-3801

Private Agencies

Adoption Options
  118 South Colonial Avenue,
  Suite 300
Charlotte, NC 28207
(702) 344-8003

AGAPE of N.C., Inc.
302 College Road
Greensboro, NC 27410
(336) 855-7107
(800) 330-9449

Amazing Grace Adoptions
1215 Jones Franklin Road,
  Suite 205
Raleigh, NC 27606
(919) 858-8998

Another Choice for Black Children
3028 Beatties Ford Road
Charlotte, NC 28216
(704) 394-1124
(800) 774-3534

Bethany Christian Services, Inc.
PO Box 15569
Asheville, NC 28813-0569
(828) 274-7146

Caring for Children, Inc.
50 Reddick Road
PO Box 19113
Asheville, NC 28815
(828) 298-0186

Carolina Adoption Services, Inc.
120 West Smith Street
Greensboro, NC 27401-2028
(336) 275-9660

Catholic Social Ministries of the
  Diocese of Raleigh, Inc.
226 Hillsborough Street
Raleigh, NC 27603-1724
(919) 832-0225

Catholic Social Services of the
  Diocese of Charlotte, Inc.
1123 South Church Street
Charlotte, NC 28203-4003
(704) 370-6155

Children's Home Society
  of North Carolina, Inc.
604 Meadow Street
PO Box 14608
Greensboro, NC 27415
(336) 274-1538

A Child's Hope
Two Hannover Square, Suite 1860
Raleigh, NC 27601
(919) 839-8800

Christian Adoption Services
624 Matthews-Mint Hill Road,
  Suite 134
Matthews, NC 28105
(704) 847-0038

Christian World Adoption
303 7th Avenue
Hendersonville, NC 28792
(828) 685-3225
(888) 972-3678

The Datz Foundation
2 Hanover Square, Suite 1860
Raleigh, NC 27601
(919) 839-8800

Faith Works Unlimited, Inc.
PO Box 14847
Raleigh, NC 27620
(919) 833-5220

Family Services, Inc.
610 Coliseum Drive
Winston-Salem, NC 27106-5393
(336) 722-8173

Frank Adoption Center
2840 Plaza Place, Suite 325

Raleigh, NC 27612
(919) 510-9135
(800) 597-9135

Gladney Center For Adoption
235 Commerce Street
Greenville, NC 27858
(252) 355-6267

Independent Adoption Center
3725 National Drive, Suite 219
Raleigh, NC 27612
(919) 789-0707
(800) 877-6736

LDS Social Services
5624 Executive Center Drive,
 Suite 109
Charlotte, NC 28212-8832
(704) 535-2436

Lutheran Family Services
 in the Carolinas, Inc.
112 Cox Avenue,
PO Box 12287
Raleigh, NC 27605
(919) 832-2620

Mandala Adoption Services
6601 Turkey Farm Road
Chapel Hill, NC 27514
(919) 942-5500

Methodist Home for Children
1300 St. Mary's Street
PO Box 10917
Raleigh, NC 27605-0917
(919) 828-0345

Nathanson Adoption Services, Inc.
6060 JA Jones Drive, Suite 504
Charlotte, NC 28287
(704) 553-9506

Nazareth Children's Home
PO Box 1438

Rockwell, NC 28138
(704) 279-5556

New Life Christian Adoptions
500 Benson Road, Suite 202
Garner, NC 27529
(919) 779-1004

Saint Mary International
 Adoptions, Inc.
528 East Boulevard, Suite 105
Charlotte, NC 28203
(704) 375-6531

Yahweh Center, Inc.
PO Box 10399
Wilmington, NC 28404-0399
(910) 675-3533

A Way for Children
1811 Sardis Road
Charlotte, NC
(704) 846-9824

NORTH DAKOTA

North Dakota Department of
 Human Services
600 East Boulevard Avenue
Bismarck, ND 58505
(701) 328-4805
(800) 245-3736

Private Agencies

AASK (Adults Adopting
 Special Kids)
1325 South 11th Street, Box 389
Fargo, ND 58103
(800) 551-6054

The Adoption Option
1201 25th Street South
PO Box 9859
Fargo, ND 58106-9859
(701) 235-6433

Catholic Family Service
1809 South Broadway, Suite W
Minot, ND 58703
(701) 852-2854

Catholic Family Service
2537 South University
Fargo, ND 58103
(701) 235-4457

Christian Family Life Services
203 South 8th Street
Fargo, ND 58103
(701) 237-4473

LDS Social Services
PO Box 3100
Bismarck, ND 58502-3100
(763) 560-0900

OHIO

Ohio Bureau of Family Services
Office for Children and Families
255 East Main Street, Fourth Floor
Columbus, OH 43215
(614) 466-9274

Private Agencies

A.C.T.I.O.N.
6000 Philadelphia Drive
Dayton, OH 45415
(937) 277-6101, Ext: 1

Adopt America Network
AASK Midwest
1025 North Reynolds Road
Toledo, OH 43615-4753
(419) 534-3350

Adoption at Adoption Circle
2500 East Main Street, Suite 103
Columbus, OH 43209
(614) 237-7222
(800) 927-7222

Adoption by Gentle Care
17 East Brickel Street
Columbus, OH 43215-1501
(614) 469-0007

The Adoption Center, Inc.
12151 Ellsworth Road
North Jackson, OH 44451
(330) 547-8255

Adoption Connection
11223 Cornell Park Drive,
 Suite 201
Cincinnati, OH 45242
(513) 489-1616

Adoption Specialists, Inc.
3373 East Scarborough
Cleveland Heights, OH 44118
(216) 932-2880, Ext: 880

Adriel School, Inc
414 North Detroit Street
West Liberty, OH 43357
(937) 465-0010

AGAPE for Youth, Inc.
8067 McEwen Road
Dayton, OH 45458
(937) 439-4406

American International
 Adoption Agency
7045 County Line Road
Williamsfield, OH 44093
(330) 876-5656

Applewood Centers, Inc.
2525 East 22nd Street
Cleveland, OH 44115
(216) 741-2241

Baptist Children's Home and
 Family Ministries, Inc.
1934 South Limestone Street
Springfield, OH 45505
(937) 322-0006

Beacon Agency
1836 Euclid Avenue, Suite 500
Cleveland, OH 44115
(216) 574-0300

Beech Acres
6881 Beechmont Avenue
Cincinnati, OH 45230
(513) 231-6630

Berea Children's Home
 and Family Services
202 East Bagley Road
Berea, OH 44017
(440) 234-2006

Building Blocks Adoption
 Service, Inc.
PO Box 1028
Medina, OH 44258
(330) 725-5521
(866) 321-2367

Caring Hearts Adoption
 Agency Inc.
771 Martin Street, Suite 2
Greenville, OH 45331
(937) 316-6168
(937) 548-7414

Catholic Charities Diocese
 of Toledo
1933 Spielbusch Avenue
PO Box 985
Toledo, OH 43624
(419) 244-6711

Catholic Charities Family
 Center of Elyria
628 Poplar Street
Elyria, OH 44115
(440) 366-1106

Catholic Community
 Services of Warren
1175 Laird Avenue NE, Third Floor

Warren, OH 44483
(216) 393-4254

Catholic Service League, Inc.
 of Ashtabula County
4200 Park Avenue, Third Floor
Ashtabula, OH 44004
(216) 992-2121

Catholic Social Services, Inc.
197 East Gay Street, Second Floor
Columbus, OH 43215-3229
(614) 221-5891

Catholic Social Services of
 Cuyahoga County
7800 Detroit Avenue
Cleveland, OH 44102-2814
(216) 631-3499

Catholic Social Services
 of Lake County
28706 Euclid Avenue
Wickliffe, OH 44092
(216) 946-7264

Catholic Social Services
 of Southwest Ohio
100 East Eighth Street
Cincinnati, OH 45202
(513) 241-7745

Children's Home of Cincinnati
1811 Losantiville Avenue,
 Suite 250
Cincinnati, OH 45237
(513) 272-2800

A Child's Waiting Foster Care
 and Adoption Program
710 Salisbury Way
Copley, OH 44321
(330) 665-1811

Christian Children's Home of Ohio
2685 Armstrong Road
Wooster, OH 44691

(330) 345-7949
(800) 643-9073

Cleveland Christian Home, Inc.
1700 Denison Avenue, #203
Cleveland, OH 44109
(216) 416-4266

Crittenton Family Services, Inc.
1414 East Broad Street
Columbus, OH 43215
(614) 265-9124

Diversion Adolescent Foster
2215 North Main Street
Findlay, OH 45840
(419) 422-4770
(800) 824-3007

European Adoption Consultants
9800 Boston Road
North Royalton, OH 44133
(440) 237-3554
(800) 533-0098

Family Adoption Consultants
8536 Crow Drive
Macedonia Professional
  Building #230
Macedonia, OH 44056
(330) 468-0673

Family Services Association
212 East Exchange Street
Akron, OH 44304
(330) 376-9494

Focus on Youth, Inc
2718 East Kemper Road
Cincinnati, OH 45241
(513) 771-4710

Harbor House Adoptions
PO Box 357
Celina, OH 45822
(419) 586-9029

Jewish Family Services of Toledo
6525 Sylvania Avenue
Sylvania, OH 43560
(419) 885-2561

LDS Social Services
4431 Marketing Place
Groveport, OH 43125
(614) 836-2466

Lighthouse Youth Services, Inc.
1501 Madison Road
Cincinnati, OH 45206
(513) 221-3350

Lutheran Social Services of
  Columbus
750 East Broad Street
Columbus, OH 43205
(614) 228-5200

Lutheran Social Services of Findlay
115 East Lima Street
Findlay, OH 45840
(419) 422-7917

Lutheran Social Services of
  Fremont
512 East State Street
Fremont, OH 43420-4259
(419) 334-3431

Lutheran Social Services
  of Mid-America
3131 South Dixie Drive, Suite 300
Dayton, OH 45439
(937) 643-0020

Lutheran Social Services
  of Mid-America
11370 Springfield Pike
Cincinnati, OH 45246
(513) 326-5430

Lutheran Social Services of
  Northwest Ohio, Inc.
2149 Collingwood Boulevard

Toledo, OH 43620
(419) 243-9178

Lutheran Social Services of
  Perrysburg
1011 Sandusky, Suite 1
Perrysburg, OH 43551
(419) 872-9111

Lutheran Social Services
  of the Miami Valley
204 North Fountain Avenue
Springfield, OH 45502
(937) 325-3441

Mathias Care
1191 Galbraith Road
Cincinnati, OH 45231
(513) 522-7390

Mid-Western Children's Home
4581 Long Spurling
PO Box 48
Pleasant Plain, OH 45162
(513) 877-2141

New Hope Adoption International
101 West Sandusky Street,
  Suite 311
Findlay, OH 45840
(419) 423-0760

Northeast Ohio Adoption Services
5000 East Market Street, Suite 26
Warren, OH 44484
(330) 856-5582
(800) 686-4277

Options for Families and Youth
5131 West 140th Street
Brook Park, OH 44142
(216) 267-7070

A Place to Call Home, Inc
36 Central Station Place
Johnstown, OH 43031
(740) 967-2167

St. Aloysius Orphanage
4721 Reading Road
Cincinnati, OH 45237
(513) 242-7600

Spaulding Adoption Program
  Beech Brook
3737 Lander Road
Pepper Pike, OH 44124
(216) 831-0638

Specialized Alternatives for
  Families and Youth
10100 Elida Road
Delphos, OH 45833
(419) 695-8010
(800) 532-7239

The Twelve Inc.
619 Tremont Avenue SW
Massillon, OH 44647
(330) 837-3555

United Methodist Children's Home
1033 High Street
Worthington, OH 43085-4054
(614) 885-5020

Westark Family Services, Inc
325 Third Street SE
Massillon, OH 46646
(216) 832-5043

OKLAHOMA

Oklahoma Department
  of Human Services
Division of Children
  and Family Services
2400 North Lincoln Boulevard
PO Box 25352
Oklahoma City, OK 73125
(405) 521-2475

Private Agencies

Adoption Affiliates
6136 East 32nd Place
Tulsa, OK 74135
(918) 664-2275
(800) 253-6307

Adoption Center of Northeastern
  Oklahoma
6202 South Lewis, Suite Q
Tulsa, OK 74136
(918) 748-9200

Adoption Choices
1616 East 19th Street, Suite 101
Edmond, OK 73120
(405) 715-1991

Adoption Pathways
1616 East Bryant
Edmond, OK 73013
(405) 715-1991

Baptist Children's Home
16301 South Western Avenue
Oklahoma City, OK 73170
(405) 691-7781

Bethany Adoption Service
3940 North College
Bethany, OK 73008
(405) 789-5423

Bless This Child, Inc.
Route 4, Box 1005
Checotah, OK 74426
(918) 473-7045

Catholic Social Services
739 North Denver Avenue
PO Box 6429
Tulsa, OK 74106
(918) 585-8167

Chosen Child Adoption Agency
PO Box 55424

Tulsa, OK 74155-5424
(918) 298-0082

Christian Homes
802 North 10th Street
Duncan, OK 73533
(405) 252-5131

Christian Services of Oklahoma
2221 East Memorial Road
Oklahoma, OK 73136
(405) 478-3362

Cradle of Lawton
902 NW Kingswood Road
Lawton, OK 73505
(580) 536-2478

Deaconess Home Pregnancy
  and Adoption Services
5300 North Meridian Avenue,
  Suite 9
Oklahoma City, OK 73112
(405) 949-4200

Dillon International, Inc.
3227 East 31st Street, Suite 200
Tulsa, OK 74105
(918) 749-4600

Eagle Ridge
601 NE 63rd
Oklahoma City, OK 73105
(405) 840-1359

The Elizaveta Foundation
6517 South Barnes Avenue
Oklahoma City, OK 73159
(405) 681-2722

Foundations for Families, Inc.
6202 South Lewis, #C
Tulsa, OK 74106
(918) 592-0539

Foundations for Families, Inc.
6202 South Lewis, #C

Tulsa, OK 74136
(918) 748-9177

Fresh Start
2115 North Boston Place
Tulsa, OK 74106
(918) 592-0539

Gladney Center for Adoption
6300 John Ryan Drive
Fort Worth, TX 76132-4122
(817) 922-6088
(800) 452-3639

Heritage Family Services
5200 South Yale #300
Tulsa, OK 74135
(918) 491-6767

LDS Social Services of Oklahoma
4500 South Garnett, Suite 425
Tulsa, OK 74146
(918) 665-3090

Lutheran Social Services
3000 United Founders Boulevard,
 Suite 141
Oklahoma City, OK 73112-4279
(405) 848-1733

Natasha's Story, Inc.
1554 South Yorktown Place
Tulsa, OK 74104
(918) 747-3617

Oklahoma Home Study
1820 Threestars Road
Edmond, OK 73034

Pathways International, Inc.
1616 East 19th, Suite 101B
Edmond, OK 73013
(405) 216-0909

SAFY of America
1209 Sovereign Row
Oklahoma City, OK 73108
(405) 942-5570

Small Miracles International
1148 South Douglas Boulevard
Midwest City, OK 73130
(405) 732-7295

OREGON

Oregon Department
 of Human Services
Office of Permanency
 for Children of Training
500 Summer Street, NE
Salem, OR 97301-1068
(503) 945-5677

Oregon State Office for Service
 to Children and Families
Eastern Region Office
20310 Empire Blvd, Suite A-100
Bend, OR 97701-5723
(541) 388-6414

Oregon State Office for Service to
 Children and Families
Metro Region Office
827 NE Oregon, Suite 250
Portland, OR 97232-2108
(503) 731-3075

Oregon State Office for Service
 to Children and Families
Western Region Office
15875 SW 72nd Avenue
Tigard, OR 97224
(503) 431-2339

Private Agencies

Adventist Adoption and Family
 Services Program
6040 SE Belmont Street
Portland, OR 97215
(503) 232-1211

All God's Children International
4114 NE Fremont, Suite 1

Portland, OR 97212
(503) 282-7652
(800) 214-6719

Associated Services for
  International Adoption (ASIA)
5935 Willow Lane
Lake Oswego, OR 97035-5344
(503) 697-6863

Bethany Christian Services
21125 NW West Union Road
Hillsboro, OR 97124-8543
(503) 533-2002

The Boys and Girls Aid
  Society of Oregon
018 SW Boundary Court
Portland, OR 97201
(503) 222-9661
(800) 932-2734

Cascade International
  Children's Services, Inc.
133 SW 2nd
Troutdale, OR 97060
(503) 665-1589

Casey Family Program
3910 SE Stark Street
Portland, OR 97214
(503) 239-9977

Catholic Charities, Inc.
Pregnancy Support & Open
  Adoption Services
231 SE 12th Avenue
Portland, OR 97214-9813
(503) 231-4866

China Adoption Services
PO Box 19699
Portland, OR 97280
(503) 245-0976

Columbia Adoption Services, Inc.
1445 Rosemont Road

West Linn, OR 97068-2395
(503) 655-9470

Dove Adoptions International, Inc.
3735 SE Martins
Portland, OR 97202
(503) 774-7210

Families Are Forever
4114 NE Fremont Street
Portland, OR 97212
(503) 282-7652

Give Us This Day, Inc.
333 NE Russell Street, Suite 205
Portland, OR 97212-3763
(503) 282-1123

Heritage Adoption Services
10011 SE Division Street,
  Suite 314
Portland, OR 97266
(503) 233-1099

Holt International
  Children's Services
1195 City View
PO Box 2880
Eugene, OR 97402
(541) 687-2202

Journeys of the Heart
  Adoption Services
PO Box 39
Hillsboro, OR 97123
(503) 681-3075

LDS Family Services
7410 SW Beveland Road
Tigard, OR 97223-8658
(503) 581-7483

Lutheran Community Services
  Northwest
605 SE 39th Avenue
Portland, OR 97214
(503) 231-7480

Medina Children's Services
123 16th Avenue
Seattle, WA 98122
(206) 260-1700
(800) 239-9238

New Hope Child and
  Family Agency
2611 NE 125th Street, Suite 146
Seattle, WA 98125
(206) 363-1800

New Hope Child & Family Agency
4370 NE Halsey Street, Suite 215
Portland, OR 97213
(503) 282-6726
(800) 228-3150

Northwest Adoptions and
  Family Services
PO Box 5724
Salem, OR 97304
(503) 581-6652

Open Adoption & Family
  Services, Inc.
5200 SW Macadam, Suite 250
Portland, OR 97201
(503) 226-4870

Orphans Overseas
14986 NW Cornell Road
Portland, OR 97229
(503) 297-2006

Plan Loving Adoptions
  Now (PLAN) Inc.
203 East 3rd Street, Second Floor
PO Box 667
McMinnville, OR 97128
(503) 472-8452

Tree of Life Adoption Center
9498 SW Barbur Boulevard,
  Suite 304
Portland, OR 97219
(503) 244-7374

PENNSYLVANIA

Allegheny County Children & Youth
400 North Lexington Street
Pittsburgh, PA 15208
(412) 473-2300

Indiana County Children & Youth
Indiana County Courthouse
825 Philadelphia Street
Indiana, PA 15701
(724) 465-3895

Lackawanna County Children
  & Youth
200 Adams Avenue, Fourth Floor
Scranton, PA 18503
(570) 963-6781

Pennsylvania Department
  of Public Welfare
Office of Children, Youth and
  Families
7th & Forster Street
PO Box 2675
Harrisburg, PA 17105-2675
(717) 705-2912

Private Agencies

AAA Transitions Adoption Agency
355 West Lancaster Avenue
Haverford, PA 19041
(610) 642-4155

Adelphoi Village
1003 Village Way
Latrobe, PA 15650
(724) 520-1111

Adopt America Network
1020 Manesville Road
Shippensburg, PA 17257
(717) 532-9005

Adopt-A-Child
6315 Forbes Avenue, Suite L-111

Pittsburgh, PA 15217
(412) 421-1911
(800) 246-4848

Adoption ARC, Inc.
4701 Pine Street, J-7
Philadelphia, PA 19143
(215) 844-1082
(800) 884-4004

Adoption by Choice
2503 West 15th Street, Suite 4
Erie, PA 16509
(814) 836-9887

The Adoption Connection
709 Third Avenue
New Brighton, PA 15066
(724) 846-2615

Adoption Horizons
899 Petersburg Road
Carlisle, PA 17103
(717) 249-8850

Adoption Services, Inc.
28 Central Boulevard
Camp Hill, PA 17011
(717) 737-3960

Adoption Services of the Lutheran
  Home at Topton
Diakon Lutheran Social Ministries
One South Home Avenue
Topton, PA 19562-1317
(610) 682-1504
(888) 582-2230

Adoption Unlimited
2148 Embassy Drive
Lancaster, PA 17603
(717) 431-2021

Adoptions From The Heart
9 Claremont Drive
Greensburg, PA 15601
(724) 853-6533

Adoptions From The Heart
30-31 Hampstead Circle
Wynnewood, PA 19096
(610) 642-7200

Adoptions From The Heart
800 Main Street, Suite 101
Hellertown, PA 18055
(610) 838–9240

Adoptions From The Heart
1525 Oregon Pike, Suite 401-402
Lancaster, PA 17601
(717) 399-7766

Adoptions International Inc.
601 South 10th Street
Philadelphia, PA 19147
(215) 627-6313

American Friends of Children
619 Gawain Road
Plymouth Meeting, PA 19464
(610) 828-8166

Asian Angels
124 Chestnut Street, Suite 2
Philadelphia, PA 19106
(215) 733-0494

Asociacion Puertorriquenos
  en Marcha
2147 North Sixth Street
Philadelphia, PA 19122
(215) 235-6788

The Bair Foundation
241 High Street
New Wilmington, PA 16142
(724) 946-8711
(800) 543-7058

Bennett and Simpson Enrichment
  Services Adoption
4300 Monument Road
Philadelphia, PA 19131
(215) 877-1925

Best Nest
325 Market Street
Williamsport, PA 17701
(570) 321-1969

Best Nest
1335-37 Pine Street
Philadelphia, PA 19107
(215) 546-8060

Bethany Christian Services
550 Pinetown Road, Suite 100
Fort Washington, PA 19034-2606
(215) 628-0202
(800) 215-0702

Bethany Christian Services of
  Central Pennsylvania
1681 Crown Avenue
Lancaster, PA 17601
(717) 399-3213

A Brave Choice
1011 Cedargrove Road
Wynnewood, PA 19096
(610) 642-7182

Catholic Charities Counseling and
  Adoption Services
90 Beaver Drive, Suite 111B
Dubois, PA 15801-2424
(814) 371-4717

Catholic Social Agency
2147 Perkiomen Avenue
Reading, PA 19606
(610) 370-3378

Catholic Social Services
81 South Church Street
Hazleton, PA 18201
(570) 455-1521

Catholic Social Services
102 Warren Street
Tunkhannock, PA 18657
(570) 835-1101

Catholic Social Services
411 Main Street
Stroudsburg, PA 18360
(570) 476-6460

Catholic Social Services
  of Luzerne County
33 East Northampton Street
Wilkes-Barre, PA 18701-2406
(570) 822-7118

Catholic Social Services of
  Lycoming County
1201 Grampian Blvd, Suite 2G
Williamsport, PA 17701-1900
(570) 322-4220

Catholic Social Services of the
  Archdiocese of Philadelphia
222 North 17th Street
Philadelphia, PA 19103
(215) 587-3900

Catholic Social Services of the
  Diocese of Altoona-Johnstown
1300 Twelfth Avenue
PO Box 1349
Altoona, PA 16603
(814) 944-9388

Catholic Social Services of the
  Diocese of Scranton
400 Wyoming Avenue
Scranton, PA 18503
(570) 346-8936

Cherubs for Us
494 Regionald Lane
Collegeville, PA 19426
(610) 489-8590

Children's Aid Society in
  Clearfield County
1008 South Second Street
Clearfield, PA 16830
(814) 765-2685

Children's Choice
2909 North Front Street
Harrisburg, PA 17110
(717) 230-9980

Children's Choice
International Plaza II, Suite 325
Philadelphia, PA 19119
(610) 521-6270

The Children's Home Society
  of New Jersey
771 North Pennsylvania Avenue
Morrisville, PA 19067
(215) 736-8550

The Children's Home of Pittsburgh
5618 Kentucky Avenue
Pittsburgh, PA 15232
(412) 441-4884

Church of the Brethren Youth
  Services
1417 Oregon Road
Leola, PA 17540
(717) 656-6580

Common Sense Adoption Services
5021 East Trindle Road
Mechanicsburg, PA 17050
(717) 766-6449
(800) 445-2444

Community Adoption Services of
  Heavenly Vision Ministries
6513 Meadow Street
Pittsburgh, PA 15206
(412) 661-4774

Covenant Family Resources
743 Roy Road
King of Prussia, PA 19406
(610) 354-0555

Delta Community Supports
2210 Mt. Carmel Avenue,
  Suite 105

Glenside, PA 19038
(215) 887-6300

Diversified Family Services
3679 East State Street
Hermitage, PA 16148
(724) 346-2123

The Eckels Adoption Agency
994 Vallamont Drive
Williamsport, PA 17701
(570) 323-2520

Families Caring for Children
96 Front Street
Nanticoke, PA 18634
(570) 735-9028

Families United Network
Brinton Avenue
PO Box 144
Trafford, PA 15085
(412) 373-2355

Family Adoption Center
960 Penn Avenue, Suite 600
Pittsburgh, PA 15222
(412) 288-2130

Family Service
630 Janet Avenue
Lancaster, PA 17601
(717) 397-5241

Family Services and Children's Aid
  Society of Venango County
716 East Second Street
Oil City, PA 16301
(814) 677-4005

Family Services of Western
  Pennsylvania
3230 William Pitt Way
Pittsburgh, PA 15238
(412) 820-2050
(888) 222-4200

Friends Association for the Care
and Protection of Children
206 North Church Street
PO Box 439
West Chester, PA 19381
(610) 431-3598

Friendship House
1561 Medical Drive
Pottstown, PA 19464
(610) 327-2200

Genesis of Pittsburgh
PO Box 41017
Pittsburgh, PA 15202
(412) 766-2693

Heart to Heart Adoption
Services, Inc.
Fox Lure Building
504 Benner Pike
Bellefonte, PA 16823
(814) 355-4310

ILB Adoption Agency
734 Melbourne Street
Pittsburgh, PA 15217
(412) 521-2413

International Assistance Group
531 Fifth Street
Oakmont, PA 15139
(412) 828-5800
(800) 720-7384

International Families Adoption
Agency
518 South 12th Street
Philadelphia, PA 19147
(215) 735-7171

Jewish Family and Children's
Service
5743 Barlett Street
Pittsburgh, PA 15217
(412) 428-7200

Jewish Family and Children's
Service of Philadelphia Inc.
10125 Verree Road, #200
Philadelphia, PA 19116
(215) 698-9950

KidsPeace National Centers for
Kids in Crisis
5300 KidsPeace Drive
Orefield, PA 18069
(800) 854-3123

La Vida International
150 South Warner Rd., Suite 144
King of Prussia, PA 19406
(610) 688-8008

LDS Social Services
46 School Street
Greentree, PA 15205
(412) 921-8303

Little Emperor Adoption Services
202 Berkshire Lane
Royersford, PA 19468
(610) 409-9711
(800) 670-4114

Living Hope Adoption Agency
PO Box 439
Telford, PA 18969
(215) 672-7471
(888) 886-8086

Love the Children
221 West Broad Street
Quakertown, PA 18951
(215) 536-4181

Madison Adoption Associates
2414 Blueball Avenue
Boothwyn, PA 19061
(610) 459-4970

New Beginnings Family and
Children's Services
8 Pennsylvania Avenue

Matamoras, PA 18336
(570) 491-2366

New Foundations
6801-17 North 16th Street
Philadelphia, PA 19126
(215) 424-1144

Northeast Treatment Center
493 North 5th Street, Suite A
Philadelphia, PA 19123
(215) 574-9500

One Another Adoption Program
50 Market Street
Hellam, PA 17406
(717) 600-2059

Open Door Children and Youth
  Services
606 Court Street, Suite 404
Reading, PA 19601
(610) 372-2200

PAACT
703 North Market Street
Liverpool, PA 17045
(717) 444-3629

Perl, Inc.
434 West Carpenter Lane
Philadelphia, PA 19119
(215) 849-8072

Pinebrook Services for Children
  & Youth
402 North Fulton Street
Allentown, PA 18102-2002
(610) 432-3919

Plan-It For Kids, PC
501 Main Street, Suite 101
Berlin, PA 15530
(814) 267-3182
(888) 810-5727

Presbyterian Children's Village
452 South Roberts Road

Rosemont, PA 19010
(610) 525-5400

Project STAR of Permanency
  Planning Advocates of
  Western Pennsylvania
6301 Northumberland Street
Pittsburgh, PA 15217
(412) 521-9000

Rainbow Project
120 Charles Street
Pittsburgh, PA 15238
(412) 782-4457

REJOICE
1800 State Street
Harrisburg, PA 17101
(717) 221-0722

A Second Chance
1964 Hawthorne Lane
Hatfield, PA 19440
(215) 412-2966

The Social Work Agency
1158 York Road
Warminster, PA 18974
(218) 343-8500

Spectrum Family Network
  Adoption Services
415 Gettysburg Street
Pittsburgh, PA 15206
(412) 362-3600

Tabor Children's Services
601 New Britain Road
Doylestown, PA 18901-4248
(215) 348-4071

Three Rivers Adoption Council
Black Adoption Services
307 4th Avenue, Suite 710
Pittsburgh, PA 15222
(412) 471-8722

Tressler Lutheran Services
836 South George Street
York, PA 17403
(717) 845-9113

Try-Again Homes
365 Jefferson Avenue
PO Box 1228
Washington, PA 15301
(724) 225-0510

Welcome House Adoption Program
 of Pearl S. Buck International
520 Dublin Road
PO Box 181
Perkasie, PA 18944
(215) 249-0100

World Links
1418 Main Street
Blakely, PA 18452
(570) 344-8890

RHODE ISLAND

Rhode Island Department of
 Children, Youth and Families
530 Wood Street
Bristol, RI 02805
(401) 254-7010

Private Agencies

Adoption Network, Ltd.
PO Box 195
Wakefield, RI 02880-0195
(800) 285-0450

Alliance for Children
500 Prospect Street
Pawtucket, RI 02860
(401) 725-9555

American-International
 Children's Alliance, Inc. (AICA)
1445 Wampanoag Trail, Suite 101

East Providence, RI 02915
(866) 862-3678

Bethany Christian Services
706 Warwick Avenue
PO Box 8939
Warwick, RI 02888
(401) 467-1395

Catholic Social Services
Reaching Out Adoption
 & Foster Care
311 Hooper Street
Tiverton, RI 02878
(401) 624-0970

Children's Friend & Service
153 Summer Street
Providence, RI 02903
(401) 331-2900

Communities for People
221 Waterman Street
Providence, RI 02906
(401) 273-7103

Friends in Adoption
PO Box 1194
Newport, RI 02840-0012
(401) 831-1120
(800) 982-3678

Gift of Life Adoption Services, Inc.
1051-1053 Park Avenue
Cranston, RI 02910
(401) 943-6484

International Adoptions
726 Front Street
Woonsocket, RI 02895
(401) 767-2300

Jewish Family Services/
 Adoption Options
229 Waterman Avenue
Providence, RI 02906
(401) 331-5437

Links to Adoption
21 Carlton Avenue
East Providence, RI 02916
(401) 434-1353

Little Treasures Adoption Services
PO Box 20555
Cranston, RI 02920
(401) 828-7747

Lutheran Social Services
 of New England
Rhode Island Adoption Program
116 Rolfe Street
Cranston, RI 02910
(401) 785-0015
(800) 286-9889

A Red Thread Adoption Services
333 Westminister Street
Providence, RI 02903
(888) 871-9699

Urban League of
 Rhode Island, Inc.
Minority Recruitment and
 Child Placement Program
246 Prairie Avenue
Providence, RI 02905
(401) 351-5000

Wide Horizons for Children
245 Waterman Street, Suite 504
Providence, RI 02906
(401) 421-4752

SOUTH CAROLINA

South Carolina Department of
 Social Services
Division of Human Services
PO Box 1520
Columbia, SC 29202-1520
(803) 898-7707
(800) 922-2504

Private Agencies

Adoption Center of South Carolina
PO Box 5961
Columbia, SC 29250
(803) 771-2272

Bethany Christian Services
1411 Barnwell Street
Columbia, SC 29201-2300
(803) 779-0541
(800) 922-0682

Bethany Christian Services
4605-C Oleander Drive
Myrtle Beach, SC 29577
(843) 839-5433
(800) 922-0682

Bethany Christian Services
2141 B Hoffmeyer Road
Florence, SC 29501-4077
(843) 629-1177
(800) 922-0682

Bethany Christian Services
620 East Washington Street
Greenville, SC 29601-2995
(864) 235-2273
(800) 922-0682

Carolina Hope Christian
 Adoption Agency
300 Yorkshire Drive
Greenville, SC 29615
(864) 268-0570

Catholic Charities of Charleston
1662 Ingram Road
Charleston, SC 29407
(843) 769-4466

Child of the Heart
741 Johnnie Dodds Boulevard,
 Suite 207
Mt. Pleasant, SC 29407
(843) 881-2973

Children First
PO Box 11907
Columbia, SC 29211
(803) 771-0534

Children Unlimited, Inc.
The Attachment Center of South
  Carolina
1825 Gadsden Street
Columbia, SC 29211
(803) 799-8311
(800) 822-0877

A Chosen Child Adoption Services
415 King Charles Circle
Summerville, SC 29485
(843) 851-4004

Christian Family Services
2166-A Gold Hill Road, #A
Fort Mill, SC 29708-9351
(803) 548-6030

Christian World Adoption, Inc.
111 Ashley Avenue
Charleston, SC 29401
(843) 722-6343

Epworth Children's Home
2900 Millwood Avenue
PO Box 50466
Columbia, SC 29250
(803) 256-7394

LDS Social Services
5624 Executive Center Drive,
  Suite 109
Charlotte, NC 28212-8832
(704) 535-2436

Reid House
169 St. Phillip Street
PO Box 22132
Charleston, SC 29413
(843) 723-7138
(888) 651-3240

Southeastern Children's
  Home, Inc.
155 Children's Home
Duncan, SC 29334
(864) 439-0259

SOUTH DAKOTA

South Dakota Department
  of Social Services
Child Protection Services
700 Governor's Drive
Kneip Building
Pierre, SD 57501-2291
(605) 773-3227

Private Agencies

Bethany Christian Services
625 South Minnesota Avenue,
  Suite 103
Sioux Falls, SD 57104
(605) 336-6999

Bethany Christian Services
2525 West Main Street, #309
Rapid City, SD 57702-2443
(605) 343-7196

Catholic Family Services
Catholic Diocese of Sioux Falls
523 North Duluth Avenue
Sioux Falls, SD 57104-2714
(605) 334-9861

Catholic Social Services
918 Fifth Street
Rapid City, SD 57701-3798
(605) 348-6086

Child Protection Program
Sisseton Wahpeton Dakota Nation
PO Box 509
Agency Village, SD 57262-9802
(605) 698-3992

Children's Home Society
PO Box 1749
Sioux Falls, SD 57101-1749
(605) 334-3431

LDS Social Services
2525 West Main Street, #310
Rapid City, SD 57702-2443
(605) 342-3500

Lutheran Social Services
705 East 41st Street, Suite 200
Sioux Falls, SD 57105-6048
(605) 357-0100
(800) 568-2401

New Horizons Adoption Agency
27213 473rd Avenue
Sioux Falls, SD 57106
(605) 332-0310

Yankton Sioux Tribal Social
  Services
PO Box 248
Marty, SD 57361-0248
(605) 384-3804

TENNESSEE

Department of Children's Services
Mid-Cumberland/Davidson Region
Center for Adoption
1210 Foster Avenue
Nashville, TN 37243
(615) 253-3311
(800) 362-2071

Tennessee Department of
  Children's Services
436 Sixth Avenue North
Cordell Hull Building, Eighth Floor
Nashville, TN 37243-1290
(615) 532-5637

Tennessee Department of
  Children's Services
Eastern Tennessee Region

182 Frank L. Diggs Drive,
  Suite 100
Clinton, TN 37716
(865) 425-4400
(877) 357-0014

Tennessee Department of
  Children's Services
Knox Region
531 Henley Street, Suite 403
Knoxville, TN 37902
(423) 594-6633
(877) 357-0012

Tennessee Department of
  Children's Services
Northeast Region
PO Box 2120
Johnson City, TN 37605
(423) 434-6921
(877) 357-0011

Tennessee Department of
  Children's Services
Shelby Region
170 North Main Street,
  Seventh Floor
Memphis, TN 38103
(901) 578-4254
(877) 822-0015

Tennessee Department of
  Children's Services
South Central Region
Maury County DCS
PO Box 800
Columbia, TN 38402
(931) 380-3311
(800) 362-2071

Tennessee Department of
  Children's Services
Upper Cumberland Region
1300 Salem Road
Cookeville, TN 38501
(931) 646-3005
(888) 335-9486

Private Agencies

Adoption Advantage, Inc.
1661 International Drive,
Suite 400
Memphis, TN 38120
(901) 758-2997

Adoption Place, Inc.
505 Oak Forest Circle
Antioch, TN 37013
(615) 365-7020

Adoption Resource Services, Inc.
218 South Third Street, #2
Elkhard, IN 46516
(800) 288-2499

AGAPE Child and
  Family Services, Inc.
111 Racine Street
Memphis, TN 38111
(901) 323-3600

Associated Catholic Charities
  of the Diocese of Memphis
St. Peter's Home
3060 Baskin Street
Memphis, TN 38127-7799
(901) 354-6300

Bethany Christian Services
400 South Germantown Road
Chattanooga, TN 37411-5025
(423) 622-7360
(800) 765-7335

Catholic Charities of
  Tennessee, Inc.
30 White Bridge Road
Nashville, TN 37205
(615) 352-3087
(800) 227-3002

Child and Family Services, Inc.
201 North Royal Street
Jackson, TN 38301-6331
(615) 422-1107

Child and Family Services
  of Knox County
901 East Summit Hill Drive
Knoxville, TN 37915
(865) 524-7483

A Child's Dream
1346 Quai Valley Trail
Apison, TN 37302-9533
(423) 236-4509

Children's Hope International
7003 Chadwick Drive, Suite 350
Brentwood, TN 37027
(615) 309-8109

Christian Children's Homes
  of Tennessee
2600 State Line Road
PO Box 285
Elizabethton, TN 37644
(423) 542-4245

Christian Counseling Services
515 Wood Land Street
Nashville, TN 37206

Family and Children's
  Services–Center for Adoption
1210 Foster Avenue
Nashville, TN 37243
(615) 253-3289
(800) 807-3228

Family and Children's Services of
  Chattanooga, Inc.
1800 McCallie Avenue
Chattanooga, TN 37403
(423) 755-2800

Frontier Health
Traces
2001 Stonebrook Place
Kingsport, TN 37660
(424) 224-1067

Global Village International
  Adoptions
615 Tides Ridge Court
Murfreesboro, TN 37128
(615) 848-5278

Greater Chattanooga Christian
  Services and Children's Home
744 McCallie Avenue, Suite 329
Chattanooga, TN 37403
(423) 756-0281

Guardian Angel International
  Adoptions
408 Douglass Drive
Lawrenceburg, TN 38464
(931) 766-5277

Happy Haven Homes, Inc.
2311 Wakefield Drive
Cookeville, TN 38501
(931) 526-2052

Harmony Adoptions of
  Tennessee, Inc.
311 High Street
Maryville, TN 37804
(865) 892-5225

Heaven Sent Children, Inc.
PO Box 2514
Murfreesboro, TN 37130
(615) 898-0803

Holston United Methodist Home
  for Children, Inc.
404 Holston Drive
PO Box 188
Greeneville, TN 37744
(423) 638-4171
(800) 628-2986

International Assistance and
  Adoption Project
1210-G Taft Highway
Signal Mountain, TN 37377

Jewish Family Services, Inc.
6560 Poplar Avenue
Memphis, TN 38138
(901) 767-8511

Knoxville Family Service Center
9915 D Kingston Pike
Knoxville, TN 37992
(865) 691-9963

Life Choices, Inc.
813 Timbercreek Drive
PO Box 806
Cordova, TN 38018
(901) 323-5433

Madison Children's Home
616 North Dupont Avenue
PO Box 419
Madison, TN 37116-0419
(615) 860-4461

Memphis Family Service Center
2969 South Mendenhall
Memphis, TN 38115
(901) 636-1189

Mid-Cumberland Children's
  Services, Inc.
106 North Mountain Street
Smithville, TN 37166
(615) 597-7134

Mid-South Christian Services
1044 Brookfield Road, Suite 102
Memphis, TN 38119
(901) 818-9996

Northeast Region Adoption
213 West Maple Street
PO Box 2120
Johnson City, TN 37601
(423) 434-6921

Omni Visions
101 Lea Avenue
Nashville, TN 37210

(615) 726-3603
(800) 851-6108

Porter-Leath Children's Center
868 North Manassas Street
Memphis, TN 38107-2516
(901) 577-2500
Fax: (901) 577-2506

Small World Adoption Programs
401 Bonnaspring Drive
Hermitage, TN 37076
(615) 883-4372
(800) 544-5083

Smoky Mountain Children's Home
449 McCarn Circle
PO Box 4391
Sevierville, TN 37864-4391

Tennessee Baptist Children's
  Homes, Inc.
PO Box 2206
Brentwood, TN 37024-2206
(615) 376-3140
(800) 624-8591

Tennessee Children's Home
1115 Ranch Road
Ashland City, TN 37015
(615) 307-3205

Williams-Illien Adoptions, Inc.
3439 Venson Drive
Memphis, TN 38135

Williams International
  Adoptions, Inc.
5100 Stage Road, Suite A
Memphis, TN 38134
(901) 373-6003

Zambo Counseling and
  Consulting Services
20796 East Main Street
Huntingdon, TN 38344
(731) 986-2001

TEXAS

Texas Department of Protective and
  Regulatory Services
PO Box 149030, E-557
Austin, TX 78717-9030
(512) 438-3412

Private Agencies

AAA-Alamo Adoption Agency
PO Box 781
Adkins, TX 78101-0781
(210) 967-5337

ABC Adoption Agency, Inc.
417 San Pedro Avenue
San Antonio, TX 78212
(210) 227-7820

Abrazo Adoption Associates
10010 San Pedro
San Antonio, TX 78216
(210) 342-5683
(800) 454-5683

Adoption-A Gift of Love
PO Box 50384
Denton, TX 76206
(817) 387-9311

Adoption Access
8330 Meadow Road, Suite 222
Dallas, TX 75231
(214) 750-4847

Adoption Advisory, Inc.
3607 Fairmount Street
Dallas, TX 75219
(214) 520-0004

Adoption Advocates, Inc.
328 West Mistletoe Avenue
San Antonio, TX 78212
(210) 734-4470

Adoption Affiliates, Inc.
215 West Olmos Drive
San Antonio, TX 78212
(210) 824-9939

The Adoption Alliance
7303 Blanco Road
San Antonio, TX 78216
(210) 349-3991

Adoption Angels, Inc.
118 Broadway, Suite 517
San Antonio, TX 78205
(210) 227-2229

Adoption As An Option
12611 Kingsride Lane
Houston, TX 77024
(713) 468-1053

Adoption Family Service
5402 Arapaho
Dallas, TX 75240
(972) 437-9950

Adoption Information
 and Counseling
2020 Southwest Freeway,
 Suite 326
Houston, TX 77098
(713) 529-5125

Adoption Services Associates
5370 Prue Road
San Antonio, TX 78240
(800) 648-1807

Adoption Services, Inc.
3500 Overton Park West
Fort Worth, TX 76109
(817) 921-0718

Adoption Services Worldwide, Inc.
7300 Blanco Road, Suite 206
San Antonio, TX 78216
(210) 342-0444

Adoptions International, Inc.
6510 Abrams Road, Suite 600
Dallas, TX 75231
(214) 342-8388

All Church Home for Children
1424 Summit Avenue
Fort Worth, TX 76102
(817) 335-4041

Andrel Adoptions
3908 Manchaca
Austin, TX 78704
(512) 448-4605

Angel Adoptions of the Heart
2715 Bissonet #221
Houston, TX 77005
(713) 523-2273

Atlantis Foundation
2800 NASA Road One,
 Suite 1406
Seabrook, TX 77586
(281) 326-1201

Bethany Christian Services of
 North Texas
10310 North Central Expressway
Building III, Suite 360
Dallas, TX 75231-8627
(214) 373-8797
(800) 650-6226

Buckner Adoption and
 Maternity Services Inc.
4830 Samuell Boulevard
Dallas, TX 75228
(214) 381-1552

Catholic Counseling Services
PO Box 190507
Dallas, TX 75219-0507
(214) 526-2772

Catholic Family Service
PO Box 15127

Amarillo, TX 79105
(806) 376-4571

Catholic Social Services of Laredo
PO Box 3305
Laredo, TX 78044
(210) 722-2443

Child Placement Center
2212 Sunny Lane
Killeen, TX 76541
(254) 690-5959

Children and Family Institute
5787 South Hampton Road,
  Suite 360
Dallas, TX 75232
(214) 337-9979

Children's Home of Lubbock
PO Box 2824
Lubbock, TX 79408
(806) 762-0481

Chosen Heritage -
  Christian Adoptions
121 NE Loop 820
Hurst, TX 76053
(817) 589-7899

Christian Homes
PO Box 270
Abilene, TX 79604
(915) 677-2205
(800) 592-4725

Christian Services of the Southwest
6320 LBJ Freeway, Suite 122
Dallas, TX 75240
(972) 960-9981

Counsel for Adoption Resources
1201 South W.S. Young Drive,
  Suite F
Killeen, TX 76541
(254) 690-2223

A Cradle of Hope
311 North Market Street,
  Suite 300
Dallas, TX 75202
(214) 747-4500

Cradle of Life Adoption Agency
245 North Fourth Street
Beaumont, TX 77701
(409) 832-3000
(800) 456-8001

DePelchin Children's Center
100 Sandman Street
Houston, TX 77007
(713) 730-2335
(888) 730-2335

El Paso Adoption Services, Inc.
905 Noble Street
El Paso, TX 79902
(915) 542-1086

El Paso Center for Children
3700 Altura Boulevard
El Paso, TX 79930
(915) 565-8361

Gladney Center for Adoption
6300 John Ryan Drive
Fort Worth, TX 76132-4122
(817) 922-6088
(800) 452-3639

Great Wall China Adoption
248 Addie Roy Road, A102
Austin, TX 78746
(512) 323-9595

Homes of Saint Mark
3000 Richmond Avenue,
  Suite 570
Houston, TX 77098
(713) 522-2800

Hope Cottage, Inc.
Circle of Hope

4209 McKinney Avenue
Dallas, TX 75205
(214) 526-8721

Hope Cottage Pregnancy and
  Adoption Center
4209 McKinney Avenue
Dallas, TX 75205
(214) 526-8721

Hope International
311 North Market Street,
  Suite 300
Dallas, TX 75202
(214) 672-9399

Hope for Tomorrow
1305 Early Boulevard
Early, TX 76802
(915) 646-4673

Inheritance Adoptions
PO Box 2563
Wichita Falls, TX 76307
(817) 322-3678

J&B Kids, Inc. Placing Agency
Route 1, Box 173 F
Yorktown, TX 78164
(512) 564-2964

LDS Social Services-Texas
1100 West Jackson Road
Carrollton, TX 75006
(972) 242-2182

Lena Pope Home, Inc.
3131 Sanguinet Street
Fort Worth, TX 76107
(817) 731-8681

LIMIAR
111 Broken Bough
San Antonio, TX 78231
(210) 479-0300

Los Ninos International
  Adoption Center
2408 Timberloch Place, Suite D1
The Woodlands, TX 77380
(281) 363-2892

Loving Alternatives Adoptions
PO Box 131466
Tyler, TX 75713
(903) 581-7720

Lutheran Social Services
  of Texas, Inc.
PO Box 40589
Austin, TX 78765

Lutheran Social Services
  of the South, Inc.
8305 Cross Park Drive
PO Box 140767
Austin, TX 78714
(512) 459-1000
(800) 938-5777

Marywood Children and Family
  Services
510 West 26th Street
Austin, TX 78705
(512) 472-9251
(800) 251-5433

Methodist Children's Home
1111 Herring Avenue
Waco, TX 76708
(254) 750-1260

New Life Children's Services
19911 State Highway 249
Houston, TX 77070
(713) 955-1001
(800) 432-9124

Orphan Voyage
Linda Crenwelge
1305 Augustine Court
College Station, TX 77840
(409) 764-7157

PAC Child Placing Agency
4655 South FM 1258
Amarillo, TX 79118-7219
(806) 335-9138

Read Adoption Agency, Inc.
1011 North Mesa
El Paso, TX 79902
(915) 533-3697

Smithlawn Maternity Home
  and Adoption Agency
PO Box 6451
Lubbock, TX 79493
(806) 745-2574

Spaulding for Children
8552 Katy Freeway, Suite 300
Houston, TX 77024
(713) 681-6991

Texas Baptist Children's Home
PO Box 7
Round Rock, TX 78664
(512) 388-8256

Unity Children's Home
12027 Blue Mountain
Houston, TX 77067
(713) 537-6148

UTAH

The Adoption Exchange
Utah Office
1065 East 3300 South
Salt Lake City, UT 84106
(801) 412-0200

Utah Department of
  Human Services
Division of Child and
  Family Services
120 North, 200 West
PO Box 45500

Salt Lake City, UT 84103
(801) 538-4078

Private Agencies

Adopt an Angel
  254 West 400 South, Suite 320
Salt Lake City, UT 84101
(801) 537-1622

Adoption Center of Choice, Inc.
241 West, 520 North
Orem, UT 84057
(801) 224-2440

Catholic Community Services
2570 West 1700 South
Salt Lake City, UT 84104
(801) 977-9119

A Cherished Child Adoption Agency
2120 Willow Park Lane
Sandy, UT 84093
(801) 947-5900

Children of Peace
715 East, 3900 South, Suite 203
Salt Lake City, UT 84107-2182
(801) 263-2111

Children's Aid Society of Utah
652 26th Street
Ogden, UT 84401
(801) 393-8671

Children's House International
1236 North, 150 West
American Fork, UT 84003
(801) 756-0587

Children's House International
PO Box 2321
Salt Lake City, UT 84110
Children's Service Society
124 South, 400 East, Suite 400
Salt Lake City, UT 84111

(801) 355-7444
(800) 839-7444

Families for Children
PO Box 521192
Salt Lake City, UT 84152-1192
(801) 467-3413

Family and Adoption
  Counseling Center
211 East Highland Avenue
Sandy, UT 84070
(801) 568-1771

Heart to Heart Adoptions, Inc.
PO Box 57573
Murray, UT 84157
(801) 270-8017

LDS Family Services
10 E. South Temple, Suite 1200
Salt Lake City, UT 84111
(801) 240-6500

LDS Family Services
55 West, 100 North
Richfield, UT 84701
(435) 896-6446

LDS Family Services
95 West, 100 South, Suite 340
Logan, UT 84321
(435) 752-5302

LDS Family Services
294 East, 100 South
Price, UT 84501
(435) 637-2991

LDS Family Services
625 East, 8400 South
(801) 566-2556

LDS Family Services
1190 North, 900 East
Provo, UT 84604
(801) 378-7620

LDS Family Services
1400 West State Street
Pleasant Grove, UT 84062
(801) 796-9509

LDS Family Services
1466 North Highway 89,
  Suite 220
Farmington, UT 84025-2738
(801) 451-0475

LDS Family Services
1525 Lincoln Avenue
Ogden, UT 84404
(801) 621-6510

LDS Social Services
2202 North Main Street,
  Suite 301
Cedar City, UT 84720-9790
(435) 586-4479

LDS Family Services
2480 East Redcliff Drive
St. George, UT 84790
(435) 673-6446

LDS Family Services
4250 West, 5415 South
Kearns, UT 84118
(801) 969-4181

Premier Adoption Agency
952 South Freedom
  Boulevard #26
Provo, UT 84601
(801) 808-9738

West Sands Adoption
  and Counseling
461 East 2780 North
Provo, UT 84604
(801) 377-4379

VERMONT

Vermont Department of Social and
  Rehabilitation Services
103 South Main Street
Waterbury, VT 05671
(802) 241-2142

Vermont Division of Social and
  Rehabilitation Services
Central Office
103 South Main Street
Waterbury, VT 05671-2401
(802) 241-2131
(800) 241-2131

Private Agencies

Acorn Adoption, Inc.
278 Pearl Street
Burlington, VT 05401-8558
(802) 865-3898

Adoption Advocates
521 Webster Road
Shelburne, VT 05482-6513
(802) 985-8289

Angels' Haven Outreach
PO Box 53
Monkton, VT 05469
(802) 453-5450

Bethany Christian Services
1538 Turnpike Street
North Andover, MA 01845-6221
(978) 794-9800
(800) 941-4865

Casey Family Services
60 South Main Street
Waterbury, VT 05676
(802) 244-1408
(800) 244-1408

Casey Family Services
160 Palmer Court
White River Junction, VT 05001-
  3323
(802) 649-1400
(800) 607-1400

Friends in Adoption
44 South Street
PO Box 1228
Middletown Springs, VT 05757-
  1228
(802) 235-2373

Friends in Adoption
The Maltex Building
431 Pine Street, #7
Burlington, VT 05401-4726
(802) 865-9886

LDS Social Services
547 Amherst Street, Suite 404
Nashua, NH 03063-4000
(603) 889-0148
(800) 735-0419

Lund Family Center
76 Glen Road
PO Box 4009
Burlington, VT 05406-4009
(802) 864-7467
(800) 639-1741

Vermont Catholic Charities
24 1/2 Center Street
Rutland, VT 05701
(802) 773-3379

Vermont Catholic Charities
351 North Avenue
Burlington, VT 05401-2921
(802) 658-6110, Ext: 312

Vermont Children's Aid Society
32 Pleasant Street
Woodstock, VT 05091
(802) 457-3084

Vermont Children's Aid Society
79 Weavers Street
Winooski, VT 05404
(802) 655-0006
(800) 479-0015

Vermont Children's Aid Society
207 West Main Street
PO Box 4085
Bennington, VT 05201
(802) 422-7901
(802) 422-0974

Wide Horizons For Children
PO Box 53
Monkton, VT 05469
(802) 453-2581

VIRGINIA

Virginia Department of Social
  Services
Central Regional Office
1604 Santa Rosa Road
Wythe Building, Suite 130
Richmond, VA 23229
(804) 662-7653

Virginia Department Of Social
  Services
Division of Family Services
730 East Broad Street
Richmond, VA 21219-1849
(804) 692-1290

Virginia Department of
  Social Services
Eastern Regional Office
Pembroke IV Office Building,
  Suite 300
Pembroke Office Park
Virginia Beach, VA 23462
(757) 491-3999

Virginia Department of
  Social Services
Piedmont Regional Office
Commonwealth Building,
  Suite 100
210 Church Avenue SW
Roanoke, VA 24011
(540) 857-7920

Virginia Department of
  Social Services
Northern Regional Office
170 West Shirley, Suite 31
Warrenton, VA 20186
(540) 347-6300

Virginia Department of
  Social Services
Western Regional Office
19 Patton Street
Abingdon, VA 24210
(540) 676-5490

Private Agencies

ABC Adoption Services, Inc.
4725 Garst Mill Road
Roanoke, VA 24018
(540) 989-2845

Adoption Center of Washington
100 Daingerfield Road, Suite 101
Alexandria, VA 22314
(703) 549-7774
(800) 452-3878

Adoption Service Information
  Agency, Inc. (ASIA)
1305 North Jackson Street
Arlington, VA 22201
(703) 312-0263

Adoptions From the Heart, Inc.
625 Water Oak Court
Chesapeake, VA 23322
(757) 546-3874

America World Adoption
  Association
6723 Whittier Avenue, Suite 406
McLean, VA 22101
(703) 356-8447
(800) 429-3369

Barker Foundation
2955 Monticello Drive
Falls Church, VA 22042
(703) 536-1827
(800) 673-8489

Beam of Hope
13801 Village Mill Drive
Midlothian, VA 23114
(804) 594-3737
(877) 263-4673

Bethany Christian Services, Inc.
287 Independence Boulevard,
  Suite 241
Virginia Beach, VA 23462-2956
(757) 499-9367

Bethany Christian Services, Inc.
10378-B Democracy Lane
Fairfax, VA 22030-2522
(703) 385-5440

Bethany Christian Services, Inc.
1924 Arlington Boulevard,
  Suite 101
Charlottesville, VA 22903
(804) 979-9631

Catholic Charities of Hampton
  Roads, Inc.
1301 Colonial Avenue
Norfolk, VA 23517
(757) 625-2568

Catholic Charities of
  Hampton Roads, Inc.
3757 Poplar Hill Road, Suite A
Chesapeake, VA 23321
(757) 484-0703

Catholic Charities of
  Hampton Roads, Inc.
4855 Princess Anne Road
Virginia Beach, VA 23462-4446
(757) 467-7707

Catholic Charities of
  Hampton Roads, Inc.
12829-A Jefferson Avenue,
  Suite 101
Newport News, VA 23608
(757) 875-0060

Catholic Charities of the
  Diocese of Arlington, Inc.
200 North Glebe Road, Suite 506
Arlington, VA 22203
(703) 841-3830

Catholic Charities of the
  Diocese of Arlington, Inc.
612 Lafayette Boulevard, Suite 50
Fredericksburg, VA 22401
(540) 371-1124

Catholic Charities of the
  Diocese of Arlington, Inc.
1011 Berryville Avenue, Suite 1
Winchester, VA 22601
(540) 667-7940

Children's Home Society
  of Virginia, Inc.
1620 Fifth Street, SW
Roanoke, VA 24016
(540) 344-9281

Children's Home Society
  of Virginia, Inc.
4200 Fitzhugh Avenue
Richmond, VA 23230
(804) 353-0191

Children's Services of Virginia, Inc.
PO Box 2867
Winchester, VA 22602
(540) 667-0116

Children's Services of Virginia, Inc.
Harrisonburg Branch Office
PO Box 660
Harrisonburg, VA 22803
(540) 801-0900

Children's Services of Virginia, Inc.
Manassas Branch Office
7547 Presidential Lane
Manassas, VA 20109
(703) 331-0075

Commonwealth Catholic Charities
302 McClanahan Street SW
Roanoke, VA 24014
(540) 344-0411

Commonwealth Catholic Charities
1024 Park Avenue NW
PO Box 826
Norton, VA 24273
(540) 679-1195

Commonwealth Catholic Charities
1512 Willow Lawn Drive
Richmond, VA 23230-0565
(804) 285-5900

Commonwealth Catholic Charities
3901 Melvern Place
Alexandria, VA 22312
(703) 256-4530

Commonwealth Catholic Charities
Charlottesville
1859-C3 Seminole Trail
Charlottesville, VA 22901
(804) 974-6880

Commonwealth Catholic Charities
Staunton
St. Francis of Assisi
  Catholic Church
121 North Augusta
Staunton, VA 24401-3636
(800) 974-4494

Datz Foundation
311 Maple Avenue West, Suite E
Vienna, VA 22180
(703) 242-8800

Family Life Services
1971 University Boulevard,
  Building 61-B
Lynchburg, VA 24502
(804) 582-2969

Holston United Methodist Home
  for Children
115 East Main Street
Abingdon, VA 24210
(276) 628-1023

Holy Cross Child Placement
  Agency Inc.
400 South Washington Street
Alexandria, VA 22314
(703) 356-8824

Jewish Family Service
  of Tidewater, Inc.
168 Business Park Drive,
  Suite 104
Virginia Beach, VA 23462
(757) 473-2695

Jewish Family Service
  of Tidewater, Inc.
7300 Newport Avenue
Norfolk, VA 23505
(757) 489-3111

Jewish Family Service
  of Tidewater, Inc.
United Jewish Community Center
  of the Virginia Peninsula
2700 Spring Road
Newport News, VA 23606
(757) 489-3111

Jewish Family Services, Inc.
6718 Patterson Avenue

Richmond, VA 23226
(804) 282-5644

LDS Social Services
  of Virginia, Inc.
8110 Virginia Pine Court
Richmond, VA 23237
(804) 743-0727

Loving Families, Inc.
101 South Whiting Street,
  Suite 212
Alexandria, VA 22304
(703) 370-7140

Lutheran Family Services, Inc.
2609 McVitty Road SW
PO Box 21609
Roanoke, VA 24018-0574
(540) 774-7100

Lutheran Social Services of the
  National Capital Area
9506-A Lee Highway
Fairfax, VA 22031
(703) 273-0303

People Places
1215 North Augusta Street
Staunton, VA 24401
(540) 885-8841

Rainbow Christian Services
6004 Artemus Road
Gainesville, VA 20156
(703) 754-8516

Shore Adoption Services, Inc.
113 Holly Crescent, Suite 102
Virginia Beach, VA 23451
(757) 422-6361

United Methodist Family
  Services of Virginia
205 South Main Street
Harrisonburg, VA 22801

(540) 438-1577
Fax: (540) 438-8467

United Methodist Family
  Services of Virginia
715 Baker Road, Suite 201
Virginia Beach, VA 23462
(757) 490-9791

United Methodist Family
  Services of Virginia
3900 West Broad Street
Richmond, VA 23230
(804) 353-4461

United Methodist Family
  Services of Virginia
4621 Carr Drive
Fredericksburg, VA 22408
(540) 898-1773

United Methodist Family
  Services of Virginia
6335 Little River Turnpike
Alexandria, VA 22312
(703) 941-9008

Virginia Baptist Children's Home
  and Family Services
700 East Belt Boulevard
Richmond, VA 23224
(804) 231-4466

Virginia Baptist Children's Home
  and Family Services
860 North Mt. Vernon Lane
Salem, VA 24153
(540) 389-5468

Welcome House of the
  Pearl S. Buck Foundation Inc.
9412 Michelle Place
Richmond, VA 23229
(804) 740-7311
(800) 220-2825

WASHINGTON

Washington Department of
  Social and Health Services
Children's Administration
PO Box 45713
Olympia, WA 98504
(360) 902-7959

Private Agencies

Adoption Advocates International
401 East Front Street
Port Angeles, WA 98362
(360) 452-4777

Americans Adopting Orphans
12345 Lake City Way NE, #2001
Seattle, WA 98125
(206) 524-5437

Catholic Children and Family
  Services of Walla Walla
Drumheller Building, Suite 418
Walla Walla, WA 99362
(509) 525-0572

Catholic Children's Services of
  Northwest Washington
1133 Railroad Avenue, Suite 100
Bellingham, WA 98226
(360) 733-5800

Catholic Community Services
100 23rd Avenue South
Seattle, WA 98144
(206) 323-1950

Catholic Family and Child Service
1023 Riverside Avenue
Spokane, WA 99201
(509) 358-4260

Catholic Family and Child Service
  of Wenatchee
23 South Wenatchee, #209

Wenatchee, WA 98801
(509) 663-3182

Catholic Family and Child Service
  of Yakima
5301-C Tieton Drive
Yakima, WA 98908
(509) 965-7108

Catholic Family and Child Services
2139 Van Giesen
Richland, WA 99352
(509) 946-4645

Children of the Nations
  International Adoptions, Inc.
PO Box 3970
Silverdale, WA 98383
(360) 598-5437

Children's Home Society
  of Washington
Regional Headquarters
3300 NE 65th Street
Box 15190
Seattle, WA 98115-0190
(206) 695-3200

Children's House International
PO Box 1829
Ferndale, WA 98248
(360) 380-5370

Faith International Adoptions
535 East Dock Street, Suite 103
Tacoma, WA 98402
(253) 383-1928

International Children's Care
2711 NE 134th Street
Vancouver, WA 98682
(360) 573-0429
(800) 422-7729

Lutheran Community Services
  North West
433 Minor Avenue N

Seattle, WA 98109
(206) 694-5700

Lutheran Community
  Services North West
Symons Building, Suite 200
Spokane, WA 99204
(509) 747-8224

Lutheran Social Services of
  Washington, Southeast Area
3321 Kennewick Avenue
Kennewick, WA 99336
(509) 735-6446

Medina Children's Services
123 16th Avenue
Seattle, WA 98122
(206) 260-1700
(800) 239-9238

New Hope Child and
  Family Agency
2611 NE 125th Street, Suite 146
Seattle, WA 98125
(206) 363-1800

World Association for Children and
  Parents (WACAP)
PO Box 88948
Seattle, WA 98138
(206) 575-4550

WEST VIRGINIA

West Virginia Department of Health
  and Human Resources
Office of Social Services
350 Capitol Street, Room 621
Charleston, WV 25301-3704
(304) 558-4303

Private Agencies

Adoptions From The Heart
7014 Grand Central Station

Morgantown, WV 26505
(304) 291-5211

Burlington United Methodist
  Family Services
PO Box 370
Scott Depot, WV 25560-0370
(304) 757-9127
(800) 296-6144

Burlington United Methodist
  Family Services
Route 3, Box 346A
Grafton, WV 26354
(304) 265-1575

Burlington United Methodist
  Family Services
Route 3, Box 3122
Keyser, WV 26726
(304) 788-2342

Childplace, Inc.
5101 Chesterfield Avenue SE
Charleston, WV 25304
(304) 757-0763

Children's Home Society
  of West Virginia
1145 Greenbriar Street
Charleston, WV 25311
(304) 345-3891

Children's Home Society
  of West Virginia
316 Oakvale Road
PO Box 5533
Princeton, WV 24740
(304) 425-8438

LDS Social Services
4431 Marketing Place
Groveport, OH 43125
(614) 836-2466

WISCONSIN

Wisconsin Department of
  Health and Family Services
Division of Child and Family
  Services
PO Box 8916
Madison, WI 53708-8916
(608) 266-3595

Wisconsin Division of Children
  and Family Services
Eastern Office
200 North Jefferson, Suite 411
Green Bay, WI 54301
(414) 448-5312

Wisconsin Division of Children and
  Family Services
Fond du Lac Office
485 South Military Road
Fond du Lac, WI 54935-4800
(920) 929-2985

Wisconsin Division of Children and
  Family Services
North Central Office
1853A North Stevens
PO Box 697
Rhinelander, WI 54501
(715) 365-2500

Wisconsin Division of Children
  and Family Services
Southeastern Office
141 NW Barstow Street
Waukesha, WI 53188
(262) 548-8692

Wisconsin Division of Children
  and Family Services
Western Office
610 Gibson Street, Suite 2
Eau Claire, WI 54701-3687
(715) 836-3399

Wisconsin Division of Children
  and Family Services
Wisconsin Rapids Office
2811 Eighth Street South,
  Suite 70
Wisconsin Rapids, WI 54495
(715) 422-5080

Private Agencies

Adoption Advocates, Inc.
2601 Crossroads Drive, Suite 173
Madison, WI 53704
(608) 246-2844

Adoption Choice
924 East Juneau Avenue, #813
Milwaukee, WI 53202-2748
(414) 276-3262
(800) 255-6305

Adoption Services Inc.
911 North Lynndale Drive,
  Suite 2-C
Appleton, WI 54914
(920) 735-6750

Bethany Christian Services
2312 North Grandview Boulevard,
  Suite 207
Waukesha, WI 53188-1606
(414) 547-6557
(800) 238-4269

Catholic Charities, Inc.
128 South 6th Street
PO Box 266
LaCrosse, WI 54602-0266
(608) 782-0704

Catholic Charities
Diocese of Milwaukee
2021 North 60th Street
Milwaukee, WI 53208
(414) 771-2881

Catholic Social Services -
  Green Bay
PO Box 23825
Green Bay, WI 54305-3825
(920) 437-6541

Children's Home Society
  of Minnesota
1605 Eustis Street
St. Paul, MN 55108-1219
(651) 646-7771
(800) 952-9302

Children's Service Society of
  Wisconsin
1212 South 70th Street
Milwaukee, WI 53214
(414) 453-1400

Community Adoption Center
3701 Kadow Street
Manitowoc, WI 54220
(920) 682-9211

Crossroads Adoption Services
911 Fourth Street, Suite B5
Hudson, WI 54016
(715) 386-5550

Evangelical Child and Family
  Agency, District Office
1617 South 124th Street
New Berlin, WI 53151-1803
(414) 789-1881

LDS Social Services
1711 University Avenue
Madison, WI 53705
(608) 238-5377

Lutheran Counseling and
  Family Services
3800 North Mayfair Road
PO Box 13367
Wauwatosa, WI 53222
(414) 536-8333

Lutheran Social Services of
  Wisconsin and Upper Michigan
647 West Virginia Street,
  Suite 300
Milwaukee, WI 53204-1535
(414) 281-4400
(800) 488-5181

Pauquette Children's Services, Inc.
315 West Conant Street
PO Box 162
Portage, WI 53901-0162
(608) 742-8004

Special Children, Inc.
15285 Watertown Plank Road,
  Suite 3
Elm Grove, WI 53122-2339
(414) 821-2125

Van Dyke, Inc.
1224 Weeden Creek Road, Suite 4
Sheboygan, WI 53081-7850
(920) 452-5358

WYOMING

Wyoming Department of
  Family Services
2300 Capitol Avenue
Hathaway Building, Third Floor,
  Room 376
Cheyenne, WY 82002-0490
(307) 777-3570

Wyoming Department of
  Family Services
District 1 - Laramie
1710 Capitol Avenue
Cheyenne, WY 82002
(307) 777-7921

Wyoming Department of
  Family Services
District 2 - Albany
710 Garfield Street, Suite 200

Laramie, WY 82070
(307) 745-7324

Wyoming Department of
  Family Services
District 2 - Carbon
PO Box 2409
Rawlins, WY 82301
(307) 328-0612

Wyoming Department of
  Family Services
District 3 - Sublette
Box 1070, 111 North Sublette
Pinedale, WY 82941
(307) 367-4124

Wyoming Department of
  Family Services
District 3 - Sweetwater
1682 Sunset Drive
Rock Springs, WY 82901
(307) 362-5630

Wyoming Department of
  Family Services
District 4 - Johnson
Box J, 381 North Main
Buffalo, WY 82834
(307) 684-5513

Wyoming Department of
  Family Services
District 5 - Big Horn
616 Second Avenue North
Greybull, WY 82426
(307) 765-9453

Wyoming Department of
  Family Services
District 5 - Hot Springs
403 Big Horn
Thermopolis, WY 82443
(307) 864-2158

Wyoming Department of
  Family Services
District 5 - Park
1301 Rumsey Street
Cody, WY 82414
(307) 587-6246

Wyoming Department of
  Family Services
District 6 - Crook
102 North Fifth, Box 57
Sundance, WY 82729
(307) 283-2014

Wyoming Department of
  Family Services
District 7 - Natrona
851 Werner Court, Suite 200
Casper, WY 82601
(307) 473-3900

Wyoming Department of
  Family Services
District 8 - Goshen
1618 East M Street
Torrington, WY 82240
(307) 532-2191

Wyoming Department of
  Family Services
District 10 - Lincoln/Afton
631 Washington, Box 1336
Afton, WY 83110
(307) 886-9232

Private Agencies

A.D.O.P.P.T., Inc.
7860 Chukar Drive
Gillette, WY 82716
(307) 687-7147

Casey Family Program
130 Hobbs Avenue
Cheyenne, WY 82009
(307) 638-2564

Catholic Social Services
of Wyoming
2121 Capitol Avenue
PO Box 1026
Cheyenne, WY 82003
(307) 638-1530
(800) 788-4606

Focus on Children
405 Sage Street
Cokeville, WY 83114
(307) 279-3434
(888) 801-7295

Global Adoption Services, Inc.
50 East Loucks, Suite 205
Sheridan, WY 82801
(307) 674-6606

LDS Family Services
7609 Santa Marie Drive
Cheyenne, WY 82009
(307) 637-8929
(800) 537-2229

Wyoming Children's Society
716 Randall Avenue
PO Box 105
Cheyenne, WY 82003
(307) 632-7619
(800) 584-9384

Wyoming Parenting Society
PO Box 3774
Jackson, WY 83001
(307) 733-5680

INTERNATIONAL ADOPTION AGENCIES IN THE UNITED STATES

NATIONWIDE

Across the World Adoptions
(800) 610-5607
http://www.adopting.com/atwa

Adopt An Angel International
http://www.AdoptAnAngel.org

Adoptions From The Heart
http://www.adoptionsfromtheheart
.org/

Bethany Christian Services
http://www.bethany.org

Children of the World
http://www.childrenoftheworld.com

Genesis Adoptions
http://www.GenesisAdoptions.org

Hope for Children, Inc.
http://www.hopeforchildren.org

Illien Adoptions International Inc.
http://www.illienadopt.com

Open Door Adoption Agency, Inc.
http://www.opendooradoption.com

Ventures for Children International
http://www.venturesforchildren.org

World Partners Adoption, Inc
http://www.worldpartnersadoption
.org

CANADIAN ADOPTION AGENCIES

ALBERTA

Alberta Children's Services
Ninth Floor
7th St. Plaza
10030-107 Street
Edmonton, AB T5J 3E4
(780) 422-5641

Private Agencies

Adoption By Choice
315, 908 17 Avenue SW

Calgary, AB T2T 0A3
(403) 245-8854

Adoption By Choice
14030 106 Avenue
Edmonton, AB T5N 1B2
(780) 448-1159

Adoption Options
202, 1228 Kensington Road NW
Calgary, AB T2N 3P7
(403) 270-8228

Adoption Options
304–10109 106 Street
Edmonton, AB T5J 3L7
(780) 433-5656

Catholic Social Services
5104 - 48 Avenue
Red Deer, AB T4N 3T8
(403) 347-8844

Catholic Social Services
8815 - 99 Street
Edmonton, AB T6E 3V3
(780) 432-1137

Christian Adoption Services
204, 11625 Elbow Drive SW
Calgary, AB T2W 1G8
(403) 256-3224

LDS Family Services
1625 Cedar Road South
Lethbridge, AB T1K 4W6
(403) 328-8263

LDS Family Services
7040 Farrell Road SE
Calgary, AB T2H 0T2
(403) 255-0153

BRITISH COLUMBIA

Ministry for Children & Family
  Development
PO Box 9705, Station
Provincial Government
Victoria, BC V8W 9S1
(250) 387-2281

Private Agencies

The Adoption Center
255 Lawrence Avenue
Kelowna, BC V1Y 6L2
(250) 763-8002

Choices Adoption and Counseling
  Services
850 Blanshard Street, Suite 100
Victoria, BC V8W 2H2
(250) 479-9811

Family Services of Greater
  Vancouver
#205
1600 West 6th Avenue
Vancouver, BC V6J 1R3
(604) 736-7613

Hope Services
#200
2975 Gladwin Road
Abbotsford, BC V2T 5T4
(800) 916-4673

LDA Adoption Services
#10122
140th Street
Surrey, BC V3T 4M9
(604) 585-7735

Sunrise Adoption Centre
171 West Esplanade, Suite 102
North Vancouver, BC V7M 3J9
(604) 984-2488

MANITOBA

Family Services & Housing Child
 Protection & Support Services
Suite 201
114 Garry Street
Winnipeg, MB R3C 4V5
(204) 945-1186

Private Agencies

CAFAC Inter-Country Adoption
 Agency
PO Box 1587
Minnedosa, MB R0J 1E0

NEW BRUNSWICK

Department of Family and
 Community Services
Second Floor
551 King Street
Fredericton, NB E3B 1E7
(506) 444-4516

NEWFOUNDLAND AND LABRADOR

Child, Youth & Family Services
PO Box 8700
St. John's, NL A1B 4J6
(709) 729-6721

NORTHWEST TERRITORIES

Northwest Territories Department
 of Health & Social Services
Sixth Floor
Centre Square Tower, Box 1320
Yellowknife, NT X1A 2L9
(867) 873-7943

NOVA SCOTIA

Department of Community Services
Family and Children's Services
 Division
PO Box 696
Hailfax, NS B3J 2T7
(902) 424-3205

Family and Children's
 Services Division
Department of Community Services
PO Box 696
Halifax, NS B3J 2T7
(902) 424-3205

Private Agencies

Children from China
6528 London Street
Halifax, NS B3L 1X6
(902) 454-5559

Children of Choice Consulting
2466 Connaught Avenue
Halifax, NS B3L 2Z4
(902) 422-9881

ONTARIO

Ontario Ministry of Children and
 Youth Services
Seventh Floor
Hepburn Block
Grosvenor Street
Toronto, ON M7A 1E9
(416) 327-4730

Private Agencies

Adoption Agency & Counseling
 Services
2349 Fairview Street

Burlington, ON L7R 2E3
(905) 634-0009

Adoption Horizons
7 Sunforest Court
North York, ON M2R 3W3
(416) 512-7591

Adoptionworxs
1594 Islington Avenue
Toronto, ON M9A 3M6
(416) 236-7337

Canadian International
  Adoption Services
297 Sheppard Avenue West,
  Suite 202
Toronto, ON M2N 1N4
(416) 250-0520

Canadians Adopt Romanian
  Children
203 Holmes Avenue
Toronto, ON M2N 4N9
(416) 224-9642

Caring Homes for Orphan Children
3727 Chesswood Drive
Toronto, ON M3J 2P6
(416) 630-2472

Children's Bridge
#221
1400 Clyde Avenue
Nepean, ON K2G 3J2
(613) 226-2112

Children's Resource and
  Consultation Centre
21 Price Street
Toronto, ON M4W 1Z1
(416) 923-7771

Cornerstone Adoption Agency
4121 Lawrence Avenue East,
  Suite 108

Toronto, ON M1E 2S2
(416) 283-7239

Family Outreach International
19-575 Old St. Patrick Street
Ottawa, ON K1N 9H5
(613) 789-8677

Global Village Adoption Agency
14 Crescent Road
Rockcliffe, ON K1M 0N3
(613) 748-1689

Loving Heart International
  Adoption Inc.
36 Canary Crescent
Toronto, ON M2K 1Z1
(416) 223-4997

Mission of TEARS
50 Gervais Drive, Suite 223
Toronto, ON M3C 1Z3
(416) 449-0018

OANA Inter-Country Adoptioins
7 St. Dennis Drive, Suite 1416
Toronto, ON M3C 1E4
(416) 425-0785

Open Arms to International
  Adoption
14 Roxborough Street West
Toronto, ON M5R 1T8
(416) 966-0294

St. Anne Adoption Center
56 Albert Street
Stratford, ON N5A 6T7
(519) 273-7121

Ukrainian Cradle Adoption Agency
3 Saffron Crescent
Toronto, ON M9C 3T8
(416) 622-0853

World View Adoption Agency
130 Westmore Drive, Suite 5

Toronto, ON M9V 5E2
(416) 745-9777

PRINCE EDWARD ISLAND

Prince Edward Island Department
 of Health & Social Services
Box 2000
Charlottetown, PEI C1A 7N8
(902) 368-6514

SASKATCHEWAN

Family & Youth Division
Saskatchewan Social Services
Twelfth Floor
1920 Broad Street
Regina, SK S4P 3V6
(306) 787-5698

QUEBEC

Ministere de la Sante et des
 Services sociau
Bureau 1.02
201, boulevard Cremazie Est
Montreal, QC H2M 1L2
(514) 873-4747 (French)
(800) 561-0246 (English)

Private Agencies

Acueillons un Enfant
Bureau 306
2900 Quatre-Bourgeois
Ste-Foy, QC G1V 1Y4
(418) 651-2608

Appel Inc.
5089 rue Mills
Rock Forest, QC J1N 3B6
(819) 564-2843

Au Berceau de la Vie
120 Ferland Street, PHB
Montreal, QC H3E 1L1
(877) 363-0292

Enfant sans Frontiere
566 boulevard St. Martin Quest
Laval, QC H7X 3S4
(514) 952-9441

Enfants d'Orient
11664 Racette
Montreal North, QC H1G 5J5
(514) 881-1514

Enfants du Monde
1600 Henri-Bourassa Quest
Montreal, QC H3M 3E2
(800) 381-3588

Societe Formons Une Famille Inc.
3700 rue Berri, Suite 450
Montreal, QC H2L 4G9
(514) 287-7290

Soleil des Nations
6 rue de Laval
Pont-Rouge, QC G0A 2X0
(819) 376-1775

Terre Des Hommes Canada, Inc.
2520 rue Lionel-Groulx, Suite 5
Montreal, QC H3J 1J8
(514) 937-3325

YUKON TERRITORY

Yukon Territory Family
 & Children's Services
Royal Bank Building
414-4th Avenue, Suite 401
Whitehorse, YT Y1A 4N7

Bibliography

BOOKS

Ackerman, Marc J., and Andrew Kane. *Psychological Experts in Divorce, Personal Injury and Other Civil Actions.* New York: Wiley & Sons, 1993.

Ainsworth, M. D. *Patterns of Attachment.* Hillsdale, NJ: Erlbaun, 1978.

Apgar, V., and J. Beck. *Is My Baby All Right?* New York: Trident, 1973.

Aries, Philippe. *Centuries of Childhood: A Social History of Family Life.* New York: Vintage, 1965.

Bachrach, Arthur J., and Gardner Murphy, eds. *An Outline of Abnormal Psychology.* New York: Modern Library, 1954.

Barron-Cohen, Simon. *The Essential Difference: The Truth about the Male and Female Brain.* New York: Perseus, 2003.

Biddulph, Steve. *Raising Boys.* Berkeley: Celestial Arts, 1998.

Biller, Henry. *Fathers and Families: Paternal Factors in Child Development.* Westport, CT: Auburn House, 1993.

Biller, Henry, and Dennis Meredith. *Father Power.* New York: David McKay, 1974.

Biller, Henry, and Robert J. Trotter. *The Father Factor: What You Need to Know to Make a Difference.* New York: Pocket Books, 1994.

Blankenhorn, David. *Fatherless America: Confronting Our Most Urgent Social Problem.* New York: Harper Perennial, 1995.

Blau, Theodore H. *The Psychologist as Expert Witness.* New York: John Wiley & Sons, 1988.

Bower, T. *Development in Infancy.* San Francisco: Freeman, 1981.

Brazelton, T. B. *The Infant Neonatal Assessment Scale.* Philadelphia: Lippincott, 1984.

Brodzinsky, David M. *The Psychology of Adoption.* New York: Oxford University Press, 1990.

Brooks, R. and Sam Goldstein. *Raising Resilient Children: Fostering Strength, Hope, and Optimism in your Child.* New York: McGraw-Hill, 2002.

Burns, Ailsa, and Cath Scott. *Mother-Headed Families and Why They Have Increased.* Hillsdale, NJ: Lawrence Erlbaum Associates, 1994.

Caldwell, Bettye M., and Henry N. Ricciuti, eds. *Child Development and Social Policy.* Vol. 3. Chicago: University of Chicago Press, 1973.

Canfield, Ken R. *The 7 Secrets of Effective Fathers.* Wheaton, IL: Tyndale House, 1992.

Daly, Martin, and Margo Wilson. "Risk of Maltreatment of Children Living with Stepparents." In *Child Abuse and Neglect: Biosocial Dimensions*, edited by R. Gelles and J. Lancaster. New York: Aldine de Gruyter, 1987.

Dickerson, James L. *Faith Hill: Piece of My Heart.* New York: St. Martin's Press, 2001.

Ekman, Paul. *Emotions Revealed.* New York: Henry Holt and Company, 2003.

Eliot, Lise. *What's Going on in There?: How the Brain and Mind Develop in the First Five Years of Life.* New York: Bantam, 1999.

Empfield, Maureen, and Nicholas Bakalar. *Understanding Teenage Depression.* New York: Henry Holt, 1999.

———. *Identity and the Life Cycle.* New York: W. W. Norton, reissued 1980.

Erickson, E. H. *Childhood and Society.* New York: W. W. Norton, 1963.

Fahlberg, Vera I. *A Child's Journey through Placement.* Indianapolis, IN: Perspective Press, 1991.

Foli, Karen J., and John R. Thompson. *The Post-Adoption Blues: Overcoming the Unforeseen Challenges of Adoption.* USA: Rodale, 2004.

Furstenberg, Frank F., and Andrew J. Cherlin. *Divided Families: What Happens to Children When Parents Part.* Cambridge, MA: Harvard University Press, 1991.

Garfinkel, Irwin, and Sara S. McLanahan. *Single Mothers and Their Children.* Washington, DC: The Urban Institute Press, 1986.

Gelles, R., and J. Lancaster, eds. *Child Abuse and Neglect: Biosocial Dimensions.* New York: Aldine de Gruyter, 1987.

Gray, Deborah D. *Attaching in Adoption: Practical Tools for Today's Parents.* Indianapolis, IN: Perspectives Press, 2002.

Hauser, Thomas. *Muhammad Ali: His Life and Times.* New York: Touchstone, 1991.

Hetherington, E. Mavis. *For Better or For Worse.* New York: W. W. Norton, 2002.

Ingersoll, Barbara D., and Sam Goldstein. *Lonely, Sad and Angry.* New York: Doubleday, 1995.

Kidman, Antony. *Family Life.* Sydney: Biochemical and General Services, 1995.

Kindlon, Dan, and Michael Thompson. *Raising Cain: Protecting the Emotional Life of Boys.* New York: Ballantine Books, 2000.

Klaus, M. H., and J. H. Kennell. *Maternal-Infant Bonding.* St. Louis: Mosby, 1976.

Krementz, Jill. *How It Feels to Be Adopted.* New York: Alfred A. Knopf, 1988.

Lamb, Michael. *The Role of the Father in Child Development.* New York: John Wiley, 1997.

Lamb, Michael, and Ann Browns, eds. *Advances in Developmental Psychology.* Hillsdale, NJ: Erlbaun, 1986.

Levine, Mel. *A Mind at a Time.* New York: Simon & Schuster, 2002.

Maas, Henry S., and Richard E. Engler. *Children in Need of Parents.* New York: Columbia University Press, 1954.

Macoby, Eleanor. *Social Development, Psychological Growth and Parent-Child Relations.* New York: Harcourt Brace Jovanovich, 1980.

Macoby, Eleanor and Carol Nagy Jacklin. *The Psychology of Sex Differences.* Stanford: Stanford University Press, 1974.

McLanahan, Sara, and Gary Sandefur. *Growing Up with a Single Parent.* Cambridge, MA: Harvard University Press, 2001.

Maddi, Salvatore R. *Personality Theories: A Comparative Analysis.* Homewood, IL: Dorsey Press, 1976.

Melina, Lois Ruskai. *Raising Adopted Children: Practical Reassuring Advice for Every Adoptive Parent.* New York: HarperPerennial, 1998.

Murphy, James M. *Coping with Teen Suicide.* New York: Rosen Publishing Group, 1999.

Neal, J. H. "Children's Understand of Their Parents' Divorces." In *Children and Divorce: New Directions for Child Development*, edited by L. Kurdek. San Francisco: Jossey-Bass, 1983.

Osofsky, Joy. *Handbook of Infant Development.* New York: John Wiley & Sons, 1987.

Pertman, Adam. *Adoption Nation.* New York: Basic Books, 2000.

Piaget, Jean. *The Moral Judgment of the Child.* New York: Macmillan, 1932.

————. *Six Psychological Studies.* New York: Random House, 1967.

Popenoe, David. *Life Without Father.* New York: Martin Kessler Books/Free Press, 1996.

Prokop, Michael S. *Kids' Divorce Workbook.* Warren, OH: Alegra House, 1986.

Pruett, Kyle D. *The Nurturing Father: Journey Toward the Complete Man.* New York: Warner Books, 1988.

Rotundo, E. Anthony. *American Manhood.* New York: Basic Books, 1993.

Stolk, Mary Van. *The Battered Child in Canada.* Toronto: McClelland and Stewart, 1972.

Tanner, J. *Education and Physical Growth.* London: Hodder and Stoughton, 1978.

Teyber, Edward. *Helping Children Cope with Divorce.* San Francisco: Jossey-Bass, 1992.

Thomas, M. *Comparing Theories of Child Development.* New York: W. W. Norton, 1996.

Thompson, Clara, Milton Mazer, and Earl Witenberg. *An Outline of Psychoanalysis.* New York: Modern Library, 1955.

Thompson, Michael. *Speaking of Boys.* New York: Ballantine Books, 2000.

Wachtel, Ellen F. *Treating Troubled Children and Their Families.* New York: Guilford Press, 1994.

Wallerstein, Judith, and Sandra Blakeslee. *Second Chances: Men, Women, and Children a Decade After Divorce.* Boston: Houghton Mifflin, 1996.

Wallerstein, Judith, Julie M. Lewis, and Sandra Blakeslee. *The Unexpected Legacy of Divorce.* New York: Hyperion, 2000.

Wodrich, David L. *Children's Psychological Testing: A Guide for Nonpsychologists.* Baltimore: Paul H. Brookes Publishing, 1984.

PERIODICALS

Abrahamson, Amy C., and Laura A. Baker. "Rebellious Teens? Genetic and Environmental Influences on the Social Attitudes of Adolescents." *Journal of Personality and Social Psychology* 83, no. 6 (2002).

Alessandri, Steven M., and Robert H. Wozniak. "The Child's Awareness of Parental Beliefs Concerning the Child: A Developmental Study." *Child Development* 58 (1987).

Amato, Paul R. "Parental Divorce and Attitudes toward Marriage and Family Life." *Journal of Marriage and the Family* (May 1988).

Amato, Paul R., and Alan Booth. "The Legacy of Parents' Marital Discord: Consequences for Children's Marital Quality." *Journal of Personality and Social Psychology* (October 2001).

Belsky, Jay. "Parent, Infant, and Social-Contextual of Father-Son Attachment Security." *Developmental Psychology* 32, no. 5 (September 1, 1996).

Duyme, Michel. "School Success and Social Class: An Adoption Study." *Developmental Psychology* (vol. 24, no. 2, 1988).

Feigelman, William and Gordon E. Finley. "Youth Problems Among Adoptees Living in One-Parent Homes: A Comparison With Others From One-Parent Biological Families." *American Journal of Orthopsychiatry* (vol. 74, 2002).

Harris, Judith Rich. "The Outcome of Parenting: What Do We Really Know?" *Journal of Personality* (June 2000).

Heinman, Toni. "A Boy and Two Mothers: New Variations on an Old Theme or a New Story of Triangulation?" *Psychoanalytic Psychology* (vol. 21, no. 1, 2004).

Hofferth, Sandra L., and Kermyt G. Anderson. "Are All Dads Equal? Biology Versus Marriage as a Basis for Paternal Investment. *Journal of Marriage and Family* (February 2003).

Kerig, Patricia K., Philip A. Cowan, and Carolyn Pape Cowan. "Marital Quality and Gender Differences in Parent-Child Interaction." *Developmental Psychology* (November 1, 1993).

Kroska, Amy. "Investigating Gender Differences in the Meaning of Household Chores and Child Care." *Journal of Marriage and Family* (May 2003).

Montague, Diane P. F., and Arlene S. Walker-Andrews. "Mothers, Fathers, and Infants: The Role of Person Familiarity and Parental Involvement in Infants' Perception of Emotion Expressions." *Child Development* (September/October 2002).

Murphy, Julie A, Edna I. Rawlings and Steven P. Howe. "A Survey of Clinical Psychologists on Treating Lesbian, Gay, and Bisexual Clients." *Professional Psychology: Research and Practice* (vol. 33, no. 2, 2002).

National Institute of Child Development (NICHD). "Do Children's Attention Processes Mediate the Link Between Family Predictors and School Readiness?" *Developmental Psychology* (May 1, 2003).

Pachankis, John E., and Marvin R. Goldfried. "Clinical Issues in Working with Lesbian, Gay, and Bisexual Clients." *Psychotherapy: Theory, Research, Practice, Training* (vol. 41, no. 3, 2004).

Pettit, Gregory S., and Kenneth A. Dodge. "Violent Children: Bridging Development, Intervention, and Public Policy." *Developmental Psychology* (March 1, 2003).

Phares, Vicky. "Where's Poppa? A Relative Lack of Attention to the Role of Fathers in Child and Adolescent Psychopathology." *American Psychologist* (1992).

Poole, Shelia M. "Canadians Look South to Adopt Black Kids." *Atlanta Journal-Constitution* (August 24, 2004).

Shinyei, Marilyn. "Alberta Down to Five Licensed Agencies." *Adoption Canada* (August 2003).

Solomon, Sondra E., Esther D. Rothblum and Kimberly F. Balsam. "Pioneers in Partnership: Lesbian and Gay Male Couples in Civil Unions Compared with Those Not in Civil Unions and Married Heterosexual Siblings." *Journal of Family Psychology* (vol. 18, no. 2, 2004).

Stansm Geert-Jan J. M., Femmie Juffer and Marinus H. van IJzendoorn. "Maternal Sensitivity, Infant Attachment, and Temperament in Early Childhood Predict Adjustment in Middle Childhood: The Case of Adopted Children and Their Biologically Unrelated Parents. *Developmental Psychology* vol. 38, no. 5 (2002).

Walton, G. E., N. J. Bower, and T. G. Bower. "Recognition of Familiar Faces by Newborns." *Infant Behavior and Development* 15 (1992), 265-269.

Wolf, Jeanne. "Keeping the Faith." *Redbook*, June 2000.

STATISTICAL AND INTERNET RESOURCES

United States

Evan B. Donaldson Adoption Institute. "Why the ICPC?" http://www.adoptioninstitute.org/policy/inters2.html.

Mississippi Department of Human Services. "Licensing Standards for Child Placing Facilities" (1986; revised 1992)

Reasononline http://www.reason.com/0508/fe.js.all.shtml

U.S. Department of State. "Hague Convention on Intercountry Adoption." http://www.travel.state.gov.

————. "Immigrant Visas Issued to Orphans Coming to the U.S." http://www.state.gov/orphan_numbers.html

————. "International Adoption." http://www.travel.state.gov.

————. "International Adoption Safeguards." http://www.travel.state.gov/family/adoption/info/info_450html.

Canada

Adoption Council of Canada. http://www.adoption.ca.

Alberta Ministry of Children's Services. http://www.child.gov.ab.ca.

British Columbia Ministry of Children and Family Development http://www.mcf.gov.bc.ca/adoption/index.htm.

Canadian Government "Ontario Child and Family Services Act." Revised 1990 (March 14, 2003)

Dave Thomas Foundation for Adoption. "A Child is Waiting: A Beginner's Guide to Adoption." http://www.DaveThomasFoundationForAdoption.org.

Families with Children from China. "Overview of Adoption in China from a Canadian Perspective." http://www.fwcc.org/canadian.html.

Family and Children's Services of Brockville and the United Counties of Leeds and Grenville. Annual Reports 1969/70; 2003/04.

Government of Canada. "Child and Family Services Statistical Report: 1998–1999 to 2000–2001–January 2005."http://www.11.sdc.fc.ca/en/cs/sp/sdc/socpol/publications/statistics/2oo4-002599/page00.shtml.

Manitoba Department of Family Services & Housing. http://www.gov.mb.ca/services/famyouth/Adoption/index.html.

Ministry for Children and Families. "British Columbia Adoption." *Practice Standards and Guidelines for Adoption.*

Newfoundland and Labrador Department of Health and Community Services. http://www.gov.nl.ca/health.

New Brunswick Department of Family and Community Services. http://www.gnb.ca/0017/adoption.

Northwest Territories Department of Health and Social Services. http://www.hlthss.gov.nt.ca.

Nova Scotia Department of Community Services. http://www.gov.ns.ca/coms/files/adopindx.asp.

Nunavut Department of Health and Social Services. http://www.gov.nu.ca.

Ontario Ministry of Children and Youth Services. http://www.children.gov
.on.ca/CS/en/programs/Adoption.

————. "How to Adopt a Child in Ontario." http://www.children.gov.on.ca.

_____. "International Adoption: A Guide for Ontario Families." Manage-
ment Support Branch / Adoption Unit (March 2001). http://www.
children.gov.on.ca/CS.

Prince Edward Island Department of Health and Social Services. http://
www.gov.pe.ca.

Quebec Ministere de Sante et des Services Sociaux. http://www.adoption
.gouv.qc.ca/fr/.

Saskatchewan Department of Community Resources and Employment.
http://www.dcre.gov.sk.ca.

Index

About the Authors

JAMES L. DICKERSON is a professional writer. He is a former social worker who was in charge of foster care and adoptions.

MARDI ALLEN is a psychologist. She was the 2002–2003 president of the Association of State and Provincial Psychology Boards (ASPPB), an alliance of state, provincial, and territorial agencies responsible for the licensure and discipline of all psychologists throughout the United States and Canada.